★ ★ ★ ILLUSTRATED ★ ★ ★

WORLD WAR II

ENCYCLOPEDIA

VOLUME **23**

★ ★ ★ ILLUSTRATED ★ ★ ★

WORLD WAR II

ENCYCLOPEDIA

AN $\mathcal{U}$NBIASED ACCOUNT OF THE MOST DEVASTATING
WAR KNOWN TO MANKIND . . . CONTAINS THE ORIGINAL TEXT PREVIOUSLY PUBLISHED IN
THE UNITED KINGDOM PLUS BACKGROUND ARTICLES BY A GROUP OF DISTINGUISHED
HISTORIANS . . . ENLIVENED WITH COLOR PHOTOGRAPHS RECENTLY UNCOVERED

BASED ON THE ORIGINAL TEXT OF
Lieutenant Colonel Eddy Bauer

EDITOR-IN-CHIEF
Brigadier Peter Young, DSO, MC, MA

CONSULTANT EDITORS
Brigadier General James L. Collins, Jr. U.S.A.
CHIEF OF MILITARY HISTORY, DEPARTMENT OF THE ARMY

Correlli Barnett
FELLOW OF CHURCHILL COLLEGE, CAMBRIDGE

EDITORIAL DIRECTOR
Brian Innes

H. S. STUTTMAN INC. *Publishers*

CONTENTS

Illustrated World War II Encyclopedia
ISBN 0-87475-520-4

Printed in the United States of America
3P(0194)15-50

The American fighting man

The mass production and big business skills which were employed in the production and distribution of weapons, ammunition, and equipment were also used in training, posting, and employment of the American soldier in World War II.

Aware of his status in a military chain of production and consumption, the U.S. soldier gave himself the nickname "G.I.", taken from the initials stamped on his equipment. He was "Government Issue".

As America moved steadily towards war in 1940 and 1941, she began to increase her war production and expand her forces. On August 27, 1940, Congress authorised the President to call up the National Guard and other reserves for active duty for a year. On September 16, the Burke-Wadsworth Bill provided for selective service for a year. These men, however, could only be employed in the western hemisphere and the possessions of the United States.

There were optimistic plans for training conscripts in special recruit cadres, but the limited facilities meant that they went straight into Regular Army divisions who had both to train them and also engage in advanced exercises themselves.

When Major-General Lesley McNair came away from one unit in September 1940, he said he had the impression of the "blind leading the blind, and officers generally elsewhere". Despite this, the ground was being prepared for greater expansion and the system could already claim some success: the quality of the young officers produced by the Reserve Officers' Training Corps. At the end of

1941 General Marshall called them "probably our greatest asset during this present expansion".

But what of the draftees, the men who had been called up, and had come "to get the job done".

By about April 1941, recruits were no longer being sent from reception centres directly into tactical units, but to Replacement Training Centers for 13 weeks' basic training. G.H.Q. added three additional phases of training to follow systematically: small unit training, combined training with the various weapons of the regiment, and division and large-unit manoeuvres.

There were proficiency tests at every stage and an emphasis on elementary training and general proficiency. Exercises were free and not rigorously con-

trolled but could include live firing to simulate battle conditions. De-briefs and meticulous umpiring reinforced lessons learned in the field.

Road runs, physical training, and the assault course hardened up the young men who now began to be inducted into the forces in greater numbers. The Army too began to lose its surplus fat.

The infantry division revamped

Under General McNair, Chief of Army Ground Forces, the infantry division, which had a full strength of 15,500 men in 1942, lost 1,250 men in the reforms. The chief savings were in defensive weapons and specialists. Infantrymen were expected to take on a variety of tasks which had been the reserve of specialists: they became radio operators, truck drivers, did simple mine-clearing, and took on enemy tanks with their rocket launchers.

Major tank attacks or complex engineering operations could be handled by the specialists who had been pooled in non-divisional units. The task of the infantry division was to advance, and so it was equipped with weapons which were mobile or man-portable.

A division had 27 rifle companies totalling 5,184 men. Each company had three rifle platoons and a weapons platoon. The rifle platoon contained three squads of 12 men armed with ten M1 Garand rifles, one automatic rifle, and one Model 1903 Springfield rifle. The weapons platoon contained two .30-inch light machine guns, three 60-mm mortars, three anti-tank rocket launchers, and one .50-inch machine gun which was intended for anti-aircraft defence, but could fire armour-piercing ammunition.

Three rifle companies were grouped with a heavy weapons company to form an infantry battalion. The heavy weapons company contained 162 officers and men with six 81-mm mortars, eight .30-inch medium machine guns, seven anti-tank rocket launchers, and three .50-inch heavy machine guns.

The battalion headquarters company had had an anti-tank platoon armed with three 37-mm anti-tank guns (later replaced by 57-mm guns), three .30-inch machine guns, one .50-inch machine gun, and eight rocket launchers.

Three infantry battalions with a headquarters company (supported by six 105-mm howitzers, a service company, and an anti-tank company with 12 guns, one .50-inch and four .30-inch machine guns) made up the infantry regiment.

Three infantry regiments were supported by three artillery battalions to make up the combat elements of a division. The artillery battalions contained one 155-mm howitzer battery with 12 guns, two 105-mm howitzer batteries with 36 guns, and a headquarters and a service battery.

Support elements

The division was supported by engineer, signal, ordnance, quartermaster, medical, and military police units, with a head-

▷ The crew of a 40-mm light anti-aircraft gun drills during an exercise near Barstow, California. It is hard to see how the crew's eyes could have become adjusted to the dark, however, with the cameraman's lights pointing in their eyes!

▽ Working his way up from the bottom: Private Francis Warren Pershing, son of General of the Armies John Pershing, learns the tricks of the machine gunner's trade with Private Jacob Kruithop (right) at Fort Belvoir, Virginia.

quarters company and a mechanised reconnaissance troop. In practice the infantry division operated in the field with a tank battalion and other supporting elements semi-permanently attached.

The division remained a standardised unit throughout the war, and was kept up to strength by a steady stream of replacements, or "reppl's" in Army slang. In three months of heavy fighting, an infantry regiment could suffer 100 per cent casualties. By early 1945, 47 infantry regiments in 19 divisions had suffered 100, and in some cases over 200, per cent casualties.

Men, like equipment, made their way through a series of depots and staging posts between the United States and arriving at the front. In McNair's words there was always "the invisible horde of

people going here and there but seemingly never arriving".

Whatever the flair and skill of generals, without these nameless men, the G.I.s, the war could never have been brought to a successful conclusion. Many already possessed skills they had learned in the city or on the farm. Trucks and cars, and their engines and maintenance, were no novelty. These men came from a gadget-minded nation, and many had used rifles and shotguns from an early age.

General George S. Patton asserted "The soldier is the Army. No army is better than its soldiers. The soldier is also a citizen. In fact, the highest obligation and privilege of citizenship is that of bearing arms for one's country. Hence it is a proud privilege to be a soldier – a good soldier."

The U.S. Army also held some of the

▽ *American infantry exercise in Northern Ireland (note the early pattern British-style steel helmets). Although the first U.S. troops arrived in Great Britain in 1942, most of them had to wait until Operation "Overlord" in 1944 before getting their first taste of action.*

*◁ The spoils of war?
Americans relax on the shores of
Wansee Lake in Berlin with local
girls after the war.
△ American soldiers entertain
themselves with the help of
equipment supplied by the Young
Men's Christian Association in
the Woking area of Surrey,
England.*

*◁ American troops in Great
Britain at an alfresco
entertainment show.
▷ Home-from-home: American
soldiers enjoy themselves at a
party given by Mrs. Rees Evans
of the Finchley Road in London.
Such hospitality by their hosts
played an important part in
making American troops feel at
home on "alien" shores.*

▷ *Preparations for war: men of the U.S. Marine raider battalion that invaded Makin Island, under Lieutenant-Colonel Evans F. Carlson, train for their big day.*

world's most educated and best informed soldiers, and General Bradley explained that in Sicily they had their own opinions about Patton.

"George irritated them by flaunting the pageantry of his command. He travelled in an entourage of command cars followed by a string of nattily uniformed staff officers. His own vehicle was gaily decked with oversize stars and the insignia of his command. These exhibitions did not awe the troops as perhaps Patton believed. Instead, they offended the men as they trudged through the clouds of dust left in the wake of that procession."

Army newspapers

The soldiers had their own newspapers, *Yank* and *The Stars and Stripes*, and most divisions and higher commands produced their own duplicated news sheets, using the journalistic talent that had been drafted into the Army. In addition there was the Armed Forces Radio, which provided news and music.

The American public demanded and received news coverage of their forces abroad which emphasised a human interest angle. Men were named in photographs and stories and their home town and state included. For as Bradley learned, for the 80,000 men in his corps there were "better than a quarter-million fathers, mothers, wives, and what-have-you in the United States, all of them worrying about these men. A good many of them are probably asking themselves: What sort of a guy is this Omar Bradley? Is he good enough to take care of my man?"

Surprisingly, this literate, democratic, and well-informed army made war as effectively as many more autocratic forces. One of the chief reasons for this was the feeling that they were fighting a just war. Japan had made a treacherous attack at Pearl Harbor and, after swallowing up Europe, Germany had declared war on the United States. Both countries were aggressors, and the war was being waged to beat them and bring peace to Europe and Asia.

The Army was well paid; by British standards the men seemed very well off,

▽ *A battalion of American infantry sets off on a route march, preparing for the day when long-distance movement would be the order of the day against the forces of the Axis.*

△ Lt.-Col. James A. Clark (with map), deputy commander of the 4th Fighter Group, briefs his pilots at Debden before a sweep over France on April 10, 1944. Two of the "aces" in the photograph are Captain Don S. Gentile (extreme right) and Major James A. Goodson (on Clark's right). During the sweep, 28 German aircraft were downed.

△▷ Corporal W. H. Porter, U.S.M.C., is eased onto a stretcher-blanket after being wounded in the battle for Iwo Jima.

▷ Mail-call for Marines of the 2nd Marine Division on Tinian island in the Marianas.

for a staff sergeant could take home as much as a British Army captain. Serving overseas, a private made $60 a month, roughly three times as much as his British counterpart. In a country that had been denuded of its men, the invasion by large numbers of comparatively wealthy young men was welcomed by many British girls. The "G.I. brides" who were carried off to the United States at the end of the war bore witness to the charms of these friendly invaders.

However, before he landed in Britain, the U.S. serviceman was given a 32-page booklet, *A Short Guide to Great Britain*. It warned him against such social blun-

ders as stealing a British soldier's girl and spending his money too freely, and added the following admonition: "The British don't know how to make a good cup of coffee. You don't know how to make a good cup of tea. It is an even swap."

But these domestic and social subtleties were only light relief for soldiers who continued their training in Britain in preparation for D-Day.

Infantry assault tactics had evolved from the covering-fire tactics of World War I. Each 12-man rifle squad had a two-man scout section, a four-man fire section, and a five-man manoeuvre and assault section. In theory the squad leader and scout section would locate the enemy, and while one section with Browning Automatic Rifles pinned down the enemy, the third section would advance.

This theory, however, only used a small part of the squad's fire-power, and often the squad leader was pinned down with his scout section. In practice the infantry often worked with tanks–between three and seven tanks were assigned to an infantry company. Sometimes the armour went at point, sometimes with the infantry (in extended line), and when there was little resistance expected, the infantry rode on them.

The tanks would take on the centres of resistance, the infantry would attack the anti-tank guns.

As an alternative to this system there was the "marching fire offensive" employed by Patton. It was costly, but could yield dramatic results. The infantry advanced in a skirmish line with close tank support. With them went all the portable weapons, including the B.A.R.s and .30-inch machine guns. All available fire would be directed at centres of resistance; this had a favourable effect on the assault troops, and looked and sounded terrifying to the defenders. Artillery and mortars would be brought forward behind this line to give supporting fire if necessary.

Good rations for the fighting man

In the field the G.I. usually received at least one hot meal a day, but sometimes he had to fall back on the three varieties of emergency rations. The K-ration came in a small cardboard box which held a can of cheese, ham and egg mixture, or beef hash, a fruit bar or hard candy, four cigarettes, hard crackers, a few sheets of lavatory paper, and coffee or fruit juice concentrate.

The C-ration included a can of meat stew, hamburger, or spaghetti with sauce. The "10-in-1" ration held dehydrated or canned food in a large carton which fed ten men for a day. A less popular item was the D-ration, which was a protein enriched bar of bitter hard chocolate.

While air force units had satisfactory washing facilities, front line soldiers had to make do with their helmets as wash basins until they visited the shower tent. Here they could leave their soiled clothes

Previous page: *Men of Company 1 of the 129th Infantry Regiment (37th Division) with their 37-mm gun during the fighting for Manila, spring 1945. This was the only true street fighting of the Pacific campaign.*
▽ *G.I.s advance over the ruins of German pillboxes in the Brest area in September 1945.*

at one entrance and at the exit collect a clean uniform.

Medical care was excellent, for many doctors, nurses, and dentists had been drafted. Each company or equivalent unit had a medical aid man, or corpsman, trained in first aid. If a man was hit or trod on a mine, the corpsman would give emergency treatment and attach a tag to him, giving details of the wound. The casualty would be sent back to the battalion aid station, where a doctor was equipped to do limited emergency surgery. A motor ambulance would then move the casualty to a division collecting company, where more sophisticated emergency surgery would be performed, then to a "field" or "evacuation" hospital. More serious cases passed on further to the rear to a "station" hospital and in some cases by air or ship to the United States.

In some theatres, specialised medical

△ ◁ A Browning .50-inch
machine gun crew in Italy. On
the left is Pfc James E. Rhodes of
Hayesville, South Carolina, and
on the right Private Casimer W.
Bielic of Niagara Falls, New
York. The two men have coffee
and doughnuts provided by the
U.S. front line services.
  ◁ ◁ A bazooka team lurks in
wait for a German tank in the
Forêt d'Andaine in France.
  △ Men of Company K of the
398th Infantry Regiment (100th
Division) ready themselves for
action in the Rosteic area in
France.
  ◁ A Negro patrol probes into a
French village.

△ *American infantry move up through Caiazzo, north of the Volturno river, in Italy. This was yet another theatre where the huge American presence was felt.*

units were moved close to the front. At Cassino, where many men were wounded in the head by flying stones and mortar fragments, eye specialists and neurosurgeons were moved up to the front line. The prompt use of their skills could save the life or sight of a soldier who would not have survived if he had been sent back through the normal medical chain.

Out of all the U.S. Army and Army Air Force casualties who received medical treatment at battalion level or above, the mortality rate was 4.5 per cent. In World War I this rate had stood at 8.1 per cent. Most of the wounded men were returned to their units after treatment, some even after their second and third wounds.

Proper burial

For those men who were killed in action there was the assurance that their body would receive a proper burial. Each man's identity tags, "dog tags", worn round his neck listed his name, serial service number, religion, and next of kin. In the event of death he could be identified, and one tag left with the body. After his personal effects had been checked for damage or blood stains, they were sent with the identity tag to the next of kin. With a mattress cover as a shroud, the body was buried in a temporary cemetery, and after

the war it could be sent home to a permanent cemetery if the relatives so wished.

The combat infantryman was faced with the grim prospect of death or wounds as the only permanent break from fighting at the front. Though he might be rotated back to a rest camp, he did not have the 30 missions and the opportunity to return home which was the prerogative of air crew in the Army Air Forces.

In the end a scheme was introduced, but it was the exception rather than the rule that men could return to the United States, for they had to fulfill a number of strict requirements before they were considered.

In the Pacific a whole unit could be pulled out for a spell in a rest camp, but in Europe only small groups would be sent back to enjoy the simple but very welcome luxuries of beds with sheets, baths, films, and hot food served on plates. The camp would be located beyond the range of enemy artillery fire, but the soldier's stay was only about 48 hours. Some men, however, did get brief passes to the cities of Australia, to London, Paris, and Rome.

An efficient mail service made up a little for the enforced separation of the war. Officers and men enjoyed a free service for their outgoing letters. Those of the enlisted men were subject to censorship, but officers were relied on to observe security restrictions–though their letters were given a random spot-check within the postal service. The quickest way to send or receive letters was by the V-mail, a special form which was microfilmed and reconstituted at the receiving end. There was one letter however which was not welcome. "Dear John", which was the title of a popular song, became the name of the letter from the G.I.'s girl friend in the United States writing to say that she had found a new boy.

Increased age and maturity

In World War I America had raised a force of 5,000,000 men, composed very largely of young men. They tripled that figure in World War II and took men aged up to 45, thus raising the average age of the Army to 26.

One service policy which remained unchanged in both wars was the segregation of Negroes. Although they were employed largely in service units, there were also tank and tank destroyer battalions, chemical mortar and artillery battalions, a fighter-bomber group, and two infantry divisions, one of which fought in Italy and the other in the Pacific.

The training of these units in the United States caused some racial tension and outbursts, particularly when the camps were situated near small provincial towns in the southern states. An added complication was that Negro Military Police were usually unarmed. Dramatic and often biased accounts in the local press served to inflame further the Negro soldiers and white community.

With the exception of the fighter-bomber group and some individual battalions, the record of these combat units has become a matter of controversy.

However, if their performance was unsatisfactory, an experiment forced on the U.S. Army in Europe in the winter of 1944–45 proved that integrated fighting

▽ *The end of the long road in the European theatre: American soldiers greet their Russian counterparts on a shattered bridge over the Elbe on April 28, 1945.*

units were just as efficient as many all-white ones. Some 4,500 Negro volunteers, many taking reductions from ranks as high as master sergeant to private soldier, fought in the 6th Army Group as provisional companies attached to infantry regiments and in the 12th Army Group as extra platoons attached to companies. The service of these units, particularly the platoons, led to the post-war policy of integrated units.

Distinct national units

There were other racially separate units in the U.S. Army. One infantry battalion contained Norwegian-Americans who spoke little or no English. Japanese-Americans, after some confusion in the early years of the war, formed an effective combat team which fought in Italy, France, and Germany. The Philippine Scouts and other units of the Philippine Army fought under American command in both the regular and irregular war against the Japanese. At the beginning of the war, some National Guard divisions reflected their regional background, but

reinforcements and replacements soon blurred any distinction between Regular, National Guard, and selective service, or draftee, divisions.

The United States Army Air Forces

In the first War Powers Act of 1941, the United States Army Air Forces became autonomous in all but name. Between 1939 and 1945 they expanded enormously: in July 1939 there were only 3,991 Air Corps personnel abroad, at the end of the war the total strength of the U.S.A.A.F. stood at 2,253,000 men and women.

Though effectively a separate organisation, this did not prevent the G.I. from envying his brother in the air. There were simple things, like the way they were permitted to shape and batter their issue caps, and the more profound suspicion that the air force had an easier war. Their pay was good, the food and living quarters at their bases seemed luxurious to the front line soldier and the promotion policy was more liberal.

Undoubtedly the Army Air Forces enjoyed all these privileges, but theirs was no easy war. The bomber and fighter crews needed a special sort of courage to take their aircraft deep into enemy territory. In early operations over Germany, before the advent of long range escort fighters, B-17 Flying Fortresses suffered heavily from German *Flak* and fighter attacks. In the Schweinfurt raid, 60 bombers out of a force of 291 failed to return, but the next day the remaining aircraft were readied, the formations adjusted, and the crews briefed in preparation for their next mission. In May 1944 one bomber would be lost for every 13 damaged by *Flak* in operations by the 8th Army Air Force.

Non-combat deaths

Sometimes the violent death caused by *Flak* or fighters was preferable to ditching at sea. In the later months of the war German civilians attacked crewmen who had parachuted from their burning aircraft. Of the eight men captured by the Japanese in the Doolittle Raid on April 18, 1942, three were executed and one died

▽ *Cheerful faces around one of the most dangerous positions in the Boeing B-17 Flying Fortress – the ventral ball turret. In the turret is Technical Sergeant Robert Myllyskoski of Painsville, Chicago, and on the right is Staff Sergeant H. Jessup of Union City, Indiana.*

of malnutrition, and others were to die for daring to trespass in "Imperial airspace".

The ground crews too were sometimes at the wrong end of air raids. In Europe the severely-stretched Luftwaffe still managed to mount attacks on advanced air strips. At Pearl Harbor, sailors, soldiers, and airmen were all victims of the Japanese air assault.

In the fighting in the Bataan Peninsula in January 1942, a handful of obsolescent Curtiss P-40's fought an unequal battle with faster Japanese Zeros and Betties. Though the aircraft had fuel, the pilots and ground crews were suffering from intense fatigue and malnutrition, but despite this they kept the P-40's flying. In the end, the Japanese overran the extemporised landing grounds, and the remaining personnel were caught in savage close-quarter fighting.

Enemy action was not the only cause of casualties. Aircrew died when their oxygen failed, or suffered frost-bite in the grim high altitude raids over Germany. Crash-landings by damaged aircraft could be as dangerous to the crash crew as they fought the fire as to the escaping air crew or pilot. More dangerous still was the crash on take-off by a loaded bomber.

Though it was the man on the ground who guaranteed the ultimate victory, the Army Air Forces were responsible for

△ *Loading the rear turret of a B-26 Marauder. From left to right the men are Technical Sergeant Robert P. Morris of Wheeling, West Virginia, Staff Sergeant Francis C. Barabe of Detroit, Michigan, and Staff Sergeant John T. McQueeney of Washington, D.C.*

▷ *Ground crew prepare a B-26 for a sortie from England. On the left, Lieutenant Glenn Abbot of Akron, Ohio, checks the bomb-load, with the help of Staff Sergeant Gustav J. Sylvan of Columbia, South Carolina.*

▽ *Thunderbolt pilots pose on the wing of one of their aircraft. These were the men, with the Mustang pilots, who defended the American daylight bomber fleets.*

◁ *Before a 9th Air Force sortie: from left to right the men are Major Robert Keller of Lititz, Pennsylvania, Captain Samuel Monk of Memphis, Tennessee, Lieutenant Thomas James of Ashville, North Carolina, Lieutenant George Hines of Knoxville, Tennessee, and Captain George Kunde of Milwaukee, Wisconsin.*

some war-winning blows. The most obvious examples are the two atomic bomb attacks on Hiroshima and Nagasaki. However, post-war evaluation of the B-29 Blitz shows that the atomic bombs were the final blow in a campaign that was already forcing Japan towards annihilation or surrender. Even the vanguard of the massive Tokyo fire raids, the comparatively modest Doolittle Raid, prompted the Japanese fleet to sail to their defeat at Midway.

In Europe the U.S.A.A.F. made two major raids on the Rumanian oil fields at Ploiești, and their later attacks on the German synthetic oil plants led to the slow immobilisation of the enemy mechanised forces.

Fighters and fighter-bombers perfected ground attack operations which made enemy movement in daylight almost impossible. And Lockheed P-38 Lightnings were responsible for the death of Admiral Yamamoto, the Japanese naval leader who had planned the Pearl Harbor attack.

It was a plodding, unglamorous, but no less courageous job that fell to the transport pilots who flew "over the Hump" to China. Their comrades in Europe earned lasting respect and admiration from ground forces for their delivery of arms and supplies, notably at Bastogne.

Throughout the war, in many lands, the G.I. remained unmistakable. Like any army, his contained a few men who committed grave crimes. They looted, turned away from the enemy, raped, or murdered. But in Europe these men represented only one half of one per cent of all the U.S. forces employed in that theatre. No army is guiltless in any war, but the U.S. Army had one of the best records in World War II.

In this war the G.I. was typified less by the impetuous "Lafayette here we come!" attitude than his father's generation in World War I. Major-General Carl Spaatz spoke for most U.S. servicemen on June 18, 1942, when at Bushy Park in England he said: "We won't do much talking until we've done more fighting. We hope that when we leave you'll be glad we came. Thank you."

In the light of subsequent events, Western Europe and the countries of the Far East have much to thank America for.

▽ *Apparently unruffled, members of the crew of a heavily-damaged Marauder pose in their aircraft. From left to right they are Lieutenant Tom Trainer (navigator) of Haverill, Massachusetts, Lieutenant Jim Davis (pilot) of Elligay, Georgia, Staff Sergeant Ritcher King (gunner) of Dallas, Texas, Staff Sergeant Joseph G. White (radio operator) of Eureka, and Staff Sergeant George Lemberger (gunner) of Ashkos.*

△ *The man who coined the term "cold war"–American politician Bernard Baruch, photographed at a session of the U.N. Atomic Energy Committee in 1946. Previous page: The U.S. air base at Thule in Greenland, carved out of the perpetual ice. The U.S. needed such bases to put their bombers within range of the Soviet Union via the "over the Pole" route.*

The cold war was a war that never was. There was no declaration of war, no employment of troops in vast and bloody attacks on defended trenches, no Blitzkrieg, and no armistice or formal surrender. Equally there was no treaty of peace. The term was invented by the American politician, Bernard Baruch, to describe the very great deterioration of relations between the Soviet Union and the United States and their allies and associates after the grand alliance of the Soviet Union, the United States, and Great Britain in the war against Nazi Germany. Since it had no formal beginning and no formal end, historians are likely to argue about when it began, what it was about and when or whether it ended, for as long as relations between the Soviet Union and the non-Soviet world are based on the ideological differences that divide them.

There is one very powerful group of writers who argue that the cold war began with the Russian revolution of November 1917 and the intervention of Britain, France, the United States, Canada, and Japan in the Russian civil war that followed. This group is in turn divided. One section argues that the cold war began with the intervention by these five

powers into the Russian civil war, and that without this, the cold war would never have happened. The other replies that the leaders of the November revolution in Russia expected it to spread immediately through Europe, and that this expectation itself amounted to a declaration of "cold war". They continue to say that the failure of the revolution to spread created a situation which, according to Soviet doctrine, could not be other than warlike, since, between the states that practised capitalism and the Soviet Union, relations could not be other than hostile, it being the declared aim of Soviet political philosophy to destroy the capitalist system. In Soviet doctrine the capitalist world was certain to perish from its own internal contradictions. It was always possible, however, that capitalist political leaders might seek to avoid the internecine conflict in which their system was bound to end by seeking unity in an attack on the one state which embodied the socialist ideal. If that happened, socialism could destroy capitalism; but in the more pessimistic of doctrines derived by the Bolshevik leader, Lenin, from Karl Marx's writings, it was also possible that both systems might perish in mutual destruction. In the view of this group of writers, the Soviet leadership thought war to be the normal abiding state of relations between the Soviet Union and capitalist states. Thinking this, they conducted relations with the capitalist states on a basis of hostility which negated any attempts by individual capitalist states to put their relations with the Soviet Union on any other basis.

The difficulty which has led many historians to avoid applying the term "cold war" to the whole of the history of Soviet relations with the principal capitalist states is that a historical term which is so all-embracing becomes virtually meaningless. The majority of historians in the countries of Europe and the United States uses the term to cover relations between the Soviet Union and the states bordering on the North Atlantic from the end of the fighting in Europe in 1945 to some date in the 1950-1972 period. Some see its ending in the process of American-Soviet détente which began after the Cuban missile crisis of 1962. Some see its ending in the series of treaties concluded by the West German Government with Russia, Poland, and East Germany in 1971-72, and in the Soviet-American understanding which accompanied the

American military withdrawal from Vietnam. Others put its ending earlier.

The real point to decide is what issue was at stake in the cold war. It was basically concerned with the question of the control of central Europe, and that this issue was settled to all intents and purposes by the meeting of President Eisenhower, Sir Anthony Eden, and the Soviet leaders at the Geneva Summit Conference in 1955, at which both sides came to accept the partition of Germany into two states, one in alliance with the states of western Europe and of North America, and one in alliance with the Soviet Union and its associates. Soviet policy thereafter, with its attempt to exploit the Middle Eastern situation in 1955-56 and its opening of the question of West Berlin in November 1958, entered a quite different phase. If one is to use the term "cold war" to describe this one must distinguish between the first and the second "cold war".

If Germany was the main battlefield of the "cold war" it was not of course the only one. The civil wars in Greece in 1944-45 and 1946-48 were clearly part of the same process. The wars which began in 1946 in Indo-China and in 1950 in Korea,

though not lacking in effect on the cold war, were coincidental in time to it and not part of the same process any more than were the fighting in Palestine in the years 1947-49, in Malaya from 1949-59, the Hungarian rising of 1956, or the covert American intervention in Guatemala in 1954. The Indo-Chinese war lay between a Communist-dominated nationalist movement and its French colonial overlords and is different from the fighting in 1947-49 in Indonesia between the Indonesian nationalists and their Dutch overlords only in that the Indonesian nationalists defeated the attempts by the Indonesian Communist party to take over and dominate the Indonesian nationalist movement, while the Indo-Chinese Communist party had largely taken command of the Indo-Chinese nationalist movement before the Japanese surrender made the return of the French possible. The consequent difference, that the United States played a large part in forcing the Dutch withdrawal from Indonesia, while agreeing after 1950 to finance and support the French, is thus understandable.

As for Korea, it seems now much more likely that the sudden attack launched by North Korean troops across the 38th

One aspect of the cold war was the formation of two military "camps" in Europe – the Warsaw Pact countries in the East and the N.A.T.O. alliance in the West, dominated by the Soviet Union and the U.S.A. respectively.

△ *Foreign ministers of some of the N.A.T.O. countries take a break during a meeting in late 1952. From left to right: Secretary of State Dean Acheson, French Foreign Minister Robert Schuman, Bjorn Ole Kraft of Denmark, and the British Foreign Secretary, Anthony Eden.*

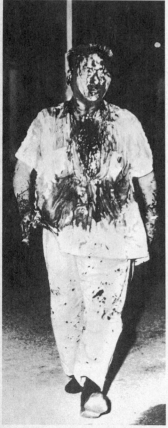

parallel against the South Korean state was not inspired by the Russians but was done to force their hand. The subsequent involvement of the Communist Chinese was a direct consequence of the decision by the American commander-in-chief of the United Nations forces not to stop after he had destroyed the bulk of the North Korean armies and driven them back across the 38th parallel, but to continue, to occupy North Korea and to unify the north and south of the country by force. If successful this would have established a state, in alliance with and dependent upon the United States, with a common frontier with China on the Yalu river. The Chinese Communist leadership, only having established their victory over the American-aided Chinese Nationalist government and forces the previous year, when the remains of the Nationalist forces withdrew to Formosa from the mainland, chose to regard this as a direct threat to the security of their new state. Their intervention prolonged the fighting for nearly four years, restored the north Korean state to its previous boundaries, and eventually resulted in the Panmunjon armistice. But it was not a direct part of the cold war between the Soviet Union,

the United States, and their allies and associates. The cold war was a European war. Korea was an American-Chinese conflict. It belongs to a quite separate set of developments which date back to the opening of Japan, the scramble of the European powers for spheres of influence in the decaying Chinese empire and the American proclamation of the Open Door which if accepted by the other powers would have put the United States on an equal if not superior footing in the scramble.

The cold war then was about the control of central Europe in general and Germany in particular. It developed quite logically out of the German attack on the Soviet Union in July 1941 and the British and American decision to treat the Soviet Union as an ally against Hitler. That decision doomed Hitler and made his defeat merely a question of time. It is possible that the Soviet Union could have defeated Nazi Germany and her allies even without British and American aid— possible but not certain. What that aid gave the Soviet Union was the food, the fuel, the raw materials, and the transportation which enabled that part of Soviet heavy industry which survived the two great German offensives of 1941-42 to concentrate on the provision of the tanks, guns, aircraft, and munitions which made the Soviet defeat of these offensives and the great counter-offensive of 1943-45 possible. Without that aid it is conceivable, no more, that a Soviet-German armistice and compromise peace might have been arranged. There certainly were clandestine Soviet-German conversations in the early part of 1943 in Stockholm, though we know very little about them beyond the fact of their occurrence.

The decision to aid Soviet Russia made the Nazi defeat inevitable. That in turn raised the question of the future of central Europe. Hitler's attack on Russia had ended a period in which Russia had advanced her frontiers westwards by annexing, with German agreement, the whole eastern section of the pre-war Polish state. In 1940 Russia had similarly occupied and annexed from Rumania the province of Bessarabia. When Hitler's forces invaded Russia, the Rumanian and Hungarian armies fought alongside them. Russia could be expected therefore to be concerned about the nature of the post-war régimes in these countries. She was equally concerned to secure from Britain

recognition of her annexation in 1939-40 of the eastern section of the pre-1939 Polish state, of the three little Baltic republics of Estonia, Latvia, and Lithuania, and of Bessarabia.

The matter was greatly complicated by two circumstances. Britain had declared war on Germany in consequence of the German attack on Poland with whom Britain had, on August 26, 1939, signed an alliance. Although Hitler had defeated the Polish forces and overrun and occupied the territory of the Polish state, there were sizable Free Polish forces fighting on the British side, and there was a Polish government-in-exile, living in London and recognised by the British and, for that matter, the Americans, as the legitimate interim government of Poland.

The German attack on the Soviet Union, the British decision to support the Soviets and, still more, the signature of the Anglo-Soviet alliance in 1942, raised the question of relations between the free Polish government-in-exile and the Soviet Union. It was an awkward question in itself. So far as the free Poles were concerned the Soviet Union had illegally occupied the eastern part of their country, had carried off into imprisonment a very sizable part

The cold war was confined to Europe, while unrest in the Far East could be attributed to a variety of factors–the success of the Communists in China, the crumbling of colonial empires, the desire for self-determination. The Japanese had proved to the people of Asia that the ruling Europeans could be defeated. Was it possible to emulate them? The Malayan peninsula, scene of one of the British Army's greatest débâcles, was a case in point. The nationalist movement was well-grounded by 1945, when the British returned, and the move to self-government and independence was delayed only by the police action against Communist guerrillas operating in the interior.
◁ *and* ◁▽ *Scenes of violent rioting in Singapore.*
▽ *R.A.F. and R.A.A.F. Avro Lincoln bombers head out for a raid on terrorists hidden in the Malayan swamps.*

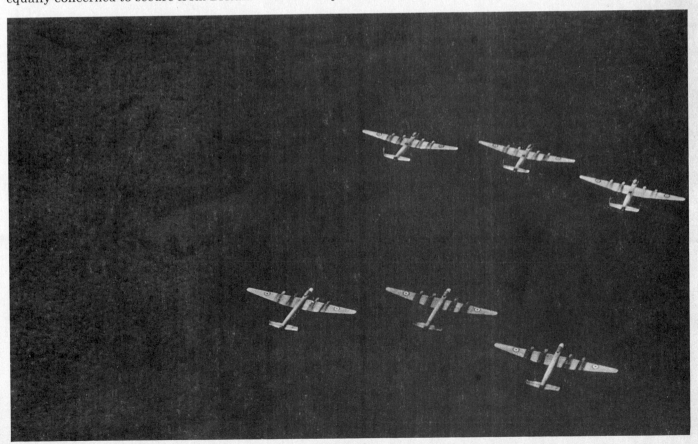

△ The result of a raid by Lincoln bombers of the R.A.F. and R.A.A.F.–a terrorist jungle camp bombed out of existence.
▷ A young Malay watches two patrols prepare to leave their base on a sweep through the jungle.

of the Polish armed forces and had stage-managed a plebiscite by which the inhabitants of these eastern areas appeared to have voted in overwhelming numbers for incorporation into the Soviet Union. The free Poles did not for a moment accept that procedure or its results as legitimate. Moreover in their view they were only an interim caretaker government. Until elections, held in a Poland free from foreign occupation, had produced a new representative government they felt, or said they felt, unable to make any far-reaching decisions about the future of any part of pre-war Poland.

There were, in the meantime, a number of practical issues on which Polish-Soviet talks could be held. Principally these concerned the whereabouts in Russia of the prisoners taken in 1939 and of their reorganisation into Polish fighting forces. Discussions were held, some though by no means all of the prisoners located, and progress made with the formation of Polish units on Russian soil. There was however far too little trust between the Polish ex-prisoners and their former Soviet captors for these units to be effective. It was decided therefore to evacuate all who wanted to go to non-Soviet territory

3115

△ The end of the line: a Tamil terrorist surrenders during an all-out police drive against insurgents in northern Malaya.

through Persia. Several thousands of former Polish citizens were evacuated and the able-bodied among them formed the Polish Corps which under General Anders played an important part in the fighting in Italy. There were, however, about 10,000 men, mainly officers, unaccounted for.

In April 1943 the German propaganda agencies announced the discovery of the bodies of over 2,000 of these officers in a series of mass graves in Belorussia near a place called Katyn. The victims had been tied together and shot. The Germans ascribed these deaths to Russian actions and produced a medical commission of the most distinguished forensic experts they could find in Europe, whose report on the corpses ascribed the date of the victims' deaths to a time when the area was under Soviet control. The Polish government-in-exile in London regarded this as confirmation of their worst fears and called for an investigation by the International Red Cross. The Soviet leadership, who had stigmatised the whole thing as a German propaganda trick, accused the London Poles of lending themselves to the purposes of Dr. Goebbels and promptly broke off relations with

them. They produced in their stead a group of Polish Communists, the pliable survivors of those who had sought refuge in Russia in the inter-war years from the dictatorship of Marshal Pilsudski, on whom the Stalinist purges of the years 1935-39 had fallen with particular severity. This group of stooges and nobodies was originally established in the Polish town of Lublin and was known as the Lublin Committee. The Soviet authorities made it clear that, so far as they were concerned, the Lublin Committee was the only acceptable representative Polish body with whom they were prepared to deal.

This was the position then when the Big Three, President Roosevelt for the United States, Prime Minister Winston Churchill for Britain, and Stalin for the Soviet Union met in late 1943 in Teheran. Their formal agenda was mainly military, as the state of the British records shows. The political discussions that took place were only preliminary. But when the meeting took place it was clear that victory was merely a matter of time. Italy had already surrendered and British and American troops were already established on the European mainland, though a long slog lay ahead up the long and mountainous Italian peninsula. The Red Army had met and defeated the last major German offensive in the East at Kursk in July, and had begun its steady and relentless westward drive. It was still a time for co-operation; but the seeds of conflict were already there.

They were to lie mainly in the overriding Soviet concern for security on her western frontier which led the Russians to insist, as they had in Poland, on a take-over by communist-dominated régimes in the countries of eastern Europe as the Red Army "liberated" them. At the same time the Russians made no effort to help or actually suppress the military and political organisations that had existed on an "underground" basis. Thus no effort was made to help the risings of the Polish Home Army in Warsaw or the Slovak rising in 1944, and British and American attempts to aid them were thwarted. Leaders of the Polish underground in the Soviet-occupied areas were arrested and six of them flown to Moscow for a "show-trial" of the 1930's kind, obviously intended to discredit them entirely. In régimes such as that which switched sides in Rumania, the Russians insisted on the control of the ministry of justice and the ministry responsible for the police being in the hands of the local Communist party.

The Communist parties of eastern Europe had never been very strong in the inter-war years. They had borne the brunt of police repression during the 1920's and of local Fascism in the 1930's. Many of their bravest and ablest men had taken part in the Communist emigration and ended up fighting in Spain or in exile in Russia. There only the most pliant had survived. The only countries where a large-scale local party with an armed resistance movement existed were those that had fought against the Nazis in 1941, Greece and Yugoslavia. In each of these, Communist partisan forces had co-existed side by side with non-Communist guerrillas. Only the most tenuous contacts with Moscow had been possible, and the parties had followed their own course of action. In each country the main source of arms and aid was the British Special Operations Executive.

The lack of contact with Moscow can be seen in the very different course followed by the Communist resistance movements in Yugoslavia and Greece. In

The Communist resistance movement in Greece, though increasingly well-armed, had done little in the way of harassing the Germans. Instead, it concentrated its efforts on eliminating the non-Communist resistance groups and – after the arrival of British troops in late 1944 – guerrilla action against these latter.
▽ *During demonstrations in Athens, a member of E.L.A.S., the armed wing of the Communist movement, is arrested by a British soldier.*

GRUSST DER SEKTOR DER FREIHEIT
DIE KÄMPFER FÜR FREIHEIT UND RECHT DER WESTSEKTOREN!

YOU ARE LEAVING
THE AMERICAN SECTOR
ВЫ ВЫЕЗЖАЕТЕ ИЗ
АМЕРИКАНСКОЙ ЗОНЫ
VOUS SORTEZ
DU SECTEUR AMERICAIN

Following complete disagreement between the Soviet Union and the Western Powers over the administration of Berlin, the Soviet Union enforced a total blockage of road, rail, and water traffic between Berlin and the West. The Western Powers replied by organising the Berlin air lift, and for almost a year flew into the beleaguered western part of the city everything required to keep its residents alive, if not in luxury.
△ *With the road blocks due to be dismantled, banners are hoisted over the Russian-American sector boundary. This one reads "The Sector of Freedom Welcomes the Fighters for Freedom and Right of the Western Sectors".*
△▷ *The first buses leave Berlin for the Western Zone after the lifting of the Soviet blockade, on May 14, 1949.*
▷ *On the same day, the first road convoy of supplies from the Western Zone to reach Berlin receives an enthusiastic welcome.*

Yugoslavia the non-Communist underground, the Četniks, did little active fighting against the German occupying authorities, for fear of provoking reprisals against the civilian population. In the Italian-occupied areas some local commanders co-existed quite peaceably with the Italians or even co-operated with them against the Communists. The Communist underground, the Partisans, by contrast, fought actively against the Germans, pinning down considerable German forces by their efforts. In Greece the opposite was the case. The Greek Communist movement, E.A.M., and its armed wing, E.L.A.S., did very little active fighting against the Germans, save when the longest and most patient of British efforts succeeded in getting them to co-operate with non-Communist forces. The rest of the time they concentrated on eliminating the non-Communist guerrillas, until the only surviving organisation of any strength was in the Peloponnese, where E.A.M. never really succeeded in establishing itself. In October 1944 when British troops landed in Greece to take over from the retreating Germans, the E.A.M. forces rose against the British and attempted to seize power.

Much of this could be explained in terms of local initiative. But it did not look that way at the time, when taken with the Soviet behaviour over Poland. A pattern of ruthless suppression of all genuine democratic forces seemed to be emerging. Both in Britain and in America, a section of the governments' advisers began to warn against what seemed to them to be a Soviet imperialism and expansionism differing little in kind from that of Hitler. Their misgivings were overruled or passed unheeded at the time, since, in the minds of Roosevelt and of the British Cabinet, no post-war security system stood a chance without Soviet participation. On the Polish issue they concentrated on trying to persuade the Russians of the need to widen the Lublin Committee to take in leading non-Communist figures both from Poland itself and from the Polish emigration. At the Yalta Conference of February 1945, they succeeded. A similar agreement was negotiated with the Russians over the Partisan régime in Yugoslavia. Stalin made no protest against the suppression of the Greek Communist revolt. His main anxieties, often brutally and roughly voiced, were that the western powers would sign

▽ *Before the blockade was lifted: a new runway being built at Gatow airfield, in the British sector.*

◁ ◁ ◁ *The millionth bag of coal to be delivered by air is lowered by Sergeant Clyde Peterson of Fairfield, California, and Group Captain B. C. Yarde, the Gatow station commander.*

◁ ◁ *One of the first cars to arrive in Berlin after the lifting of the blockade.*

◁ *Unloading supplies from an R.A.F. Sunderland on the Havel river near Berlin. The skill of pilots landing and taking off in heavily built-up areas or—as in this case—using inland waterways, was a vital factor in keeping Berlin supplied during the blockade.*

For two years the bitter fighting in Korea swept back and forth across the country as first one side, then the other, gained the upper hand.
△ *American-equipped South Korean troops march* en route *to the battle zone.*

a separate armistice with the German forces in the west, which would enable a Nazi or nationalist government to survive in Germany and turn its forces exclusively against Russia.

The main issue at Yalta was, however, territorial. Since Russia insisted on retaining the territories she had taken from Poland in 1939, Poland would have to be compensated in the west. At Teheran it had more or less been agreed that this should be at Germany's expense. Now this was settled and it was agreed that eastern Germany up to the rivers Oder and Neisse should be taken over by Poland. Königsberg was to become Russian, Danzig Polish. But this in turn had consequences. If post-war Germany was not to become inspired by the idea of recovering these territories, then she would have to have a government that the Soviet Union could rely on. For Russia this meant a Communist or fellow-travelling government. The issue of the control of Germany was raised inevitably.

Up to that point, although the Russians, alone among the belligerents, had fostered a free German movement, the Russian representatives had been committed to the idea of splitting Germany into a num-

ber of small, weak states. Only Britain had resisted this, convinced that this would not only sow the seeds of a new war, but that it would saddle Britain with the cost of supporting the economy of whatever part of Germany she occupied and make her own post-war economic recovery as well as that of Europe itself virtually impossible. After Yalta the Soviet Union sharply reversed its position. At the same time it began preparing small teams of German Communists to enter Germany behind the Red Army and set up 'anti-Fascist' committees which would serve as the centres of new German political activities under Soviet control.

It was at this point that Roosevelt died and was succeeded by Harry Truman. Roosevelt had been prepared to make very far reaching concessions to get the Soviet Union to join the United Nations and to provide a secure basis for post-war peace. Truman, as it turned out, was less inclined to make this his overriding priority and more concerned that the United States should receive their due share of respect and attention and that the post-war settlement should be based on justice and a true balance of power. Soviet action in forcing a Communist puppet government on Rumania in February 1945, and in making it virtually impossible for any western representation to move freely in Hungary or Bulgaria, struck him as being inspired by unfriendly sentiments towards America. He felt, as he said, that American "agreements with the Soviet Union so far had been a one-way street". He was "fed up", he said, "with babying the Soviets". In practice, however, there was little he could do: and as seen from London, the intense American pressure for demobilisation and an end to all wartime aid to Europe, Lend-Lease, etc., seemed to be leaving the Soviets an entirely free hand in Europe. On the ground Soviet obstruction was holding up western occupation of the zones agreed on at Yalta, in Berlin, and in Vienna. And at Potsdam the Americans in essence accepted the division of Germany into two by accepting that trade between the Soviet and non-Soviet zones should be regulated by agreement rather than be free, and accepted that the Soviets should have an entirely free hand in their own occupation zone. American conciliation of the Soviet Union was to continue until early in 1946. The Soviet satellite governments in Rumania and Hungary and Bulgaria were

recognised: and the level of economic activity in Germany was fixed at a level so low that British money continued to be necessary to keep the population of north-west Germany alive.

The turning point came in America over the winter of 1945-46. Congressional opinion was outraged by Soviet pressure on Turkey, for joint control of the Dardanelles, by the attempt to set up pro-Communist separatist states in the Soviet occupied zone in northern Persia, and by the Soviet sponsorship of a new Greek Communist rising in March 1946. Moreover, the Republican party saw a chance of making heavy inroads in the urban areas of the American midwest, with their Polish and other east European minority groups, if they attacked the American government for making concessions to the Soviets over these countries. They succeeded in causing the Truman administration to issue a number of severe moral condemnations of Russian actions. But American unwillingness to do anything more was shown conclusively in March 1946 when Winston Churchill, speaking at Fulton, Missouri, declared that the Soviet Union had divided Europe by an "iron curtain", created police states

▽ *Primitive but practical, given the terrain: a South Korean cavalry unit on the road.*

and suppressed liberty behind it, and was seeking to spread her system wherever she could. He called for a "fraternal association" of the English-speaking peoples", in close military relationship with each other, to stand up to Russia. Although he was disowned by the American government, jeered at on a drive through New York, and accused of trying to commit the United States "to the task of preserving the far flung British empire", to appease American opinion the American government adopted a much firmer, more moralistic stand. This secured some concessions from the Russians at the conference which met in Paris from April to June 1946 to draft treaties of peace with Italy, Rumania, Hungary, and Bulgaria. But American forces were still being run down in Europe. In Germany, however, the Americans ended reparation deliveries to the Soviet Union from their zone. The British followed suit and negotiations began for a fusion of the American and British zones into a single economic unit.

The change in the American position was much too slow for the realities of the power relationships in Europe. In the summer of 1946 the British had been forced to introduce bread rationing in Britain to provide any margin of food for their zone. The harvest failed in France. The winter of 1946-47 was one of the worst in recent history; the British economy came to a virtual halt. That of the Bizone broke down almost entirely. There was widespread starvation and malnutrition. The British were forced to finance the Bizone entirely. The cost of maintaining aid to Greece and Turkey, and occupation troops in Greece and northern Italy, in addition to military responsibilities the globe over, was bankrupting Britain. The British government had been driven to the reluctant conclusion in the summer of 1946 that the Soviet Union was deliberately trying to wreck the economy of Britain and western Europe so as to create conditions for the growth of Communism. In February 1947 therefore, determined to force America's hand, they informed the American government that Britain could no longer undertake the economic support of Greece and Turkey and would have to resign herself to see them go Communist unless America would intervene.

The message arrived at an auspicious moment. President Truman's relations with his Secretary of State, James Byrnes,

◄▲ *American Boeing B-29 Superfortresses in flight over Korea. These planes were still the mainstay of the U.N.'s bomber force during the Korean War.*

◄ *U.S. and South Korean captured troops being marched off the P.O.W. camp by their captors—either Chinese or North Korean.*

▲ *The Soviet Union's hierarchy on display at the funeral of Deputy Premier Andrei Zhdanov, one of the Communist Party's leading ideologists. Nearest the camera is Stalin, then Marshal Voroshilov (partly hidden), V. M. Molotov, the Foreign Minister; Georgi M. Malenkov, who succeeded Stalin as head of the Soviet government; Lazar Kaganovich, and Andreev.*

The death of Stalin, who had ruled the Soviet Union for 20 years, brought great speculation in the West about his successor.

△ The contestants stand impassively by the great dictator's coffin. From left they are: Nikita Khrushchev, Laurenti Beria, Malenkov, Marshal Nikolai Bulganin, Voroshilov, and Kaganovich.

had deteriorated throughout 1946 and toward the end of the year he had replaced him by General Marshall, the war-time chief of the American Joint Chiefs-of-Staff, whose judgement and integrity were respected by everyone. The State Department's Russian experts had been combining to warn the President against either assuming that Russia was planning an all-out war or that the Soviet judgement of the fundamental differences between the Soviet system and that of the west could be reconciled. What was needed was a policy of quiet containment, not one of self-proclaimed "toughness". At the same time a joint State-War-Navy Committee had been concerned for the better part of the past year with the possibilities of bolstering the European economy.

Between February and July 1947, five significant developments marked the change in American foreign policy. The first was the enunciation of the so-called "Truman doctrine" in President Truman's message to Congress on March 12, 1947, which declared it to be "the policy of the United States to support free peoples who are resisting attempted subjugation by armed minorities or by outside pressures"

and appropriated $400 million for economic and military aid to Greece and Turkey, two specific commitments disguised behind an open-ended undertaking to engage on an ideological crusade. The second was the establishment of the State Department Policy Planning Staff in April 1947. The third was a speech by Marshall's assistant under-secretary, Dean Acheson, at Cleveland, Mississippi, promising "top priority for American reconstruction aid" to "free peoples who are seeking to preserve their independence and democratic institutions and human freedoms against totalitarian pressures, either internal or external".

The fourth was the presentation of George Kennan's thesis on "containment" which gave the Truman administration a philosophical defence for the policy it was embarking upon. (It was published under the pseudonym "X" in the American journal *Foreign Affairs* in July 1947.) The fifth was Mr. Secretary Marshall's famous speech at the Harvard University Graduation Day ceremonies on June 5, 1947, the origin of the Marshall Plan.

In this speech General Marshall offered American aid to all nations which would co-operate in the programme. The initia-

tive in determining their needs and co-ordinating them would have to be taken by the European nations. The speech was aimed at starting a process the nature of which, even the scale of which, had not been worked out in Washington. It was not couched in terms which would exclude the Soviet Union or its satellites. But it was not expected they would go along with it.

The British Government equally had spent much of 1946 wondering how the American government could be persuaded to unlock its funds to aid Europe's economic recovery. In the autumn of 1945 the British had negotiated a seemingly immense loan from the United States: the criticism the Labour Government had had to face while Congress was ratifying this loan determined its members never to repeat the experience. Much of the loan had had to be spent buying food and raw materials for the British and American zones in Germany. But the British had found it difficult to establish friendly relations with Byrnes or his underlings. The message abandoning Greece and Turkey was a desperate attempt to shock the Americans into awareness.

The British Foreign Secretary, Ernest Bevin, therefore had devoted much of his energies to cultivating the French. For the first 18 months of the occupation of Germany, French obsession with the dangers of a German revival of power and President de Gaulle's anti-American fixations had made France and the Soviet Union natural allies in preventing any recovery of the German economy or the establishment of any central German administration. In January 1947, however, after President de Gaulle's resignation in January 1946 had removed the doctrinal obstacles to a reorientation of French foreign policy, Britain's patient cultivation of France throughout the previous year paid off in the shape of an Anglo-French alliance, the Treaty of Dunkirk. At the Moscow Foreign Ministers' Conference in March 1947, the French were finally convinced that the Soviet Union was not to be counted upon as an ally to keep Germany weak, and came to abandon their independent position and lean towards Britain.

The way was open for Bevin to seize on the Marshall speech, and, in conjunction with Bidault, the French Foreign Minister, to summon a conference of the European states in Paris. Molotov, the Soviet

3127

In the mid-1950's Marshal Bulganin, as Chairman of the Council of Ministers, and Nikita Khrushchev, as First Secretary of the Communist Party's Central Committee, travelled extensively boosting Russia's image—and trade—in many countries.

△ *A new era of good relations with Yugoslavia is opened as they are greeted at the airport in Belgrade by President Tito.*

foreign minister, attended the conference with 80 advisers, a sign that at first the Russians took the idea of participation seriously. During the meeting, however, he was instructed by Stalin to break off all participation. The British and French went ahead with a second conference a month later in Paris. Very heavy Soviet pressure had to be exerted on Czechoslovakia and Poland not to accept the invitation. As by September those nations which did attend agreed on a joint statement of their needs and the machinery to handle it, the effects of the Marshall speech were to confirm and institutionalise the division of Europe. France's agreement to merge her occupation zone in Germany with those of Britain and America translated that division into German terms.

In the winter of 1946 Soviet policy in Germany had received a serious set-back. Up to that point the Soviets had hoped to secure power by the formation of a "front organisation", the Socialist Unity Party (S.E.D.), which in their zone was composed of a fusion of the Communist party and sections of the Social Democratic, Christian Democratic, and German Liberal parties which had been allowed to restart operations in Germany in the winter of

1945-46. In October 1946, however, local government elections were held throughout the Soviet zone in Germany and in Berlin. Despite the most far-reaching assistance from the Russian occupation authorities, the S.E.D. was resoundingly defeated in Berlin, where the Social Democratic party had repudiated any links with the S.E.D. The experience made it clear to the Russians that there was no hope of the S.E.D. winning power in Germany by free elections.

Instead they determined to make an increased bid for the support of German nationalist sentiment. In March 1947 at the Moscow conference of Foreign Ministers, and again in London in November, Molotov called for an independent German government to be set up by agreement between the German political parties and alleged that west Germany was being reduced by Britain and America to the status of a colony. A People's Congress was assembled in eastern Berlin in December and prominent representatives from west Germany of the idea of a new German-Soviet agreement as the price of reunification were given their head. The Soviet appeal for a revival of German nationalism was, however, rather marred by a demand for £10,000 million in reparations.

At the same time the Soviet leadership began to tighten its hold on the satellite countries. In Poland, Rumania, and Hungary, police persecution and all kinds of other pressures were turned on the surviving non-Communist parties to force them to merge with the Communists in "united front" parties controlled by the Communists. Individual political leaders who proved recalcitrant were arrested on trumped-up charges. From Hungary, which at least had a common border with Austria, refugees flooded across into the British-occupied zone of Austria by tens of thousands throughout the summer of 1947. The Rumanians were less happily placed. And from Poland only a few of those whom the Russians had been forced to accept in 1945, including the Peasant Party leader, Mikolaczyk, managed to escape. In February 1948, the Russians staged a *coup d'état* in Czechoslovakia, the one country that they had had most trouble with over the Marshall plan. President Benes was forced, under threat of civil war, to accept a government dominated by Russian nominees. The Foreign Minister, Jan Masaryk, was found dead in suspicious circumstances. And a number of Czechs were added to those from Hungary in the

△ *Leaving the Geneva Summit Conference in July 1955; Khrushchev, Bulganin, and Marshal Zhukov, the Defence Minister.*

D.P. camps in the British and American zones in Austria and Western Germany.

The Prague coup seemed so exactly like Hitler's annexation of Austria or his occupation of Prague in March 1939 that western Europe was galvanised with activity. Mr. Bevin had been turning over plans for creating some kind of institutionalised community of western Europe since the previous summer at the very least. On January 22, 1948, speaking in the House of Commons, he had described Soviet policy as attempting to unsettle "and intimidate west Europe by political upsets, economic chaos and even revolutionary methods". In March 1948 he persuaded France and the three Benelux countries to sign a treaty establishing a western European Union, a permanent military alliance with a standing council of Foreign Ministers. The first item on the council's agenda was the setting in motion in western Germany of discussions on the drafting of a Federal constitution and the eventual establishment of a west German government.

This challenge to Soviet plans for Germany was a turning of Soviet methods against their originators. A logical corollary to this was a drastic reform of the German currency, since without this the economy in west Germany would remain dominated by barter and the black market. The admission of the "trizone" (the three western zones of occupation now shared a common administration in economic affairs) to the Marshall plan in February 1948 made this even more essential. The Soviet Union was confronted with the possibility of a west German state, strong economically and welded into western Europe, in a way which would not only put the establishment of Soviet control over it beyond all possibility but was certain to exercise a strong emotional pull on the Soviet-occupied zone.

The Soviet reply was a series of graduated measures of pressure on the western powers' occupation of Berlin. On March 20, 1948, the Soviet members walked out of the Control Commission. Road, rail, and air links with Berlin were harassed. On June 16 the Soviet representatives walked out of the Allied *Kommandatura* in Berlin. Between June 19 and July 10, 1948, they suspended all road, rail, and water communications between Berlin and western Germany.

Thus began the blockade of Berlin, a thoroughly alarming period for all con-

cerned. The Soviet Union had an almost overwhelming military superiority on land in Europe. Soviet troops only had to move westward to sweep away almost overnight the small and pathetically unprepared western occupation forces in Germany and Austria. Only one military restraint on them existed – the American possession of the atomic bomb.

The blockade was to last until May 1949. It was broken by the air lift, a massive use of air transport, heavily subsidised, to bring food, coal, raw materials, etc., into Berlin, and to bring Berlin's exports out again. Its effect was to turn the western European Union from a purely European security organisation, designed to control the new west German State and to allay the fears of those western Europeans who had only four years earlier been liberated

from German occupation, into an anti-Soviet security system under American leadership. In September 1948 the British postponed demobilisation of those conscripts whose term of service was up and secured the stationing in Britain of American aircraft, armed with atomic bombs, to be used against any Soviet aggression in Europe. In December 1948 the American government eventually committed itself to the idea of a North Atlantic alliance. The Treaty establishing N.A.T.O. was signed in April 1949.

In the meantime the Soviet Union had suffered three other serious defeats. At the beginning of October 1947 as the Marshall Plan was being organised by the west European governments, a Russian-organised conference, meeting in Warsaw, attended by delegates not only from Soviet

open. Yugoslavia was formally expelled from the Cominform, and the "Tito clique", which had isolated and arrested the Soviet cats'-paws in its midst, denounced as imperialist agents. The Yugoslav defection was followed by the collapse of the Greek Communist guerrillas, deprived of their bases in the Yugoslav mountains. The experience led Stalin to carry out a series of purges of the Communist leadership of eastern Europe, Rajk in Hungary, Gomulka in Poland, Kostov in Bulgaria, Xoxe in Albania and, lastly and most extensively, Slansky and his allies in Czechoslovakia. Only those Communist leaders, whose presence in Russia during the war years guaranteed their loyalty, were immune to this latest of the Stalinist purges.

East Germany

The formation of N.A.T.O. and the setting up of the West German Federal Republic in 1949 was answered by the establishment of an East German state, for which the Soviets had already, in 1948, begun recruiting a paramilitary armed and regimented police of 50,000 men with armoured cars and light artillery. At that point the most stringent prohibition on the establishment of any West German armed forces had been accepted by the West German Government despite the advice of the N.A.T.O. military staffs that without a sizable German military contribution western Europe could hardly be defended. In the summer of 1950 when the new Federal Chancellor, Dr. Adenauer, approached the Allied High Commissioners for permission to raise a Federal West German police force to match the armed *Volkspolizei* of the east, despite British support neither the French nor the American Governments would hear of the matter, even after the outbreak of the Korean War in July 1950.

By September, however, the American government had changed its mind. Its decision to press its N.A.T.O. allies to allow the raising of a 12-division West German army was unveiled at a special N.A.T.O. meeting in New York. The French replied by proposing that this new German army should only be allowed within the framework of a European army, the German forces being integrated at a unit level so small that no separate German army could ever come into existence. This pro-

Communist parties and those of the Russian satellites, but also from the French and Italian Communist parties, had set up the Communist Information Bureau, which had immediately called for the defeat of the Marshall Plan, "a European branch of the general world plan of expansion being realised by the United States", a declaration of political warfare against the west. An all-out campaign of general strikes and demonstrations was launched in France and Italy. It failed. A major effort was made to win the 1948 elections in Italy. Again the effort failed.

The third, and worst, failure came in the summer of 1948 when long-standing differences between the Soviet Union and Yugoslavia, stemming from Soviet efforts to establish full control over the Yugoslav Communist leadership, broke into the

△ *"K & B", as they became known to the Western press, arrive at Victoria Station at the start of an official visit to Britain in 1956. They are being greeted by Sir Anthony Eden, the Prime Minister.*

The Hungarian Rising of October-November 1956 underlined the reality of a divided Europe caught in the Cold War between the Soviet Union and the United States. Despite desperate pleas for help, the Western Powers could – or would – do nothing to help the Hungarians apart from making formal protests at the U.N. The Russians were thus able to put down the revolt, which threatened their security, unhindered.

△ Baross Strasser, scene of bitter fighting, on October 31 after the withdrawal of Russian troops from Budapest.

posal was so novel, so controversial, and so antipathetic to the British that it took from 1950 to 1952 to negotiate, the European Defence Community treaty being signed in Paris only in May of that year.

During the long debate on the setting up of the E.D.C., the Soviet Union had remained comparatively inactive on the European front. Her main attention was taken up with monitoring the Korean War and her main propaganda effort put into organising the Stockholm peace petition, a massive and fortunately quite unsuccessful attempt to arouse what was coming to be called "neutralist" opinion in Europe against the United States, where the initial stage of the Korean War had been followed in January 1951 by an enormous rearmament programme, the distribution of American strategic air command bases all round the Soviet borders and the establishment of a sizable military force and an integrated military command under General Eisenhower within N.A.T.O. The American hydrogen bomb programme had already been launched. The first test bomb was to be exploded in November 1952.

It was the prospect of West German rearmament and the E.D.C. actually

going through which stirred the Soviet Union into new diplomatic action in central Europe. In March 1952, the Soviet leadership called for a Four Power Conference to negotiate a German peace treaty and a German unification. The Soviet position was a weak one. In September 1951 the United Nations had been persuaded into appointing an international commission of neutral states to investigate the possibility of holding free elections in both parts of Germany. It had been denied entry into the Soviet occupied zone. Soviet chances of a successful appeal to German nationalism had been greatly weakened by the conclusion of a treaty between East Germany and Poland recognising the Oder-Neisse line as the frontier, something it was to take 20 years to get West German opinion to accept.

The reply of the three western occupying powers opened a period of shadow boxing. The rules of the game were that it was about the rules by which Germany was to be reunified. Was it to be by free elections to an all-German parliament that an all-German government would emerge, as the western powers demanded? Or was it to be by the prior establishment of an all-German government drawn from

the governments of the two German states, as the Soviets insisted? The first would sweep away the S.E.D. and the East German Government. The second would provide chances for all kinds of shenanigans. The aim of the western allies was to achieve a position of reasonable military strength and then, and only then, negotiate. This aim was very much that of the Federal German chancellor, Dr. Adenauer.

The shadow-boxing lasted for two years, the Soviets concentrating on delaying the ratification of the E.D.C. treaties by the French parliament, and on attempting to disrupt support for them in Germany. The Soviets had a good deal of success with both these ploys.

The players changed

Four major events, however, changed the whole thrust and scale of the game. The first was Eisenhower's election to the U.S. Presidency in November 1952 and his appointment of John Foster Dulles as Secretary of State, whose crusading anti-Communism and hostility to containment as "cringing to the Soviets" led him into a policy of diplomacy by bombastic rhetoric; phrases such as "the liberation of the captive nations", "rolling back the enemy", "massive retaliation", and "not being scared to go to the brink" concealed a gradual realisation that the limits on American action observed by the Democratic administration were objective restraints, not subjective inhibitions.

The second was the death of Stalin and the absorption of the successors in a struggle for the leadership which was to last for the next four to five years. The new leadership was originally headed by Georgi Malenkov and Molotov, the Soviet Foreign Minister, but gradually they were ousted from power by Nikolai Bulganin and his successor, Nikita Khruschev. In the struggle for power the unconscious longing for a relaxation of the tensions of Stalin's police state, at least for the Soviet élite, was Khruschev's most potent weapon.

The third event was the development of a Soviet thermo-nuclear bomb in the first year of the Eisenhower régime. The fourth was the East German rising of June 1953 which revealed both the thinness of Soviet control over its satellites and the willingness to use force, armed force, to suppress dissidence. It showed also the total inability of the west, despite all Dulles's rhodomontades, to do anything to assist popular movements within the Soviet bloc. A "balance of terror" had been established which was to prove the most stabilising factor in the new situation. It was under these circumstances that the British Government under Winston Churchill began its great drive for an armistice if not a settlement in the "cold war", to be settled "at the summit", that is by a meeting of heads of government. France duly failed to ratify E.D.C. despite Dulles's threats of an "agonising reappraisal" of American policy leading to a withdrawal from Europe. The British drive began in May 1953. Its dominant idea was a central European security pact based on mutual guarantees.

The first stage, the four-power foreign ministers' conference which met in Berlin in February 1954, was largely devoted to reiterating past proposals. It was followed by the failure of the French Assembly to ratify the E.D.C. agreements. In its place the British revived the 1948 establishment of western European Union to include West Germany. Britain broke the practice of centuries and committed a large part of her armed forces to the continent as a guarantee against France finding herself

▽ *Matyas Rakosi, 1st Secretary of the Hungarian Workers' Party just before the 1956 uprising.*

△ Russian tanks roll through the streets of Budapest, crushing the last flickers of revolt.
△ ▷ A 15-year-old freedom fighter; her fate is unknown.
△ ▷ ▷ The huge head from Stalin's statue lies in the street, decorated with a traffic sign. The vast statue symbolised the oppressive presence of the hated Russians and was toppled by cheering crowds in the early days of the Rising.
▷ Hacking the statue to pieces – parts of it were taken away as souvenirs.

alone against Germany. This the French Assembly accepted, the Germans following suit in March 1955. West Germany joined N.A.T.O. The Soviets replied in May 1955 by setting up the Warsaw Pact.

In February 1955 Bulganin replaced Malenkov as Soviet premier and Khruschev, the Party secretary, became more and more prominent. At Geneva in April 1954, Britain and Russia had collaborated in negotiating an ending to the French war in Indo-China and a prevention of its escalation into a Sino-American confrontation. The experience heartened the British foreign minister, Anthony Eden, sufficiently to play on Eisenhower's desire, the year before he was due to retire or run again for re-election, to do something serious about peace. Bulganin and Khruschev co-operated, most noticeably by proclaiming their belief in co-existence and suddenly abandoning their ten-year-old opposition to a peace treaty with Austria. At the same time, the Soviet feud with Yugoslavia was brought to an end.

The Geneva summit conference duly met in July 1955. The Soviet position was by no means a flexible one. The British hope had been that some kind of alternative security could be found to that provided

for the Soviets by the presence of 20 of their divisions in East Germany. The Soviets made it clear that only the withdrawal of American forces from Europe and the dismantling of N.A.T.O. would lead them to accept the unification of Germany. Superficially these disagreements were patched over. But when the Foreign Ministers met in Geneva in October 1955, the same problems emerged again. Nothing was achieved save an acceptance of the existence of the two German states, each integrated into the military, economic, and political systems of the two blocs. This was to be confirmed a year later with West German participation in the setting up of the Common Market. The Soviet acceptance of this was symbolised in the Soviet recognition of the Federal German Government and the invitation to Dr. Adenauer to visit Moscow.

The cold war ends

With this tacit acceptance by each side of the division of Germany, the cold war properly considered had ended. The lines

drawn in central Europe by the tripartite agreements reached at Yalta and afterwards on the zonal boundaries between the areas of Germany and Austria to be occupied by each of the four occupying powers had hardened into a division of Europe into two power blocs. No serious possibility existed of intervention across those dividing lines, extended as they were up to the north cape by the addition of Denmark and Norway to N.A.T.O. in the north, and to the Dardanelles by the entry of Greece and Turkey into N.A.T.O. in the south. Even here the line followed that agreed between Churchill and Stalin in October 1944 as dividing British and Soviet spheres of influence with Yugoslavia, divided 50:50 between the two countries in 1944, occupying since 1948 a half-way position of neutrality between the two blocs.

In this the Geneva summit and the Foreign Ministers' conference of 1955 marked a recognition of the balance of power which had existed since 1945, a balance between Soviet contentional forces and the American nuclear deterrent. The addition of N.A.T.O.'s minimal forces and the Soviet deterrent to that balance did nothing really to disturb a situation in which for once only a madman could see any profit in a new war. The near miscalculation of the 1962 Cuban missile crisis, and Khruschev's long but in the end unsuccessful attempt to exploit the weaknesses and ambiguities of the western position in Berlin only underlined the stability of the balance. Its concomitant was the western acceptance of episodes such as the bloody suppression by the Soviets of the Hungarian rising in 1956 and the Czechoslovak "liberalising" régime of Mr. Dubcek in 1968. The cold war had become a cold stalemate, an armistice which no one was really interested in breaking.

Organisationsbuch der N.S.D.A.P.
The Nazi Party Handbook

It took the compilers of the Nazi Party Handbook 550 pages to expound the intricacies of Party organisation. From this, much of which is too technical to be of general interest, only the most significant passages have been translated. It is hoped that they will provide readers with an answer to the puzzle of how the Nazis persuaded the German people that the way to a Golden Age of Teutonic glory lay in the all-embracing folds of National Socialism.

The answer emerges only too clearly from the Handbook: there existed, from 1934, an incredibly complex Party organisation, one of whose aims was the inclusion of every Aryan German within its folds. This was achieved efficiently by means of a comprehensive Party hierarchy, at the bottom of which was the Block Leader, in charge of 40 to 60 households. He knew, or soon found out, all that went on in them.

This, however, is only one aspect; plausibility is another. Very often the long-winded sentences of ideological claptrap are deceptively, insidiously persuasive: there was to be a fellowship

of the people, and in this ability, rather than standing, was to be the criterion. In this system, therefore, the Block Leader was not a snooper but a confidant and aide. Anyone who took the Block Leader into his confidence did so at his own peril, however, for the information was passed through the hierarchy and could be used to ensure the loyalty of the original informant. The whole etiquette of precedence and prerogative implicit in the system of subordinates and superordinates effectively cancelled out any supposed feeling of fellowship even in the first years of the Nazi era.

There is in the Handbook all that a German could desire: a para-military organisation, uniforms, ranks, ceremonies, rallies, and parades–the trappings of power without its responsibilities.

It is hoped that the passages chosen will illustrate the frightening completeness with which every German was caught up in the Nazi net. In translating the text, every effort has been made to preserve the crude and often clumsy sentence construction of the German original. The translation and notes are by **Suzanne Flatauer.**

1936

Commemorative badges:
△ △ △ *The S.A. Rally of 1931 in Brunswick.*
△ △ *The Coburg Decoration.*
△ *The Party Day of 1929 in Nuremberg.*

1. The National Socialist's General Conduct

Every Party member must think of himself as a servant of the Movement and of his people, and act accordingly. That applies particularly to Political Leaders, to Leaders of all Sections of the Party, to Administrators and Wardens.

It is the most important task of every National Socialist to keep alive and continually strengthen the idea of national unity within Party and State.

It is incompatible with this task to keep oneself aloof from one's fellow Party members and citizens, to imagine oneself to be superior, and thus to open up a gulf, to bridge which has caused deep-felt anguish to the best of German men. When he accepts higher office, a National Socialist accepts higher duties. He holds absolute power only to enable him to carry out his higher duties. It does not entitle him to become overbearing, arrogant, and conceited. He will never win the confidence and the ready obedience of his Junior Leaders and men by threats, tyranny, and parade-ground language.

On duty he should be a leader and supporter, off duty he should act as good companion and helper to his Junior Leaders, fellow Party members, and fellow citizens. The more his deeds are in keeping with his words, the more readily his fellow Party members as well as his fellow citizens will follow him with a will.

In his behaviour, every National Socialist must remain as simple and as modest as was customary among National Socialists during the times of struggle. He should not want to appear to be greater than he really is, and just as he will reject any obsequiousness towards those above him, he should not allow obsequiousness towards himself. A leading Party member must not be vain and sensitive at any time; he is bound to prefer a well-tried fighter's true and candid speech to the honeyed words of creatures who fawn on him.

Always he is to keep in touch with the most humble of his fellow citizens, lending a willing ear to their troubles. They will be pleased to come to him if he has remained the same as ever, and if he still moves in the same society and circles as in the times of struggle.

Political Leaders, Administrators, and Wardens should not take part in banquets; they should not go after presents and after becoming freemen of cities; they should not patronise the most expensive restaurants; and they should always behave, on duty and off duty, in the manner expected of them as representatives of the German Freedom Movement and as collaborators in the unutterably hard task of building a better Germany.

Above all they should avoid excessive consumption of alcohol at a time when there are still many German families who lack the barest necessities of life and who are bound to lose their painfully regained faith while men belonging to the Movement – possibly by breaking licensing laws – are holding drinking parties, damaging by their behaviour in a state of intoxication the reputation of the Movement.

A true National Socialist does not boast of his actions and does not demand thanks. He finds his greatest reward in the knowledge of having performed his duty, in the success of his work, and in the confidence in him of his following.

A National Socialist is bound to act correctly if he examines himself daily, asking himself if he could justify his behaviour before his Führer.

2. The Party Member

(1) Admission

Every member of the German nation, of unblemished character and of German stock, not belonging to any Masonic Lodge (or any of its subsidiary organisations), and having completed his 18th year, may become a member of the N.S.D.A.P. (*National Sozialistische Deutsche Arbeiterpartei* = National Socialist German Workers' Party) on completion of the application form of the N.S.D.A.P. and on payment of the fixed admission fee. The Party management may, at any time, impose a bar on the admission of new members, or restrict admission to certain persons. Announcements in this connection will be issued by the National Treasurer of the N.S.D.A.P. only.

Rejection of an application for admission will be made, no reasons being stated, either by the respective Leader of the local branch or by the Base Leader, as the case may be, in agreement with the competent Party Tri-bunal. There is no legal redress against rejection.

Admission has officially taken place upon issue of a membership card or a membership book. Whoever becomes a National Socialist is not merely joining an organisation, but is turning into a soldier of the German Freedom Movement, and that implies far more than simply paying one's fees and attending Party meetings. In making this step, he takes upon himself the obligation of setting aside the self and of venturing everything he possesses, himself and his property, for his people. Only he who knows how to do this should become a National Socialist: the selection has to be made with this aim in mind.

Fighting spirit
   A spirit of Sacrifice
      Strength of Character
those are the qualifications of a true National Socialist. Minor blemishes (e.g. if someone should have committed a youthful offence) may be overlooked. Performance in the struggle for Germany is all-decisive. A healthy organism will spontaneously expel what is diseased, as long as the will to be healthy has been proved through suitable leadership and achievement. Thus the criteria for admission to the Party should be not bourgeois but soldierly standpoints, and the decisive factor for judging a man's character should be his bearing when he is face to face with the enemy. The Party must always remain the élite of the people. Therefore care has to be taken as to who is admitted as a Party member, and all philistines and "big shots" who are selfish and lacking in character are to be kept out or expelled.

In order to prevent unsuitable elements from slipping through, a fellow citizen may only be admitted into and carried on the register of the Party at his place of residence. Every application form has to pass through the hands of the local Block Leader. Should the prospective member apply to the Cell, the Base, the Local Branch, the District Board, or any other place rather than directly to his Block Leader, the application form must be returned as quickly as possible to the local Block Leader for evaluation. It is the duty of the Block Leader, who knows every person in his block, to initial this application form and to forward it to the Local Branch without delay. This procedure is applicable also to people proposed for admission

△ △ and △ *The 1923 and 1925 Gau decorations for Saxony, the Bavarian Ostmark, Halle-Merseburg, Hessen-Nassau, Magdeburg-Anhalt, Mecklenburg-Lübeck, and Schwabia (the 1923 decoration only for the last named).*

to the Party by the H.J. (*Hitler-Jugend* = Hitler Youth Organisation).

(2) The Pledge

When he is given his membership card, the member will be solemnly sworn in. All new Party members will have to undertake this Binding Oath, regardless of whether they belong to the S.A. or the S.S. The Binding Oath is administered by the Local Branch Leader or the Base Leader during the meeting of Party members. In the course of a brief address, he will outline the duties of the Party member and stress the significance of the oath of allegiance. Then he himself will speak the words of the oath of allegiance, sentence by sentence. In full view of the National flag, those to be sworn in will repeat the pledge, sentence by sentence, while raising their right arm in the German Salute. The text of the oath of allegiance is as follows:

"I pledge allegiance to my Führer Adolf Hitler. I promise at all times to show respect and obedience to him and to any leaders he may appoint for me."

The handing over of the membership book by the Local Group Leader will take place in solemn style during the meeting of Party members, accompanied by the words:

"In the name of the Führer I am handing over to you your membership book. Remain as loyal to the Party as you have been up to now!"

(3) Withdrawal

Membership lapses through death, through voluntary withdrawal, through individual expulsion, and through expulsion of whole Blocks, Cells, Bases, or Local Branches. Voluntary withdrawals, caused almost invariably by personal grievances or alleged slights, prove that the person concerned is no National Socialist. Such a loss does not render the Party any poorer; on the contrary, it can only gain by it. A true National Socialist will never withdraw voluntarily, because for him National Socialism has become his purpose in and his way of life. If the withdrawal takes place in order to forestall expulsion, the regular legal proceedings of the Party will nevertheless have to be carried out.

In connection with applications for expulsion, it will be necessary to exercise the utmost care and the highest sense of responsibility. Expulsion is the most severe punishment the Party has. Today it means loss of livelihood and loss of all personal standing to the person to whom it is meted out.

Members *will* be expelled

(a) if they commit dishonourable acts, or if the fact that they committed such acts in the past comes to light;

(b) if they act contrary to the aims of the N.S.D.A.P.; and

(c) if by their moral behaviour they give offence to the Party and to the general public and thereby harm the Party.

Members *may* be expelled

(a) if within a Local Branch, a County or an Administrative District they have repeatedly been the cause of bickering and quarrelling;

(b) if, in spite of reminders, they are three months in arrears with their membership fees, without having tendered an apology; and

(c) because of lack of interest.

Should there be mitigating circumstances, a warning may be decided upon in place of expulsion and, should the occasion arise, the loss of the right to occupy posts in the Party administration for the duration of up to three years.

Based on a legally valid decision of a Party Tribunal, the following persons are qualified to order expulsion:

(a) the Local Branch Leader

(b) the County Leader

(c) the Administrative District Leader

(d) the Führer.

In the first instance, the expulsion will be executed by the Leading Functionary to whose administrative area the Party Tribunal making the application belongs.

The Party Tribunals have only the right of application for expulsion. They must send this application to the accused and to the Leading Functionary responsible. Both have the right to lodge an appeal within a period of eight days. This appeal has the effect of deferring judgement. A Leading Functionary may execute an application for expulsion by the Party Tribunal only if the Party Tribunal informs him that the accused has not made use of his right to lodge an appeal. In urgent cases the expulsion may be carried out by the Leading Functionary in agreement with the Chairman of his Party Tribunal.

Objection against this procedure is allowed within eight days. However, this objection has no deferring effect. In every case where an objection is being lodged, Party legal proceedings will have to be carried out. If in the course of these proceedings the expulsion is confirmed, the accused must be informed by the Leading Functionary that the expulsion has become final. Final judgement in all matters concerning expulsion rests with the Führer. It is he who has authority, in agreement with the Supreme Party Tribunal, to order the expulsion of complete Local Branches. In that case, their assets go to the N.S.D.A.P.

(4) Re-admission

As a rule, for Party members who left after January 1, 1932, whether they left of their own accord or through expulsion, re-admission into the N.S.D.A.P. is out of the question. In principle, re-admission of an expelled Party member will only take place in agreement with the local Party Tribunal. Extensive leniency should be exercised with expelled persons as far as is compatible with the standing and the honour of the Party.

(5) Transfer

Every Party member must know that members of the N.S.D.A.P. are obliged to notify their local Political Office of all changes of address and of personal status, including temporary changes.

(6) Duties of a Party Member

A National Socialist's commandments:

The Führer is always right!

Never offend against discipline!

Never waste your time in idle gossip or in complacent criticism, but lend a hand and work!

Be proud, but not conceited!

Let the (Party) programme be your dogma; it demands your utmost commitment to the Movement!

You are a representative of the Party, let your behaviour and appearance be determined by it!

Let loyalty and selflessness be your highest precept!

Be a loyal comrade, you are then a true Socialist!

Treat your fellow citizens as you would be treated!

In battle, be tough and silent!

Courage is not the same as brutality!

What is useful to the Movement, and thus to Germany, i.e. your country, is right!

If you act according to these commandments, you will be a true fighter for your Führer.

(7) Rules of Conduct for Members of Local Branches

The following rules of conduct are to be made known to members of both sexes, to be thoroughly memorised:

Make the work of Political Leaders easier by discharging your duties promptly.

If you are a female Party member, take part in the work of the N.S. Women's Guild. There you will find tasks awaiting you.

Do not buy from Jews!

As a token of consideration for the health of speakers and Party Members, refrain from smoking at Party meetings.

Do not become the mouthpiece of political enemies by spreading false rumours.

To be a National Socialist means to set an example!

(8) The Wearing of Badges and Uniforms by Party Members

(1) When in civilian clothes, a Party member wears his Party badge.

(2) After two years' membership, a Party member is entitled to wear a brown shirt with his

civilian clothes.

(3) Party members are allowed to wear uniforms or parts of uniforms of Political Leaders, the S.A., the S.S., the N.S.K.K. (the transport corps), and the H.J., with or without badges, only when they belong to one of the above-named units and possess a pass to that effect.

Who is entitled to issue Assessments?

Unless requests are made by higher-ranking departments of the Party, political assessments and personal character references may only be issued by Leading Functionaries from the rank of District Leader upwards.

For official or semi-official purposes as well as for the purpose of planned distribution of labour such references are to be given as a matter of principle. In all other cases the giving of references is at the discretion of the Leading Functionary.

Passport Photographs

Members of the N.S.D.A.P. or members of their units and of associated formations are not allowed to use passport photographs showing the holder of a pass in party uniform including section badges.

Conversations with Foreigners

All Party members are forbidden to hold conversations about foreign affairs with foreigners. The authority to do so belongs solely to Führer appointees.

Correspondence with Foreign Countries

All correspondence with foreign groups of the N.S.D.A.P., their associated organisations, or with Political Leaders or Party Members must be conducted via the management of the German Foreign Institute, Berlin.

Private Correspondence

In connection with private correspondence, in particular with German nationals abroad, the use of official stamps, notepaper and envelopes of Party departmental offices is not permitted.

Qualities a Party Member holding a Leading Position is expected to possess:

His leading position will be acknowledged only if the Party member is outwardly and inwardly unblemished.

If he does not behave in an obsequious manner to his superiors, if he does not give himself airs with his subordinates, if at any time he has the courage to speak the absolute truth, if he is too much on the alert ever to be misled.

Further, leading Party members in the Movement should distinguish themselves by endeavouring

to distinguish soundly between right and wrong,

to practise self-control,

to prepare their plans thoughtfully,

to carry out their tasks thoroughly,

always to keep their pledged word,

never to promise anything they cannot keep,

to be straightforward,

to win the love and respect of others through their behaviour.

Leading Party Members in the Life of the Local Branch (or of the Base)

Political Leaders, Leaders of Units, Party members holding high office in the service of the State, and full-time Party workers who are not included in the Local Branches at their place of residence, but who belong to the Section *Gauleitung* or to the Local Branch *Braunes Haus* (Brown House), are to consider it their natural duty to take part in the life of the Local Branch at their place of residence. They are to attend the functions of their Local Branch and, unless they are employed in leading posts in the Party Organisation, they are, if possible, to serve actively in the Local Branch at their place of residence.

In this connection, it is a matter of course that Junior Leaders in the Party who have as their subordinates Party members occupying, for example, high-ranking Government posts, may give orders to them only in their capacity as Party members, and may not abuse the Party authority conferred upon them to exert any influence whatever on their State and other functions.

3. Aims

I

Through efficient distribution of activities, a leading Party member working in an honorary capacity should be enabled thoroughly and conscientiously to carry out his Party activities, including those in sections and associated organisations,

Important Party banners:
△ *The banner of the* Kreis *of Munich* . . .
△▷ . . . *and that of the* Ortsgruppe *of Altdorf.*

without having to neglect his Family and his Job.

Attempts should therefore be made to reduce as far as possible the fields of action of the individual so that the above principle may be taken into account.

II
The Party's Tasks are solely ideological

Attempts must therefore be made gradually to transfer all those technical tasks which during the upheaval of organising the Reich are still being carried out by the Party, to the associated organisations or, if expedient, to Government administration. If necessary or possible, orders should be issued by the individually responsible office of the National Executive.

The Party itself as instrument of ideological education has to become the leading corps of the German people. The leading corps is responsible for the complete penetration of the German people in the National Socialist spirit and for overcoming dependence on internationally orientated forces, which is still partially rooted in the people.

Furthermore, it will be the duty of this leading corps to see that the technical and specialist tasks which are being carried out in associated organisations as well as in Government administration are in fact accomplished in alignment with National Socialist thinking.

4. The Political Leader

The basis of Party organisation is the principle of leadership. The community cannot rule itself, either directly or indirectly. Whoever is best fitted for such a job should be a leader. Such a man will be supported by the confidence of the people. All Political Leaders are held to have been appointed by the Führer and are answerable to him; towards their subordinates they enjoy full authority. What matters in the selection of Political Leaders is to place the right man in the right post. The offices of the Party vary to such a degree that the accurate selection of leaders requires considerable knowledge of human nature as well as long experience. Age and social position are irrelevant, character and aptitude alone being decisive in the selection of leaders.

In principle, it has to be observed that only he who has been trained through undertaking the painstakingly detailed work of our Party is entitled, if suitable for the purpose, to lay claim to higher posts. We can only make use of leaders who have worked their way up from the ranks. Any Political Leader who deviates from this principle should be removed or relegated for retraining to less important spheres of action (i.e. as Block or Cell Leader).

Let every Political Leader remember at all times that leader-

ship does not simply bring with it greater rights, but that, first and foremost, it imposes greater responsibility.

It is the first duty of a Political Leader, in his personal bearing and in his conception of duty, as well as in his private way of life, to be a shining example. Let him be conscious of the fact that more harm is done by the bad example of a Political Leader than can be made up for by a hundred and one admonitions. Invariably, Cells, Blocks, Bases, or Local Groups are the mirror image of their Leading Functionary. Whoever fails to do his duty in his home town or place of residence, will fail elsewhere.

His second duty is absolute justice. Nepotism must not be tolerated. Whoever sits upon able Party members because he is afraid they might outshine him, is a despicable wretch and a detriment to the Party. The Leading Functionary should not want to do everything single-handed. He must be guide, supervisor, and arbitrator. In a nutshell: the very life and soul of it all. Because he cares for his group–in many cases his own creation–the Political Leader must immediately extinguish any spark which might cause a conflagration. He must anticipate and not be caught napping. For these reasons he must not overburden himself with laborious details.

Any position of leadership demands a considerable measure of knowledge and ability. That is why every Political Leader has to keep on educating himself con-

tinuously. That is why the Party considers it to be its chief task to make possible the continuous training of all Political Leaders. It is not his commission which makes a leader, but the fact that his followers may look up to him in every respect. Not every Political Leader can be a good speaker, and yet he must be a preacher and a propagandist for the Idea.

Every Political Leader must have a strong personality. Do your duty in the place your Führer allocates to you. If you are a front-line soldier, you cannot be a general staff officer, and *vice versa*. Take care of your job, and do not take on more tasks than you are able to perform; but carry those you have accepted to completion. If the Political Leader wants to perform the tasks assigned to him correctly and thoroughly, he must not fritter away his powers. That is why membership of non-Party societies, and, in particular, taking part in their activities, is undesirable.

Each public appearance of the Party and, similarly, every internal function, such as discussion groups, indoctrination evenings, meetings of Party members, etc., must be most carefully prepared. When giving orders, give them clearly, concisely and accurately. Never say: "I think... one ought to... it is advisable...". Your opinion is immaterial; on the other hand, every one demands to know what you want. Only then may you call every one to account, only then will there be no uncertainty.

Bear this in mind: whoever cannot obey, will never be fit to give orders. Never put your own personal standing first. There is only one standing, namely that of the Movement. Carefully cultivate comradely relations with all other sections of the Party.

The typical Political Leader

From what has gone before, there emerges a picture of the typical Political Leader. The Political Leader is not a civil servant, but, at all times, the political representative of the Führer. He must see and think clearly. In times of national crisis, he must stand firm as a rock and obey orders implicitly. By means of Political Leaders we are building up the political management within the State.

The Political Leader must be preacher and soldier at one and the same time. He may never become a bureaucrat, he must always work with the people and for the people. He must be an example.

Reason is the product of instinct and intelligence. It is not absolutely necessary for the Political Leader to possess detailed technical knowledge: he has competent officials for that purpose; but his judgement must be superior. The typical Political Leader is not characterised by his office. There is no Political Leader of any one Party organisation, but only

a Political Leader of the N.S.D.A.P.

The Swearing-in of Political Leaders

The swearing-in of Political Leaders takes place annually at the same time as the swearing-in of male and female leaders of the Hitler Youth and its associated organisations.

The formula of the oath is as follows:

"I pledge unswerving loyalty to Adolf Hitler. I pledge absolute obedience to him and to any leaders he may appoint for me."

The Political Leader feels indissolubly bound up with the ideas and the organisation of the N.S.D.A.P. He may not resign from the post assigned to him without the express consent of his superior administrative office.

The oath will expire only with the death of the person sworn in, or with expulsion from the National Socialist community.

Political Leaders require the following personal documents:

(a) personal questionnaire

(b) curriculum vitae

(c) family tree as proof of Aryan origin

(d) extract from prison records (in case of criminal record)

(e) two passport photographs.

General Remarks concerning the Political Leader's Uniform

The Political Leader's uniform has been developed out of the realisation that political work for Germany is based on soldierly principles.

In creating it, the Führer has clearly expressed his wish to bring about a clear distinction between the typical Political Leader of the N.S.D.A.P. and civilian politicians of former parties and countries. The Political Leader is preacher and soldier at one and the same time; he represents that political leadership for which the German nation has fought for 2,000 years.

The Political Leader should be conscious of this lofty mission when he wears his dress of honour, awarded to him by the Führer.

Notes

Political Leader = *Politischer Leiter*. Any person in a leading position within the Party hierarchy.

Leading Functionary = *Hoheitsträger*. Alternative name for a person in charge of Nazi Party units.

5. Duty Parades

There exist Service *Section* duty parades and Service *Area* duty parades.

The following are Service Sections: Base Command, Local Group Command, District Command, Regional Command, and the Service Sections of National Command.

Service Areas, on the other hand, are: The entire area under the control of Base, Local Group, District, Region, and the Reich.

Duty Parades of Sections and Areas will take place at Bases, Local Groups, Districts, and Regions.

Service Section Duty Parade

(1) All Leading Functionaries are obliged to hold a parade for all Political Leaders of their Service Section at least once a month, in such a manner that, as far as possible, place, day and time are the same.

(2) If required, special parades may be held.

(3) All Political Leaders attached to the Service Section, regardless of rank, are obliged to attend. Non-attendance at duty parades is permissible only on the strength of express leave of absence, or requires reasonable excuse.

It is desirable that senior leaders of the S.A., S.S., N.S.K.K., and the H.J., responsible for the Region in question, should be included in these parades.

(4) The purpose of a duty parade is as follows: the Section Leader is to be given an opportunity of meeting and talking to his closest colleagues outside their daily duties; of informing them—insofar as he considers this to be necessary—of his views, wishes, and suggestions; and, above all, of getting to know them as comrades.

Political Leaders should be able to see their Section Leader; to get to know and appreciate the work their comrades are doing; and to strengthen the ties of comradeship among themselves as much as possible.

(5) As a matter of principle, service dress is worn on duty parade.

(6) The organisation of duty parade. Duty parade consists of the following:

    (a) Report to the Section Leader

    (b) Report by office holders

    (c) Comments and decisions, as well as a report on the political situation by the Section Leader

    (d) Social gathering of comrades.

Further instructions

(a) Report: A few minutes before commencement of duty parade, the officer in charge of training or, in his absence, the most senior office holder present, will order all Political Leaders to line up and ascertain the number of those present.

As the Section Leader, or his deputy, appears, the officer in charge of training will give the command "Attention!"; he then will walk up to the Section Leader, salute by raising his arm and report the number of those present, either "Political Leaders, all present and correct!" or "Political Leaders present! Absent with leave, Party Member X; absent without leave, Party Member Y." The Section Leader will thank him and command "at ease!"; then he will greet all Political Leaders with a handshake. Subsequently they will all sit down, in such a manner that

(in the case of larger staffs) members of the same office sit together.

(b) Then, one after the other, office-bearers (in Local Groups or Bases this includes Cell Leaders and, if expedient, Block Leaders) will report on their work, briefly and succinctly. If necessary, the Section Leader may order individual discussions.

(c) After receipt of reports, the Section Leader will summarise briefly the results of discussions. He will issue final instructions, and this will immediately be followed by a brief lecture on the political situation.

(d) Social gathering of comrades: gatherings after duty parade should not be held in the Section office rooms but elsewhere, since, as a rule, during the course of these gatherings, eating, drinking, and smoking take place. If the meeting place should be a public restaurant, conversations about internal Party matters will have to cease.

Notes

The hierarchy of the Party was as follows:

Block = *Block*, the smallest subdivision

Cell = *Zelle*

Base = *Stützpunkt*

Local Group = *Ortsgruppe*

District = *Kreis*

Region = *Gau*

S.A. = *Sturm-Abteilung* (Storm Troopers or Brown Shirts)

S.S. = *Schutz-Staffel* (Security or Defence Squad, Black Shirts)

N.S.K.K. = *Nationalsozialistisches Kraftfahr-Korps* (National Socialist Motor Transport Corps)

H.J. = *Hitler-Jugend* (Hitler Youth Organisation)

6. Applied Disciplinary Power

(1) Is disciplinary power necessary?

Every chief who has to carry out a task, for the execution of which he requires assistants and subordinate offices, must realize, above all else, that it is necessary, in order to solve problems, maintain discipline, and carry out normal duties, to direct the will inherent in every single assistant towards the execution of their relevant tasks.

In his consideration of the form in which the human will manifests itself, the task of the Political Leader is made easier by the fact that he deals consistently with

assistants who, by dint of the leader concept, have been pre-trained to such an extent that they have learned to regard as necessary the subordination of personal advantages to the good of the community.

The release of an act of will requires a motive, an impetus, just as it is utterly impossible for a stone to fall down from a roof without impetus. Therefore, in order to give to a person's will a certain direction, it is necessary to present it with a motive which will allow him to work in the desired direction.

This he will pursue until a stronger motive will turn him away from his original direction. In other words, an assistant will co-operate in the execution of a task; in upholding manly discipline; in the service as a whole; until he considers something else to be more important.

This something else may be a motive which approaches him from outside; on the other hand, it may be something within himself, such as, for instance, personal indolence, or becoming habituated to a vice, or similar causes. However, each of those motives which are inclined to keep an assistant from the execution of his official duties, must be curbed by the holder of disciplinary power. This is achieved by a chief, once and for all, bringing his assistant to the irrefutable conviction that his allotted task is the most important thing which has been assigned to him to be carried out in the interest of the Movement.

An assistant who has not yet grasped that the general welfare is his own welfare, cannot be regarded as such. Inner motives may be countered only by forcing to a speedy retreat that stubborn pigheadedness (so well-known to soldiers) that frequently erupts on such occasions, by threatening exceedingly uncomfortable, even unpleasant, countermeasures.

The realization that there exist measures to deter forcibly any form of egotism wishing to act anti-socially, from doing anything of the kind, has, for thousands of years, proved to be the most effective antidote for any troublesome manifestations of will, be they of selfishness or sloppiness.

(2) Prevention of situations which may necessitate the application of disciplinary power:

The best motive to give to the human will is the effect of authority. **Authority is achieved by continually giving a good example.** The leader who, in open battle, storms ahead of his troops, will have much less cause for complaint about cowardice among the ranks of his comrades than one who gives orders to attack from a safe position, having not the least intention of leaving it.

If it should happen that hours of work need to be extended over and above normal working times, and if the Section Leader is himself the last man to leave the office, no murmurings are likely to be heard, but they *will* be heard when he himself sets a job of work and then goes home before it has been finished.

In the interest of comradely co-operation, it is of great importance to avoid having to apply disciplinary power. However, this can be achieved only through most strenuous and consistent efforts on the part of the chief, by giving, in his own person, an example worth striving for, on the one hand by a blameless life, that is to say by self-discipline, on the other hand by tireless execution of his duty.

But that is not by any means enough! Any chief not well-informed about the characters of his assistants will often arrive at individually wrong methods in the handling of comrades who are his subordinates. As wrong as the widely-believed fallacy that a horse may be broken in by means of curb and spur, is the assumption that, in principle, by peremptory and harsh conduct one will have equal success with all assistants.

Indeed no, only careful study of the disposition of every single assistant will enable the chief to act correctly at all times. And that, in turn, will spur on the desire to do one's duty and reduce the necessity of meting out punishment. This study of characters should most conveniently take place by means of private social gatherings; indeed, it is their true purpose. For, conversely, by means of social intercourse the assistant, in turn, will gain better understanding of his chief, namely when he cannot

but perceive that his chief is a thoroughly good comrade, possessing far greater knowledge and ability than may be observed during daily office routine.

The best test of correct treatment of assistants is in the frequency with which disciplinary power has to be applied. The less often it puts in an appearance in well-functioning establishments, the more readily it is an indication that the chief knows how to handle his assistants psychologically correctly. It is better that actual punishment should be applied infrequently, for a knife that is seldom used keeps its edge. A penal law continuously applied quickly loses its educational value.

In order to carry out this pedagogic education of one's assistants, it is necessary that one should feel fully equal to one's job. The realisation that one has an advantage over each of one's assistants in respect of knowledge, ability, and capacity for work, is the most important basis for cordial co-operation between chief and assistant. And once that true comradeship has been achieved, everybody will anxiously guard against infringing any regulations, for, in that case, he will fear the anger of fellow workers more than the application of disciplinary power.

On the other hand, a chief's conceited and aloof conduct *vis-à-vis* his assistants demonstrates almost invariably that the chief is quite incapable, and his stand-offishness is nothing but a miserable fence which he has built round himself in order to hide his incompetence. Eighty per cent of pre-war class conceit was nothing other than fear, in case the man in the street should notice the puffed-up emptiness of so-called good society.

And yet, in the long run this fence is of no avail. Before long the assistant will have discovered that his chief knows less than he does himself, and at once his devotion to duty will diminish; at first, infringements against disciplinary regulations will occur, and presently conditions will prevail at the office which cannot but be called unpleasant. For that reason, if the head of a department should notice that he is not equal to his job, he should not attempt to stifle the justified criticism of his assistants with the help of disciplinary power, but he should resign instead. Then no one will reproach him, rather will they admire his cour-

age and readily transfer him to a more suitable post. In the other event, that is to say when, through the unpleasant conditions described above, such as constant punishments, and similar occurrences, a drastic change of head of department will be considered necessary in higher quarters, he will, of course, be regarded with justified suspicion.

We National Socialists are used to giving our opinions frankly and without diplomatic adornments. This quality, praiseworthy in itself, must not be allowed to tempt us into committing the following mistake. When corresponding with other, perhaps subordinate, offices, one may tend to forget that there another National Socialist does his duty. Our sharp tone may induce him to reply in like manner, and after a brief exchange of letters, things will frequently have come to such a pitch that disciplinary power will have to intervene.

Let everyone therefore adopt this principle: to proceed as courteously as possible when corresponding with other N.S. offices, including subordinate ones. It is easily forgotten that a harsh word on paper outweighs the spoken word three times. In principle, letters written in a harsher than usual tone should be released for despatch only one or two days after dictation, and even then only after reading them through once more.

It is gravely in conflict with maintaining one's own standing as holder of disciplinary power if that holder has two different ways of communicating with others, being rude when the letter is addressed to a subordinate office, and wheedling when writing to a superior.

Such people are called "bootlicking bullies". Their behaviour carries its own punishment, since it lends itself like nothing else to putting assistants into secret opposition and to destroying all comradeship.

(3) Application of disciplinary power:

Before meting out punishment, every punisher should ask himself the following questions:
(i) Have I listened to both parties, the accuser and the accused?
(ii) Am I in a sufficiently calm frame of mind myself to pronounce a just punishment?
(iii) According to the case in question, is a corrective or an exemplary punishment called for?

Additional notes:

(1) It is quite impossible to condemn anybody without having listened to his statement relevant to the case. Such proceedings would, after a very short time, throw open wide the gates to informers and their nefarious activities. The quality of human objectivity being defective, it is advisable always to examine carefully whether the plaintiff may not have had personal grounds which could have slightly shifted the argument to the disadvantage of the accused.

(2) The punisher will be well advised to take good heed of the principle **never to pronounce punishment immediately**, but to sleep on the case before pronouncing judgement. That will contribute a great deal towards objectivity. Punishments pronounced in the first flush of anger frequently have to be amended later on, which does not help to enhance the standing of the person holding disciplinary power.

(3) In meting out the sentence, the following should be taken heed of: **"Justice is the hardest virtue!"** (Schopenhauer). Accordingly, great pains should be taken not to assail the accused immediately – whether found guilty or having admitted his guilt – with the most severe means, but to try, through instruction and pedagogically wisely chosen punishment to restrain him from repeating his offence. In particular, dismissal from service should be applied only in most severe cases, for we must realise that a person dismissed from the Party and its organisations because of an offence will scarcely be able to find a new sphere of activity anywhere in Germany.

General remarks

In general, it will be sufficient to administer an appropriately severe reprimand to Party members or fellow citizens who have committed minor offences.

Once a punishment has been decided upon, let it be carried out without the least amendment, for it will, after all, be pronounced only after a carefully considered judgement has been arrived at. Retraction or mitigation of punishment makes the punisher appear inconsistent and, in the long run, renders illusory the preventive deterring effect of penal laws. On the other hand, the punisher and those working with him should realize that

Uniforms of Political Leaders:
◄ *A* Stellenleiter *(Section Leader) of a Regional Executive* (Gauleitung) *in walking out dress.*
▶ *An* Amtsleiter *(Department Leader) of a* Gauleitung *in walking out dress and greatcoat.*

attacks on Movement and State, which were obviously animated by a contemptible way of thinking, invariably demand most severe punishment.

A man authorised to mete out punishment must be particularly severe with himself. It is impossible to reprimand or punish an assistant for an offence of which, at all times, one is guilty oneself. The following may serve as an example: it is not possible to reprimand one's subordinate assistant X because he continually plunges his hands into his trousers pockets when, while reprimanding him, one puts one's own hands into one's pockets in agitation. This is bound to arouse in X a feeling of ridiculousness, and thus one will have achieved the opposite of what one had intended. To give another example: an assistant has been seen drunk in the street. How is it possible for an officebearer to punish that man when he himself, as is well-known to all and sundry, indulges in the same vice?

More than anyone else, therefore, the holder of disciplinary power will have to justify the great trust placed in him. Never ever, in the execution of his difficult and responsible office, may he turn his gaze away from our unique example, our Führer, Adolf Hitler!

Notes

Boot-licking bully: a free translation of the German *Radfahrernatur*, the literal meaning of which is "a person with a cyclist's mentality". This is a colloquialism much used in German: it describes – aptly – a person encountered not infrequently, especially in Germany, who cringes to those he considers his superiors, while kicking those whom he looks down upon, symbolically describing the attitude and movements of a cyclist.
Fellow citizen: *Mitbürger* would be the German equivalent of "fellow citizen". The Nazi concept of *Volksgenosse*, used throughout the text, has happily no equivalent in the English language and is thus untranslatable.

7a. Regulations concerning Complaints

Complaints may be lodged
(1) against a disciplinary decision; for instance, a reprimand, a suspension, or a dismissal from the office of Political Leader;
(2) if a Political Leader considers himself to have been injured or damaged in his service competence and authority;
(3) if a Party member believes his honour or his reputation to have been violated by actions on the part of other Party members.

Not included under (1) are judgements by Party Tribunals which have been executed by a Leading Functionary.

The Leading Functionaries of the N.S.D.A.P. or the respective responsible heads of departments are the only persons entitled to accept and deal with complaints concerning internal Party matters and Party leaders. They alone are responsible for integrity and justice in the Movement, and it is their duty conscientiously to examine, or to have examined, every complaint, whether made in writing or orally. Each case must be dealt with as speedily as possible. If the complaint is directed against a chief or a Leading Functionary, it has to be lodged with the next higher-ranking leader. Under no circumstances may the right of complaint be misused by narrow-minded people and by grousers for the purpose of unproductive arguments. Within the National Party Executive the correct procedure for complaints is via the competent departmental or head office director to the immediately superior National Director or the Deputy of the Führer.

Complaints may be made orally or in writing. Collective complaints by several Party members are inadmissible and will be punished. If any one incident should give cause for complaint to several Party members, it is up to each individual involved to make a complaint. All complaints should be made after calm and mature consideration only. If any one should, capriciously or against his better judgement, make a complaint which is based on an untrue assertion, he must expect to be disciplinarily punished himself. Should the investigation prove the complaint to have been justified, the fault which has come to light must be remedied forthwith. The head of a section is responsible for any

formal complaints within his sectional purview and, in case of complications, responsibility rests with the Leading Functionary.

If a Party member believes that his complaint has not been considered at all, or insufficiently so, he is entitled to take his complaint to the immediately superior official for settlement. The way to the Führer or to his Deputy is open to every Party member, but only if no settlement of his complaint has been forthcoming from lower departments of the Party, that is to say, Local Groups, District, or Regional directorates.

It is strictly prohibited to apply to State departments, or to individual persons, in connection with complaints concerning internal Party affairs or Party leaders. In case of contravention, expulsion from the Party will have to be faced.

Internal complaints
Insofar as technical disputes arise within an area, the decision rests with the immediately superior Leading Functionary. Insofar as the Leading Functionary is himself implicated in these disputes, and directions from a departmentally superordinate department have come to hand, the decision rests with the next superordinate Leading Functionary. For example:

The Regional Administration of the N.S.V. has issued a departmental directive to the District Administration of the N.S.V. The District Leader responsible, disagreeing with the execution of the directive for his district, appeals to his District Administrator. The District Administrator reports the appeal to his Regional Leader who is departmentally his superordinate, who, in his turn, should he insist in the execution of his directive, will get in touch with the District Leader.

If the District Leader should persist in refusing to allow execution of the directive to proceed, the Regional Leader will decide after hearing the Regional Administrator of the N.S.V. and the District Leader. If the Regional Leader should be satisfied that the proposed measures are in order, he will inform the District Leader that they should be allowed to proceed.

If the Regional Leader should agree with the District Leader, but the directive issued on the part of the Regional Adminis-

◄ *A Leader candidate (Führer-anwärter) at Training Castle (Ordensburg) in service dress. Candidates were mostly from the H.J. and destined for high posts in the Party.*
▶ *An Amtsleiter of the Reich Supreme Party (or Central) Executive (Reichsleitung) in walking out dress.*

tration of the N.S.V. corresponds with a directive of the National Administration of the N.S.V., and if the National Administrator is of the opinion that the directive will have to be carried out without fail, then the National Administrator will try to reach an agreement with the Regional Leader. Should agreement once again not be reached, the Deputy Führer will decide after hearing the National Administrator of the N.S.V. and the Regional Leader.

The right of appeal has become invalid if the dispute concerns a measure within an area, which has not been decreed by the department of a superordinate area. In this instance, the Leading Functionary of his own area has the right of making the final decision.

Notes

National Director = *Reichs-leiter*
N.S.V. = *Nationalsozialistische Volkswohlfahrt* (National Social-ist Public or People's Welfare Organisation)

7b. Party Meetings and Public Functions

Leading Party Functionaries are responsible for fixing all Party meetings and public functions planned by Party offices and af-filiated organisations. They will be authorised
(1) by the Local Group Leader, when their importance does not exceed the scope of the Local Group;
(2) by the District Leader, when their importance does exceed the scope of the Local Group; and
(3) by the Regional Leader, when they possess general political significance for the Region.

As for the rest, the organisa-tion of meetings and functions will take place according to the regulations of the department re-sponsible for organisation and propaganda.

Prior to arranging demon-

strations of general political im-portance for the country, the point of view of the National Propaganda Chief must be sought. Large meetings arranged with lightning speed may take place only with the approval of the National Propaganda Chief.

When fixing a timetable for their functions, District and Local Group Leaders must take into consideration functions planned for their Region, and, similarly, Local Group Leaders functions planned for their District.

By the twentieth of each month, Political Leaders and Adminis-trators must inform their re-sponsible Leading Functionary of all functions planned for the following month; subsequently he will, by the twenty-fifth of each month, fix and announce the overall plan. All Local Group Leaders must submit their plans for functions to their District Leaders in duplicate by the twenty-seventh of each month, who, by the last day of each month, will pass on one copy of these plans to the Regional Ad-ministration.

The current Leading Function-aries are obliged to inform re-sponsible leaders of the S.A., S.S., H.J., and N.S.K.K., about dates of functions, so that, when fixing their duty rota plans, they may enable members of the S.A., S.S., H.J., and N.S.K.K. to attend at least important meetings.

Party Tribunals, internal Leader Conferences, etc., are not affected by these regulations.

With the help of these plans, Regional Leaders, Regional In-specting Officers, Central Office Leaders, and Section Leaders of the Regional Administration, District Leaders, etc., will be able to pay unannounced visits every month to remote Local Groups, in order to obtain a clear picture concerning the state of the organisation, the suitability of Junior Leaders, and feeling among Party members and fellow citizens. The surprise appearance in a remote Local Group of a high-ranking Leader is possibly of more important and more lasting value than an important speech at an important meeting. Above all, every Political Leader and Administrator will be on his toes to keep his organisation functioning smoothly at all times, and not only when important visitors are announced. Again and again, procedure of this kind has increased the trust of the most humble Party member in his high-ranking leaders who

Political Leaders' Service Rank Insignia

Supreme Party Executive

 Reich Leader
(Reichsleiter)

 High Command Leader
(Hauptdienstleiter)

 Head Office Leader
(Hauptamtsleiter)

 Department Leader
(Amtsleiter)

 Senior Section Leader
(Hauptstellenleiter)

 Section Leader
(Stellenleiter)

Deputy Section Leader
(Hilfstellenleiter)

 Assistant
(Mitarbeiter)

Collar and cap braid

District Party Executive

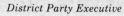

 District Leader
(Kreisleiter)

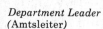 Head Office Leader
(Hauptamtsleiter)

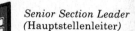 Department Leader
(Amtsleiter)

 Senior Section Leader
(Hauptstellenleiter)

 Section Leader
(Stellenleiter)

Assistant
(Mitarbeiter)

Collar and cap braid

Regional Party Executive

Regional Leader
(Gauleiter)

Deputy Regional Leader
(Stellvertreter Gauleiter)

Head Office Leader
(Hauptamtsleiter)

Department Leader
(Amtsleiter)

Senior Section Leader
(Hauptstellenleiter)

Section Leader
(Stellenleiter)

Assistant
(Mitarbeiter)

Collar and cap braid

Local Group and Base Party Executive

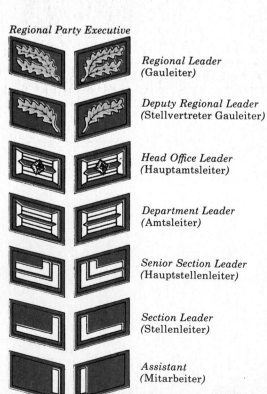

Local Group Leader
(Ortsgruppenleiter)

Base Leader
(Stützpunktleiter)

Cell Leader
(Zellenleiter)

Block Leader
(Blockleiter)

Department Leader
(Amtsleiter)

Senior Section Leader
(Hauptstellenleiter)

Section Leader
(Stellenleiter)

Assistant
(Mitarbeiter)

Collar and cap braid

Service rank insignia for Political Leaders on active service:
▽◁ *Head Office Leader of the Supreme Party Executive.*
▽ ▽ ◁ *Deputy Regional Leader.*
▽ ▷ *Department Leader of the District Party Executive.*
▽ ▽ ▷ *Senior Section Leader of the Local Group or Base Party Executive.*
Political Leaders' honour weapons:
▷ ▷ *The honour weapon, and* ▷ ▷ ▽ *holster for the honour weapon.*

Ehrenwaffe
des Politiſchen Leiters

Taſche zur Ehrenwaffe
des Politiſchen Leiters

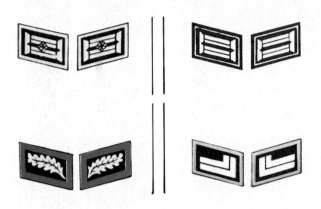

might perhaps become strangers if he should catch only a glimpse of them from afar at Regional rallies, or read about them in his newspaper.

Should the Leader of a superordinate office be present, no matter whether he is there on duty or as a guest, the function must be reported to him, in any case. If he wishes to take the floor, he will make this known during the report. The report will always be addressed to the most high-ranking Political Leader present. If, in an emergency, the Leader of a superordinate office intervenes in the management of a conference of Political Leaders, or of a meeting of members of the Party or of one of its affiliated organisations, he must do so by declaring: "I am now taking charge of the management of this function."

Should two units of equal rank organise a meeting or conference, the preparation and management will be in the hands of the most senior Political Leader. The certificate of appointment will decide seniority. If both bear the same date, seniority will have to be determined by age.

With reference to public demonstrations, meetings, parades, ceremonies, etc., public liability insurance in case of accidents will have to be taken out. In this connection, the regulations of the National Treasurer of the N.S.D.A.P. will have to be taken into consideration well before the event.

Notes

Local Group Leader = *Ortsgruppenleiter*
District Leader = *Kreisleiter*
Regional Leader = *Gauleiter*

8. Prospective Leaders and their Selection

During our Time of Struggle there existed in the N.S.D.A.P. no problem of prospective leaders as it does today. The Struggle was the most effective means of selection. Whoever did not possess unshakeable faith in the truth of our Führer's idea, as well as the fanatic will to be victorious, in addition to the general qualities of leadership demanded, was unable to stand his ground as leader in the Struggle and in that way was automatically eliminated. Besides, the Party had no well-paid posts to bestow, and its adherents in their bourgeois posts were frequently subject to persecution. Thus it was that only those Party members assumed positions of leadership who were imbued with the spirit of sacrifice and ready to toil at the work of the Führer, utterly dedicating

their entire strength to their task.

With the Assumption of Power by the Party, the selection of leaders through trial in battle ceased, naturally. And yet, it is essential that the leadership of the Party should continuously keep up its former fighting strength and buoyancy, for what is at stake is the task of safeguarding and of firmly consolidating what has been won by hard struggle. There has therefore arisen the question of prospective leaders which, especially as far as the higher-ranking, specifically political Party leadership is concerned, is to be solved as follows.

(1) Leading Functionaries, and in particular Regional Leaders, have been instructed to devote the utmost attention possible to prospective leaders.

(2) Special castles, called "*Ordensburgen*", have been created. In these castles, valuable Party members from all regions undergo three years' training as prospective leaders. Party members must be aged 25 to 30 and represent an élite, racially, physically, and mentally. In this connection, their previous occupation is immaterial. They are chosen by the National Chief of Organisation at the suggestion of their Regional Leader in conjunction with the Head Office for Public Health. Among the sub-

jects taught are History, Social Politics, Philosophy of Life, every kind of sport, as well as Deportment, etc. If necessary, training will be continued until trainee leaders can be released into the Regions as fully-trained Political Leaders.

(3) In the Regions, it is desirable that at first these Party members should be employed as Local Group Leaders, and that subsequently they should, as and when possible and necessary, work their way through all ranks of Political Leadership. These Party members will undergo continuous assessment of their abilities as Political Leaders.

(4) It is intended that Political Leaders thus trained should form a replacement nucleus for the higher-ranking and more directly politically active Party leadership.

However, attention will have to be devoted not only to future training for prospective leaders, but just as much attention will have to be given to effective utilisation of Political Leaders already serving. In that connection the following regulations exist:

(1) Higher Party leadership should be supplemented solely with Party members who have already proved their mettle in Local Groups, Districts, and Regions.

(2) Accordingly, only those Party members may be proposed by the Führer for posts as Deputy Regional Leaders who previously have held office as Local Group Leaders or District Leaders, or Local Group Administrators or District Administrators; it is most desirable that, in addition, they should also have held office as particularly politically active Regional Administrators.

(3) The following are deemed to be particularly politically active Regional Administrators: The Regional Secretary, if he deals with the entire business of the Regional Executive on behalf of the Regional Leader; the Regional Director of Organisation; the Regional Director of Personnel; the Regional Director of Training; the Regional Director of Propaganda; and the Regional Inspecting officers.

(4) Those Regional Directors mentioned under (3), from whose ranks, as from the ranks of District Leaders, are to emerge Deputy Regional Leaders, may only be proposed for approval of nomination for office, if they have been previously active as Political Leaders at Bases, Local Groups, or District Executives. Until further notice, only those Party members may be employed in offices listed under (1) who joined the Party not later than the Assumption of Power and who previously had been working actively either politically or in one of the organisations of the Party.

(5) Where from the point of view of personnel policy it can be justified, honorary District Leaders may be made full-time District Leaders, or replaced by full-time District Leaders.

(6) In order to bring continuity to the work of District Executives which, according to trends of development, must be regarded as very important areas, and also in order systematically to create prospective personnel for the offices of District Leader and for work in Regional Directorates and, beyond Regional Executives, in the National Executive, at least one full-time District Administrator will have to be appointed in District Executives. These District Administrators who may, in addition, hold one of the offices of the District Executive mentioned under (3), will have to be carefully selected by District Leaders: (a) they should have worked actively in a Local Group; (b) they should have belonged to the S.A., S.S., N.S.K.K., or H.J.; and (c) they should have shown potential for growth. In making this selection, care must be taken to avoid favouring the old. That is to say that, as far as possible, Party members who are young in years should be selected for the post of full-time District Administrator. However, it is a condition that they should have joined either the Party or the H.J. prior to the Assumption of Power.

Where financially possible, as for instance in larger Districts or Urban Districts, several full-time District Administrators should be employed.

(7) It is the duty of Regional Leaders to see to it that District Leaders, and in particular full-time District Administrators, are enabled to gain as much experience as possible by transfers within their Regional area and also by temporary secondment to Regional Executive. However, continuity of work of District Executives must not be allowed to suffer on account of these arrangements.

(8) Just as it is possible for a District Leader to become Deputy Regional Leader without first having been Regional Administrator, it is also possible that a Local Group Leader may become District Leader without first having been District Administrator. Local Group Leaders should be re-assessed regularly to ascertain to what extent they may be considered as replacements for retiring District Leaders.

(9) Broadly speaking, Regional Leaders and District Leaders must devote their utmost attention to the question of replacement of personnel right down to Bases and Local Groups.

(10) In the interest of systematic training of prospective leaders who are closely tied to their people (*volksverbunden*), careful attention to the above regulations is absolutely essential. Regions have the opportunity of selecting from among their tens of thousands of Party members those prospective leaders who, passing from Block and Local Group to Regional Executive, may be able, during temporary or permanent activity in the National Executive, to make good use of their experience gathered in every office in closest contact with our most humble fellow citizens, for the benefit of Movement and people.

At the same time, the selection of the very best human material

with respect to character, achievement, and experience is also in the interest of work in the Regions.

Personal connections, relationships, origin, and standing must never be allowed to play a part in the selection nor in the training of prospective leaders in the Party.

Political Leaders:
◄ *Section Leader of a Local Group or Base in service dress with pack.*
▷ ▷ *Senior Section Leader of a District Party Executive in service dress with greatcoat and pack.*
▷ *Items of Political Leaders' service equipment.*

(11) The National Director of Organisation, on behalf of the Deputy Führer, will supervise the execution of the above regulations.

The H.J. as source of prospective leaders

In order to safeguard from among the H.J. valuable, trained prospective leaders for the Party, suitable members of the Hitler Youth may be assigned to Leading Functionaries from Local Group Leader upwards for the purpose of training.

During their period of secondment to Party service, members of the Hitler Youth are excused from service in the H.J. The selection of youths will be undertaken jointly by the Leading Functionary and the H.J. Leader in charge. Care will have to be taken to select youths from all sectors of the community.

After 12 to 18 months' training, during which time members of the Hitler Youth must be made conversant with all official duties, they will be detailed for attending a Regional School for Leaders. On completion of his training, a detailed certificate of aptitude will be made out for each member of the Hitler Youth, to be kept at his respective personnel office. Subsequently, members of the Hitler Youth thus trained will be assigned as Block Leaders to Local Groups; it is desirable that later they should be promoted according to aptitude and opportunity.

In general, in addition to the regulations on selection recorded above, a process of selection will be established automatically because of the fact that from his earliest days, every German fellow citizen will be included in

the Party, the Party guiding and educating him.

The first occasion on which they are thus gathered together is in the *Jungvolk*, whence the young people are transferred to the Hitler Youth. A member of the Hitler Youth will then enter the S.A., the S.S., or the N.S.K.K., or he will co-operate in the work

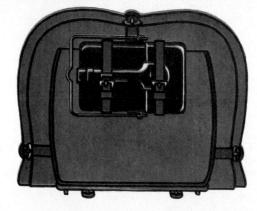

Pack with blanket, groundsheet, and mess tin

Whistle lanyard for Training Leader (Ausbildungsleiter)

Belt with double pin buckle and two D rings. 60-mm wide

Bread bag and water bottle   *Message pouch*

of affiliated organisations of the Party. After completion of his Labour Service and military service, the soldier will return for duty in the Party or its affiliated organisations.

The following will be the criteria for the Party, including all its organisations, for selecting the corps of leaders:

Character
Frankness
Honesty

Tidiness
Perceptiveness
Qualities of Leadership
Community Spirit
Reliability
Sense of Justice
Independence of Thought
    and Deed and of
    General Knowledge
Courage and Determination

Notes

The Time of Struggle = *die Kampfzeit*, a Nazi concept referring to the time before
The Assumption of Power = *die Machtübernahme* on January 31, 1933
Ordensburgen: These castles were created in imitation of the castles of the Teutonic Knights who in the 14th and 15th Centuries colonised and conquered Prussia.
Regional Administrator = *Gauamtsleiter*
Regional Secretary = *Gaugeschäftsführer*
Regional Director of Organisation = *Gauorganisationsleiter*
Regional Director of Personnel = *Gaupersonalamtsleiter*
Regional Director of Training = *Gauschulungsleiter*
Regional Director of Propaganda = *Gaupropagandaleiter*
Regional Inspecting Officer = *Gauinspekteur*
Deutsches Jungvolk = German Youth, a section of the Hitler Youth for boys between 10 and 14 years of age

9. N.S.D.A.P. Organisation

"The Party has been created by the Führer from the realisation that if our people are to live and walk towards a new Golden Age, they will have to be led according to an ideology which is true to our German nature. This ideology requires men who rise above the average, that is to say, men who, through self-discipline and self-control, through achievement and greater insight, surpass all others. Consequently, the Party will always have to represent a minority, the Order of National Socialist ideology, comprising the leadership of our people.

"For that reason, the Party consists solely of fighters, ready to undertake anything and to risk their all for the realisation of National Socialist ideology. Men and women to whom service to the people is their first and most sacred duty."

The N.S.D.A.P., being the German people's Order of Leadership, entirely dominates public life everywhere, whether—seen from the point of view of organisation—they are affiliated organisations, or organisations of the State administration, etc. In the long run, it will be impossible for leaders to remain in responsible posts anywhere, unless they are recognised by the Party. Moreover, in future suitable conditions for the systematic selection of leaders will be created by the Party.

When forming new National Socialist organisations, the following principles should be borne in mind:
(a) the Führer principle
(b) subordination to and integration with the overall organisation
(c) regional unity, and
(d) giving expression to practical community spirit.

The Führer principle

The Führer principle presupposes a pyramid-shaped organisational structure, in detail and as a whole.

At its top stands the Führer.

He appoints the leaders required for the individual spheres of action of the National Directorates of Party and State.

Thus the terms of reference for the purpose of the Party have been clearly outlined.

It is an Order of Leadership. Moreover, it is responsible for the spiritual, ideological, and National Socialist alignment of the German people.

The right to organise men for their own sake stems solely from such reasons.

Hence follows, in addition to the inclusion of men and women in the organisations of the Party, namely the S.A., the S.S., the N.S.K.K., the H.J., the N.S. League of Women, the N.S.D. Students' Association, the N.S.D. University Lecturers' Association, the justification for subordinating to the Party organisations concerned with public welfare.

The National Socialist structure of leadership is already clearly shown here.

Every single organisation is in the care of an office of the N.S.D.A.P.

In every instance, the leadership of each single organisation is supplied by the Party.

The National Director of Organisation of the N.S.D.A.P. is simultaneously leader of the D.A.F. The N.S.B.O. gives organisational support to the D.A.F.

The Director of the Head Office for Public Welfare is also Director

◄◄ *Bandmaster of a "Bandsmen's Squad" of a Regional Party Executive in service dress.*
◄ *Bandsman of a "Bandsmen's Squad" of a Regional Party Executive in service dress.*

of the N.S. People's Welfare.

The same relationship exists between

(i) the National Department of Justice (*Reichsrechtsamt*) and the N.S. Lawyers' Association (*Nationalsozialistischer Rechtswahrer-Bund*)

(ii) the Central Office for Public Health (*Hauptamt für Volksgesundheit*) and the N.S. Medical Association (*Nationalsozialistischer Aerztebund*)

(iii) the Central Office for Education (*Hauptamt für Erzieher*) and the N.S. Teachers' Association (*Nationalsozialistischer Lehrerbund*)

(iv) the Central Office for Civil Service (*Hauptamt für Beamte*) and the National Association of Civil Servants (*Reichsbund der deutschen Beamten*)

(v) the Central Office for War Victims (*Hauptamt für Kriegsopfer*) and the N.S. War Victims Welfare (*Nationalsozialistische Kriegsopferversorgung*)

(vi) the Department of Technical Science (*Amt für Technik*) and the N.S. German Technical Association (*Nationalsozialistischer Bund deutscher Technik*)

(vii) the Eugenics Office (*das Rassenpolitische Amt*) looks after the National Association of families with three or more children (*Reichsbund der Kinderreichen*)

(viii) the N.S. Women's League and the German Women's Service

Moreover, the Central Office of the N.S.D.A.P. for Agrarian Policy (*Reichsamt für Agrarpolitik der N.S.D.A.P.*) is closely connected with the National Agricultural Board (*Reichsnährstand*), a Government Department. Here, too, indirect supervision and unity of leadership are ensured.

The understructure of all affiliated organisations, as well as all Party offices, is based not only on the National leadership, but also on lower organisational levels, namely on the Regions, and then on the Districts, and furthermore, if expedient, on Local Groups or Bases. In addition, with the N.S. League of Women, the D.A.F. and the N.S.V., this also applies to Cells or Blocks. In Local administrative areas, in District sectors or District squads, which geographically correspond to Local Groups or Bases of the Party, members of affiliated organisations will automatically be included.

The Führer principle. Subordination to and integration with the overall organisational structure

However, the leadership structure would be split up if all organisations or affiliated bodies, from the smallest unit to National leadership, as far as their respective structure was concerned, were to be completely independent, and subordinate only directly to the Führer at the top.

If one takes into account the four chief areas, (Reich, Region, etc.) the situation might be compared to a four-storied house, all of whose posts and walls go right up to the roof, without shoring and connections on each floor.

Furthermore, it would be incompatible with the National Socialist Führer idea, which presupposes a complete sense of responsibility, to assume that, over and above his technical and practical responsibility, the leader of an organisation or of an affiliated body would be in a position to guarantee, from the point of view of National Leadership, the political and ideological attitude of all junior leaders down to the smallest unit.

Besides, the completely detached status of each organisation would involve each single organisation having to establish its own offices for organisation, personnel, and training. This in turn would, with the best of good will on the part of all National Leaders, Central Office chiefs and administrative leaders, in charge of the National Leadership of the Party, lead to a situation where, in the course of time, in every case, differences would arise, which, at a later date, would bring about a state of completely different systems in regional, vertical, personal, etc. respects, within the National Socialist régime.

For that reason, organisations such as the N.S. German Students' Association, the N.S. Women's League, the N.S. German University Lecturers' Association, affiliated bodies and their leaders, while, starting from the bottom, they are subordinate to the next superordinate office within their organisation, are, in the sovereign areas of the Party, disciplinarily subordinate to the responsible Leading Functionary of the N.S.D.A.P., that is to say in respect of organisation, ideology, politics, supervision, and personnel.

In this way, all organisations will be securely moored to the structure of the Party, and in all areas a firm connection with the Leading Functionaries of the N.S.D.A.P., commensurate with the National Socialist Führer principle, will have been created. The National Socialist structure of organisation will always stay alive and flexible. As it becomes expedient to do so, we shall extend the organisation, but, at the same time, we shall summon up courage, should the situation result in displacements, to reduce individual fields of duties, if necessary, or alternatively, to undertake the disbandment of individual sections of the organisation. The foundation, however, will remain untouched forever.

The practical expression of community spirit
If we National Socialists would wish to spread the National Socialist idea of solidarity among the people to replace liberalistic mentality, we shall have to build upon the community of the family, and in that way we shall achieve **the fellowship of the people.**
Fellowship of the people, however, cannot be represented by any one class or section.

A spirit of fellowship is not proved merely by the fact that one feels "compassion" for other sufferers, and is prepared to dispense "charity".

Furthermore, we shall have to recall the pronouncement of the National Director of Organisation of the N.S.D.A.P., in which he said that we should "follow the proclamation of the idea of fellowship of the people by practising that fellowship".

Hence follows the task of bodies affiliated to the N.S.D.A.P. Starting from the clear realisation that it is fundamentally wrong to organise people for technical reasons, and turning away from Ottmar Spann's idea of different "orders", the Party has set about the problem of the idea of fellowship in the field of organising men, and it has solved that problem by creating the National Socialist fellowship organisation, called "The German Labour Front" (D.A.F.).

In the German Labour Front, the fellowship spirit is practised at the place of employment. In their professions and on the shop floor, factory workers, employers, civil servants, and office workers form one single community of staff and management. The establishment is an integrated whole.

As in the field of family life, the idea of community spirit has been made secure in office and factory.

In addition, there is a revolutionary new creation, namely the care of men and women by the department of the D.A.F., entitled "The N.S. Association 'Strength through Joy'".

Here, once again, the community spirit is being practised.

Notes
N.S. League of Women = *N.S. Frauenschaft*
N.S.D. Students' Association = *Nationalsozialistischer Deutscher Studentenbund*
N.S.D. University Lecturers' Association = *Nationalsozialistischer Deutscher Dozentenbund*
National Director of Organisation = *Reichsorganisationsleiter*
German Labour Front = D.A.F.: *Deutsche Arbeitsfront*
the Administrative sub-division of the German Labour Front
Head Office for Public Welfare = *Hauptamt für Volkswohlfahrt* =
N.S.B.O.: *Nationalsozialistische Betriebszellenorganisation*

orders: the word is to be understood here in the sense in which it was used in Victorian times, i.e. "the lower orders".
Strength through Joy: Although this has become the accepted translation for *Kraft durch Freude*, perhaps on the analogy of Schiller's *An die Freude*, which is "Ode to Joy" in English, it would be more accurately translated as "Strength through Pleasure" or "Enjoyment" or even "Happiness". The aim of this organisation was to take charge of everybody's leisure time, by providing organised amusements, entertainments, and holidays for the workers, under the supervision of the Party.

10a. The Block: smallest subdivision of the N.S.D.A.P.

Organisation: The household: The household is at the bottom of the chain of communities; it forms the basis of the systems of Blocks and Cells. A household is the organisational joining together of all fellow citizens living in the same dwelling, including lodgers, domestic help, etc.

Nazi Party badges. From top to bottom these are:
National insignia (Hoheitszeichen) of the old pattern;
Party badge (Partei-Abzeichen);
National insignia of the new pattern;
S.A. badge as worn on civilian clothes;
S.S. badge as worn on civilian clothes; and
N.S.K.K. badge as worn on civilian clothes.

Example: Residing on the first floor, at 20, Senefelderstrasse, the Müller family, consisting of four members, in addition to one lodger and one domestic help—the latter, although living in the same house, occupying her own room not on the same floor—form
one Residential Community—one Household.
Whether or not the lodger finds his own board is, in this context, completely immaterial.

A N.S.D.A.P. Block consists of 40 to 60 Households
Whether the number of households included in a Block is nearer the upper or lower limit depends on the density of population or on local conditions in the area.

The combination of households to form a Block will be carried out down one side of the street; in the case of houses forming polygons (geographical triangles, squares, rectangles, etc.), it will be carried out according to the course of the street, skirting these polygons.

The size of the scheduled area must be such that it gives to the responsible Political Leaders or to Administrators and Wardens an opportunity of thorough and comprehensive canvassing.

Personnel
(*a*) A Block Leader is the most junior Leading Functionary of the N.S.D.A.P.
(*b*) Selection: A Block Leader must be a Party member. He should be chosen from among the best Party members within his Local Group. His service title is:

Block Leader of the N.S.D.A.P.
(*c*) Subordination: In his Local Group, a Block Leader is disciplinarily subordinated to the Cell Leader. In a Base, the Block Leader, in case there are no Cells, is subordinate directly to the Base Leader.
(*d*) Nomination: A Block Leader is nominated by the Local Group Leader or the Base Leader.
(*e*) Appointment: After a period of probation and production of the prescribed personal documents (proof of Aryan ancestry up to and including grandparents), and three to four months after his provisional appointment, he will be officially appointed Block Leader by the competent District Leader.
(*f*) Rank: The Block Leader holds

the service rank of Block Leader of the N.S.D.A.P.; service uniform of a Political Leader; Local Group tabs with gold corners; gold buttons, twin-tongued buckle, and cap cord.

Tasks and Responsibilities
A Block Leader is responsible for all occurrences in his area relating to the Movement; he is fully answerable to the Cell Leader, or, if in a Base, possibly directly to the Base Leader. The discharge of the following duties are incumbent upon him. At least once a month, the Block Leader must call a meeting of his disciplinarily subordinate fellow workers, or, as the case may be, Block Administrators, during the course of which reports are given on activities and on situations encountered. On this occasion, by means of discussion and agreement, directives for future work should be laid down.

The Block Leader decides upon the tasks planned for the future. In special cases, special meetings, over and above regular discussions, may be held. In this connection, it is immaterial whether the meetings take place at a restaurant or at a private residence. (It is most advisable to use different private residences in turn).

A Block Leader acts as leader of, and adviser to, all Block Administrators, etc., and Party members working in his Block area.

He has to act in an enlightening, mediating, and helpful capacity, in accordance with the principles of the Movement. He has to see that people who spread rumours are traced, and to report them to the Local Group or the Base, as applicable, so that the authorities may be informed.

Not only must a Block Leader be preacher and champion of National Socialist ideology with respect to those Party members and fellow citizens entrusted to his political care, but he must also work to achieve the practical co-operation of Party members belonging to his Block area, and, in the case of their exceptional aptitude and achievement, to introduce them to the Leading Functionary.

Again and again, the Block Leader should draw the attention of Party members to their special duties towards State and People. A Party member should not only be a contributor of membership fees, but an active comrade-in-arms and a propagandist for the

Nazi Party badges. From top to bottom these are: Honour badge (Ehrenzeichen) of the Hitlerjugend or Hitler Youth; Hitlerjugend badge; Deutches Jungvolk badge; and German Students' League (Deutsches Studentenbund) badge.

Movement (decoration of houses with flags, attending of Party meetings, co-operation, willingness to make sacrifices, etc.). Every Party member is obliged to co-operate and may be called on to give his support at any time.

The collection of membership fees on behalf of the N.S.D.A.P. will be undertaken by the Block Leader.

Although the payment of membership dues represents a debt to be discharged at the domicile of the creditor, prompt collection of dues from every Party member affords the best possible opportunity for the Block Leader to make and keep up the required personal contact with a fellow Party member. In handling the collection of membership dues it is the Block Leader's duty strictly to adhere to the instructions issued.

The card index recording membership dues, which the Block Leader is obliged to maintain and keep up to date, has to be left under lock and key and access to it may be afforded to no one except competent Political Leaders. In addition, the Block Leader will keep a record concerning each household.

As with all Political Leaders, Administrators, and Wardens, incessant training, education, and instruction, manly discipline and exemplary bearing, not only on duty, but also in his private life, are, particularly for the Block Leader, the presupposition for the accomplishment of his tasks and his weighty responsibility. On request, he must lend a hand in training, education, and functions duties, just as he will see to the participation of subordinate Political Leaders, Administrators, and Wardens, should he be ordered to do so.

When wearing service uniform, the Block Leader should apply himself at all times to displaying exceptionally correct bearing, cleanliness, and strict adherence to regulations concerning uniforms. It is the aim of the Block Leader to succeed in persuading the sons and daughters of the families in his Block area to join the relevant units of the H.J., the S.A., the S.S., and the N.S.K.K., as well as relevant affiliated bodies, such as the D.A.F.; and to see that National Socialist functions, demonstrations, and ceremonies are attended.

In brief, the Block Leader is an incessantly toiling activist and propagandist of the Movement. He has to observe and pay daily

attention to bars imposed on members, and to relevant regulations of the Party, its offices, formations, and associations. A Block Leader has to guide and supervise the activities of the Block Administrators and existing helpers. In principle, a Block Leader must attend to his official duties verbally or, as the case may be, accept and pass on messages verbally. Communications in writing will take place only in the case of absolute expediency or necessity.

Upon Party members being newly admitted, their application form passes through the Block Leader's hands.

Notes
Administrators and Wardens = *Walter und Warte.* Note the alliteration, giving the phrase that authentic Germanic flavour. A debt to be discharged at the domicile of the creditor: the German word used in *Bringschuld.* This is a strictly legal term, the English equivalent for which has been used in translation, in order to emphasise the ludicrous way in which this weighty expression has been misused to describe the process of paying one's membership dues.

The House Notice Board of the N.S.D.A.P.:
In every apartment house (corresponding to a house group) a House Notice Board will be fixed in a clearly visible place (at ground floor level), according to the regulations listed. In settlements and villages with normally not more than one to three families per house, it is advisable to put up House Boards at Parish Information Boards, Party press showcases, etc., or at any other, clearly visible, places.

The Block Leader is responsible for keeping the House Notice Board in good order; this includes putting up or removing announcements and notices, as well as keeping in order directions and personal denominations affixed.

Behaviour towards Fellow Citizens:
Work in Blocks of the N.S.D.A.P. presupposes an exceptional measure of tact, knowledge of human nature, care, and empathy towards one's fellow citizens. Any insolently peremptory behaviour and, similarly, any ingratiating behaviour, can do nothing but harm, whereas matter-of-fact behaviour, making plain one's concern for the fellow citizen under

one's care, is, for the most part, the sole means suitable to create, strengthen, and consolidate a relationship of trust with the fellow citizen.

In this connection, it is a matter of course that pride, a stainless way of life, propriety and correctness are prerequisites to the position of trust as Block Leader and Block Administrator, conferred upon a man on the part of the Party.

(a) A Block Leader spreads National Socialist propaganda. Gradually, he will awaken the understanding of those forever dissatisfied people for measures and laws of the National Socialist Government which have often been merely misinterpreted and misunderstood. He should invite fellow citizens to put questions to him; point out to them that they are welcome to unburden themselves to him freely; but, for the rest, should the occasion arise, urge them to be discreet concerning idle chatter with regard to other fellow citizens. Should complaints and belly-aching make themselves heard, it is by no means his job to agree in order to demonstrate his solidarity, but he must, in every case, endeavour to think positively and as one affirming life, and accordingly, by his confident attitude, exert an influence on the men and women in his care.

(b) Insofar as enquiries cannot be dealt with by the Block Leader, information should be given as to the place at which the problems in question could be attended to. (Office of the N.S.D.A.P.) Questions will only be answered when the correct answer is known, otherwise the answer will be put off until the proposed visit to the N.S.D.A.P. office. It is not to anyone's discredit if he admits openly that, at that moment, he is unable to answer a question clearly. On the other hand, it is to one's discredit if the questioner notices that one's answers are superficial and hasty.

(c) Any information given is not legally binding.

(d) The utmost discretion in all things is a precondition for winning the confidence of all fellow citizens. Anything which comes to the knowledge of a Political Leader in the execution of his Party duty, comes under the heading of "Official Secret" which he has to guard absolutely against everyone.

The following example is quoted to illustrate a Block Leader's field of duty, its peculiar aptness accounting for the great detail and comprehensiveness of narration.

The family N.N., living in rather wretched circumstances, and consisting of the father, an unskilled labourer, the mother, an adult son, and three daughters, aged 14, 8, and 2, suddenly loses its breadwinner through death.

The competent Block Leader (or, where suitable, the Block Administrator or Block Helper, if any) betakes himself to the widow in order to offer her his help and advice:

He informs the D.A.F. Block Administrator so that the previous contractual working conditions of the head of the family may be ascertained in order to apply to the previous employer of the head of the family for possible special assistance, or to persuade him to grant such assistance.

On that occasion he may ask for and be given information about the adult son's earning potential, since he will be temporarily the breadwinner of the family, in order to consider possibilities of how his earning opportunities may be improved.

He will help the widow in obtaining whatever legal aid is necessary in connection with insurance claims.

He will ascertain which social security or accident assurance institutions are obliged to make disbursements in this case, in order to assist the widow.

He will enquire after the state of health of the children who are minors, so that, if necessary, he may arrange for the help of the N.S.V. (and the Office for Public Health) via the responsible Block Administrator of the N.S.V.

Moreover, he will ascertain what arrangements may be made for the two school-age daughters, by making them join the B.D.M. or J.M., to work in the spirit of the Führer's youth education; and, in order to alleviate the widow's domestic cares, he will concern himself with obtaining sponsorships for membership fees and free supplies of service uniforms and equipment for both girls.

He will arrange for the widow to be looked after in purely womanly matters by the N.S. Women's League, which for example, will see to it that the 14-year-old girl, who will be leaving school shortly, will either remain at home to help her mother in the house, or, according to what is more advisable, be

Political Leaders' vehicle standards and pennants:
Top line: *Reich Leader's standard* (left) *and the pennant for a Senior Service Leader* (Hauptdienstleiter), *Senior Department Leader* (Hauptamtsleiter), *and Department Leader* (Amtsleiter) *in the* Reichsleitung.
Second line: *Regional Leader's standard and the pennant for a Deputy Regional Leader* (Stellvertreter Gauleiter) *and Department Leader in a* Gauleitung.
Third line: *District Leader's standard and the pennant for a Department Leader in a* Kreisleitung.
Fourth line: *Ordinary Party standard and pennant.*

directed to serve her compulsory year of domestic or agricultural duty, so that immediately afterwards and up to her marriage, she may be directed to a suitable opportunity of earning money.

He will endeavour to remedy unsatisfactory living accommodation.

He will arrange for the son to become a member of the D.A.F.

He will put the son, who is overworked but otherwise healthy, in touch with the K.d.F. Block Warden, so that the possibility of a cheap holiday may be discussed.

Briefly, he will make himself confidential adviser and helper of this family in the tragic loss of their father, with all their daily troubles and care, and in this way he will become the intermediary between the people and the Movement.

The deserving and modest poor should be reported to the N.S.V. Administrator for special care. Often a piece of good advice may help to convince a fellow citizen of our honest endeavour to create a State of Social Justice. The trust given to him, he will have to justify by obtaining help and advice, either in person or in mediation with the office of Party or State responsible.

Insofar as the sale of pamphlets, badges, admission tickets, etc., has been stipulated, the Block Administrator, Block Leader, etc., may under no circumstances whatever become importunate towards fellow citizens and Party members.

In principle, Political Leaders below the rank of Cell Leader are obliged to communicate not in writing, but verbally only.

Notes

B.D.M. or *Bund Deutscher Mädel* = German Girls' Association.
J.M. or *Jungmädel* = literally "Young Girls", corresponding – in age only – to Brownies.

▷ *A cadre member, or an official, of the National Socialist Students' League or N.S. Deutscher Studentenbund.*

Block Helpers

The following is recommended to all Regions to be carried through voluntarily: Over and above the arrangement outlined above for linking 40 to 60 households in one Block, it is recommended that, within any one Block, House Attendants or Block Helpers should be appointed to help out.

Tasks and Responsibilities of Block Helpers

(*a*) From time to time, Block Leaders may call in Block Helpers, if they have been found suitable, to assist them in their work.

(*b*) On behalf of the Block Leader, Block Helpers will take charge of the House Notice Board, being responsible for the display of announcements, etc.

(*c*) If instructed to do so, Block Helpers will take part in discussions arranged by the Block Leader.

(*d*) Block Helpers will attend functions arranged by the Party, especially training evenings and any training courses provided, as well as duty parades.

(*e*) Insofar as the local leader of the National Air Defence League was consulted at the time of the appointment of Block Helpers, and if, in consequence, they should, at the same time, be House Wardens of the National Air Defence League, any tasks laid down on the part of the National Air Defence League will be incumbent upon the Block Helpers.

In their service area, Block Helpers are regarded as trusted representatives of the N.S.D.A.P. and its organisations. Block Helpers should endeavour to fortify themselves ideologically; towards fellow citizens they should, at all times, do their best to behave consistently with the dignity of the Party. Confidentiality concerning official matters has to be strictly observed.

Block Administrators

Insofar as sections or affiliated bodies of the Party have developed their organisation to include the formation of Blocks, a Block Administrator is to be appointed.

Selection

The Block Administration will be run by the most suitable Party member from among the inhabitants of that particular Block Administration. If, within a Block

Administration, no Party member can be nominated for this task, the fellow citizen deemed most suitable will have to be appointed. It is, of course, essential that he should be politically reliable and of Aryan blood. The Block Administrator of the D.A.F. must be a member of the D.A.F. His service title is *Blockwalter*.

Tasks and Responsibilities
(*a*) A Block Administrator will take part in the regular or extraordinary discussions, ordered by the Block or Cell Leader, or the Local Group or Base Leader.
(*b*) Insofar as special operations render this necessary, the Block Administrator has the right to apply to the Block Leader for an extraordinary meeting of all Block workers. Insofar as the Block Leader has named place and time, the Block Administrator making the application is obliged to inform all other Block Administrators, etc. accordingly, on behalf of the Block Leader.
(*c*) The Block Administrator will visit regular training evenings or training courses, as provided, as well as duty parades.
(*d*) He is responsible for work assigned to him by the Cell Administrator in authority.
(*e*) The Block Administrator will have to keep his Block Leaders as well as his Cell Administrator informed about his activities.
(*f*) In general, Block Administrators are not allowed to correspond with Block Leaders and Cell Administrators.

10b. The Cell

Organisation
A Cell is composed of four to eight Blocks. A Cell Leader is the next highest Leading Functionary of the N.S.D.A.P.

Tasks and Responsibilities
The tasks of a Cell Leader correspond by analogy to the tasks of the Block Leader. As the Block Leader is authorised and responsible for all events in his area affecting the Party, the Cell Leader is authorised and responsible in greater measure for the area of all Blocks under his authority.
In particular, he will have to render to his Local Group Leader valuable and active support in respect of training and political work. It will be necessary therefore that he keeps his Local Group Leader informed about all events of importance to the Party. A Cell

Leader will supervise the work of Block Leaders and Cell Administrators, if necessary intervening in order to help; he will be responsible for seeing that Block Leaders are not appointed in name only, but that they in fact strive to accomplish their tasks.
With permission of the Local Group Leader, an experienced Cell Leader may or should hold Cell Evenings for all fellow citizens in his service area. It is not intended that on these Cell Evenings spirited lectures should be given, but that, for instance, a chapter from Adolf Hitler's *Mein Kampf* should be read. Subsequently, by means of questions and answers, a so-called Discussion Evening will be organised on the lines of Block Leader and Cell Leader discussions. Such Cell Evenings may be enhanced in a dignified manner by community singing and musical renderings.
The arrangements for similar evenings may be entrusted by Local Group Leaders or Base Leaders to particularly experienced Block Leaders for the benefit of fellow citizens in their area. Permission for this purpose may only be given, however, if there is incontestable evidence that the Block Leader will prove equal to the organisation of such a Block Evening.

The Cell Administrator
A Cell Administrator should be a Party member. He may, in exceptional cases, be a non-Party member. Political and personal reliability are, of course, essential.
A Cell Administrator of the D.A.F. must be a member of the D.A.F. His service title is *Zellenwalter*.

General Regulations
Questions: All fellow workers within Blocks and Cells are expected to answer questions on the part of fellow citizens and Party members only if they are in a position to answer these accurately. Otherwise a reply will have to be deferred until an opportunity should present itself again, and in the meantime, the Leading Functionary or Administrator of the Local Group, who is qualified to make a reply, will have to be consulted.

Sale of Admission Tickets, etc.: Just as no higher-ranking office is permitted to send admission tickets, pamphlets, badges, etc. to Local Group or Base Control with the instruc-

Training School uniforms:
◀ *A member attending a course for attached units of the Nazi Party.*
▶ *A member of a Regional Training School.*

tion that they must all be sold, it is absolutely forbidden that, on the part of Local Group or Base Control, admission tickets, pamphlets, badges, etc., be handed to Cell and Block Leaders or Cell and Block Administrators with the express instruction that they will have to be disposed of in their entirety.

Block Administrators, etc., are, naturally, expected to try to dispose of the tickets, etc., handed to them. However, they are under no circumstances allowed to become importunate towards fellow citizens and Party members.

Staff Records: No detailed staff records will be kept on the part of Cell and Block Leaders concerning Block Leaders, Block Administrators, and Cell Administrators, etc. If it becomes necessary, Cell or Block Leaders may be allowed inspection of the personal records of their Local Group or Base Leader.

Disagreements: In the case of disagreements and enmities, a settlement will have to be undertaken by means of personal exchange of ideas; alternatively, the Leading Functionary who is next in seniority will give a decision. Insofar as measures and reprimands should prove necessary, these will have to be administered to the person concerned in private, and never in the presence of other fellow workers.

Note
National Air Defence League = *Reichsluftschutzbund*, the German Civil Defence organisation.

11. N.S.D.A.P. Local Groups

(1) The Area defined
The area controlled by a Local Group comprises one or more communities. If necessary, towns may be divided into several areas. In principle, Local Group boundaries should not cut across community boundaries.
(*a*) A Local Group comprises a minimum of 50 Party members; it may not exceed 500 Party members. The maximum number of households in any one area, permissible only in exceptional cases,

is 3,000. No lower limit on the number of households per Local Group has been fixed.
(*b*) The units upon which the organisation of Local Groups has been based, are rated according to the following upper or lower figures:
House Group = 8 to 15 Households
Block = 40 to 60 Households
Cell = 4 to 8 Blocks

(2) The Local Group Leader
As Leading Functionary he has authority for all expressions of Party will; he is responsible for the political and ideological leadership and alignment of the area under his control. The Local Group Leader is immediately subordinate to the District Leader in authority. Subordinate to the Local Group Leader within his area, as far as discipline is concerned, are all Political Leaders and Party members as such.

Party members receiving appointments as Leaders will be sworn in by the Local Group Leader in the setting of a duty parade. Final appointments as Political Leaders will have to be made by the Local Group Leader on the occasion of a public meeting of the Local Group. The swearing in will take place in solemn manner by means of a handshake, while for a brief moment the consecrated sovereign flag is lowered onto the clasped hands.

Upon issue of a membership card, provisional admission into the Party has taken place (see discourse on "The Party Member", paragraph 2, "The Pledge"). During the course of a solemn members' parade, in full view of the sovereign flag, the membership book will be handed over by the Local Group Leader. In the introductory remarks of his brief address, the significance of Party membership will be explained. At the same time, emphasis will be put on the fact that membership of the Party is meant as preparatory to later activity in a service post of the Party's organisation. It is therefore the duty of a Party member to prepare himself unrelentingly, by training, self-discipline, and ideological attitude, for his future duties; final admission into the National Socialist German Workers' Party embodies at the same time the obligation to comply with every call by the Party.

Over and above all technical and political tasks, a Local Group Leader must be example, adviser

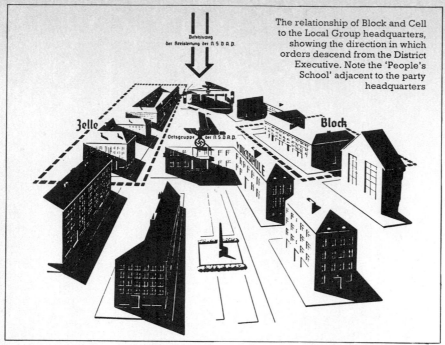

The relationship of Block and Cell to the Local Group headquarters, showing the direction in which orders descend from the District Executive. Note the 'People's School' adjacent to the party headquarters

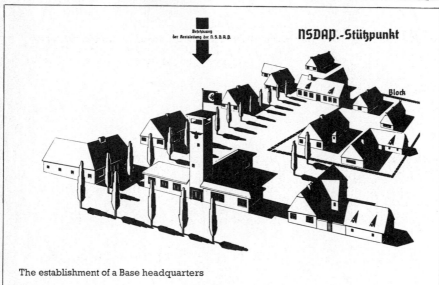

The establishment of a Base headquarters

The Nazi Ortsgruppe *or Local Base* (top) *and* Stützpunkt *or Base* (bottom). *In the first the relationship of the two lowest levels in the Nazi administration, the Block (Block) and the Cell (Zelle), to their immediate superior, the* Ortsgruppe, *is immediately apparent. It is easy to imagine how the Party could keep its eyes on the activities of even the smallest elements of the new "pan-Teutonic" fellowship or community.*

and comrade. He must see to it that strict secrecy is observed by his Political Leaders concerning all official incidents brought to their notice, and to set a good example himself in this respect.

(3) The Local Group Flag
Upon application by the District Leader, the Local Group may be granted the right to carry a sovereign flag by the Regional Leader. The sovereign flag is the

sacred symbol of the Local Group (or of the Base). It is on it that a Party member is pledged.

It will receive a place of honour at the Local Group (or Base) office. Insofar as no dignified place can be given to it, the District Leader will decide where the sovereign flag should have its place of honour. The sovereign flag may only be displayed at Party functions.

The Local Group or Base

Leader will appoint a serving Political Leader and entrust him with the honourable office of flag bearer. Only exceptionally deserving Political Leaders may be installed as flag bearers. The flag bearer must be conscious of the significance of his task. He honours the motto: "Man may fall, but the flag stands forever". Like the Local Group, the Base is an independent area under local control. The essential

points in which Base differs from Local Group are
(a) smaller membership;
(b) in suitable cases, one Political Leader holding more than one post; and
(c) limited formation of Cells.
Regulations for Local Groups apply correspondingly to Bases.

12. The District Executive

The District Executive is the most subordinate office of the Party with a full-time staff. Within the area under his control, the District Leader is responsible for the entire political, cultural, and economic development of all manifestations of life, according to National Socialist principles. If not otherwise stated, the designation "District" has, at all times, to be taken as referring to the Party District, as opposed to the State Administrative District.

The District Leader
The District Leader is directly subordinate to the Regional Leader. Technical directions issued by the Regional Administrator are binding for the District Leader. He will carry out general technical directives, taking into consideration the special nature of his area.

The following are disciplinarily subordinate to the District Leader: all Political Leaders on his staff, as well as Local Group and Base Leaders of the area under his control.

The District Leader is wholly responsible to his Regional Leader for the political and ideological education and alignment of Political Leaders and Party members, as well as the population in the area under his control.

13. The Regional Executive

The Regional Executive (the Regional Leader and his Regional Staff) has the job of politically leading a certain part of the country and of acting in a policy-forming capacity. Within the area under his control, the Regional Leader is responsible for the entire political, cultural, and economic development of all manifestations of life, according to National Socialist principles.

The Area Defined: The Region constitutes the incorporation of a number of Party Districts. The demarcation of its boundaries will be carried out, according to the Führer's directions, by the Director of Organisation.

(1) The Regional Leader

The Regional Leader is directly subordinate to the Führer, or to the Deputy Führer acting on the Führer's behalf. He is appointed by the Führer.

The Regional Leader bears overall responsibility to the Führer for the area entrusted to his control. Rights, duties, and spheres of authority of the Regional Leader arise mainly from his commission, granted by the Führer, and for the rest, from regulations laid down in detail.

The Regional Leader bears overall responsibility to the Führer for the political and ideological education and alignment of Political Leaders, Party members, as well as the population.

(2) The Deputy Regional Leader

If, through unforeseen circumstances, the Regional Leader is wholly prevented from the execution of his duties as Regional Leader, the Deputy Regional Leader will take over all rights and duties of the Regional Leader until relevant instructions from the Führer or Deputy Führer come to hand.

The principal sphere of activity of the Deputy Regional Leader is in relieving the Regional Leader. He is the Regional Leader's confidential aide, receiving his instructions from him. From this confidential relationship evolve his duties and rights.

△ ▷ *The relationship between the* Kreis *(District) and the* Gau *(Region). The illustration uses the* Kreis *of Pforzheim and the* Gau *of Baden to give reality to the example. Orders are transmitted from the* Gauleitung *to the* Kreisleitung, *and thence further down the chain of command to the* Ortsgruppen *and* Stützpunkte.
▷ *The relationship between the* Gauleitung *(Regional Party Executive) and the* Reichsleitung *(Supreme Party Executive). The* Gau *here illustrated is Saxony, with its headquarters in Dresden. In all there were 32* Gauen.

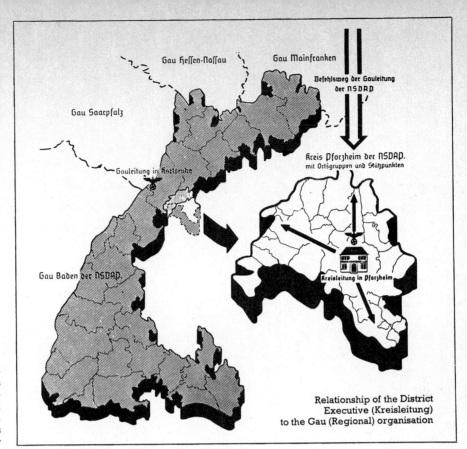

Relationship of the District Executive (Kreisleitung) to the Gau (Regional) organisation

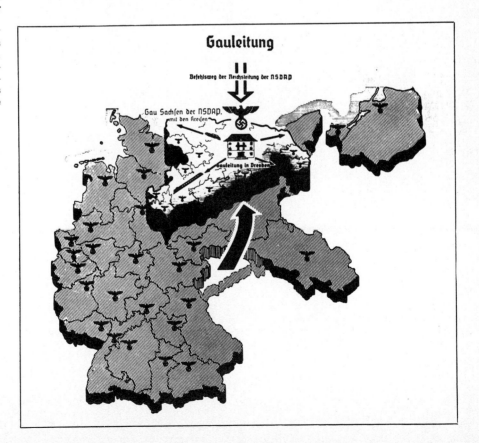

Gauleitung

(3) The Regional Inspecting Officer

The Regional Inspecting Officer is a representative of the Regional Leader. On behalf of the Regional Leader or his Deputy, it is his task to look into complaints, to carry out investigations, and to perform all kinds of special assignments.

All applications and complaints received by the Regional Executive either from the Deputy Führer or from other Party or State offices, as well as from public and private quarters, will be handled by the Regional Inspecting Officer.

It is the duty of the Regional Inspecting Officer to listen to callers visiting the Regional Offices in connection with complaints of one kind or another, and to prepare a report about the matter.

The Foreign Section: It is the task of the A.O. to win over German citizens abroad and also those employed at sea, to the National Socialist philosophy of life, and to keep alive, across class, profession, and creed, the idea of a Fellowship of the People in every single German national living abroad.

Notes

Regional Leader = *Gauleiter*
Regional Inspecting Officer = *Gauinspekteur*
A.O. = *Auslandsorganisation* (Foreign Section)
Fellowship of the People = *Volksgemeinschaftsgedanken*

14. The Central Executive

The N.S.D.A.P. represents the political conception, the political conscience, and the political will of the German nation. Political conception, political conscience, and political will are embodied in the person of the Führer. According to his directives, and conforming to the programme of the N.S.D.A.P., the German people's political aims will be guided and determined by the organs of the Central Executive. The threads of organisation of the German people and of the State meet in the Central Executive. Through the appointment of the Deputy Führer as Minister of the Reich, and through special administrative regulations, the penetration of the governmental apparatus by the political will of the Party has been ensured. It is the task of individual organs of the Central Executive, by means

of their sub-sections in the Regions, etc., to remain in the closest possible touch with the life of the people. What is observed in the Front of Battle should be compiled by the offices of the Central Executive for evaluation.

The Central Executive's structure has been planned in such a manner that the way from the most subordinate Party offices to the top makes possible the transmission of the smallest fluctuation and change in the temper of the people, and that, in turn, the moulding of will in the Central Executive brought about thereby reaches the Party's furthest command post, swiftly and unequivocally.

The Central Executive takes care, too, that reports of popular feeling should be passed upwards speedily and uninterruptedly, and that the will of the Führer should reach the outermost areas; exactly as with the healthy organism of a tree whose roots absorb nourishment from the soil, directing it to the leaves, whereas the nutritive juices formed in the leaves are sent down to the furthest roots. This interplay ensures an ever-renewed absorption of strength and an ever-increasing anchorage through the roots, and permits the crown

to spread ever more widely, to strive higher and higher and yet to defy wind and weather.

Since the National Socialist Movement evolved from within the people, it is first and foremost the task of the Central Executive to watch carefully that the strong roots of the Party, namely its bond with the people, should not wither away.

A further essential task of the Central Executive is the safeguarding of a first-class selection of leaders. The Central Executive must take care to see that in all spheres of life there exists a leadership which stands unswervingly for National Socialist ideology, working for its dissemination with all its energy.

In addition to the great general tasks which devolve upon the Central Executive, it will also have to ensure that all offices of the Party are properly organised. The National Director of Organisation, therefore, will exercise constant vigilance over the organisation of the entire Party apparatus to prevent a bureaucracy which might paralyse the Party's striking power from springing up. It is the supreme task of the National Director of Organisation always to maintain a sharp-edged sword for the Führer.

It is the purpose of the internal organisation of the Central Executive to carry out the above-named tasks. The number of its offices has been so calculated that all aspects of public life are represented in the Central Executive.

15. The Führer

It was his awareness of the deplorable state of affairs in pre-war Germany, preventing as it did the development of a genuine community of the people; his front-line experience of the Great War with its spirit of comrade-

Reichsleitung

△ *The* Reichsleitung. *This, the Party's government, was based in Munich in the* Gau *of Munich-Oberbayern. It will be remembered that the Nazi movement had started in Munich, and so its headquarters remained there.*

ship; and his loathing of a post-war Germany which was traitor-ously pacifist, that decided the Führer to enter politics and to create for the German people a new state which, for centuries to come, would safeguard their legitimate vital interests.

In order to achieve this end, the Führer created the National Socialist German Workers' Party. He imbued it with his spirit and his will, and on January 30, 1933, he seized power with its help. The will of the Führer is the Party's supreme law. As the Movement's supreme Leading Functionary he exercises the right of pardon within the jurisdiction of the Party.

By a law of August 1, 1934, concerning the head of state of the German Reich, the offices of Reich President and Reich Chancellor were merged. As a result, the former powers of the Reich President were transferred to the Führer, and now Reich Chancellor, Adolf Hitler. This law placed the leadership of Party and State into the same hands. At the Führer's wish the law was submitted to a plebiscite, held on August 19, 1934. On that day, the German people chose Adolf Hitler to be their sole leader; he is responsible only to his own conscience and to the German people.

Inside the Party the Führer is addressed as "My Führer"; on official, state and other occasions as "Führer and Reich Chancellor".

To assist him, especially in questions of Party policy, the Führer has appointed a

Deputy Fuhrer

who, in order to safeguard the closest co-operation between Party organs and public authorities, is a member (i.e. a Minister) of the Government.

In addition, the Führer has entrusted

Reich Executive Directors

within the Reich Central Executive of the N.S.D.A.P., with the implementation of specific Party tasks.

16. The Deputy Führer

The bearing of a National Socialist, his demeanour and his relationship with other Party members and with fellow citizens is supported by self-confidence and sound self-assurance, acquired during the Struggle for Power. This self-confident demeanour which a National Socialist draws from the fact that

the rules by which he lives are firmly anchored in his ideology, will impress others as genuine and natural only if it is free from any petty thirst for power and from any nervous tendency to regard as a threat to one's own job any fellow Party member who can accomplish more than one-self in some field of activity or other.

No leading Party member, because at some time his personal feelings might have been hurt, must let himself be carried away to pass an unfair judgement on a subordinate Party member.

Leadership presupposes men who follow readily, and that they will do so as long as they are conscious that their leader is a National Socialist to whom leadership means, not satisfaction of his own lust for power, but service to the Movement and commitment to his men. A junior leader who, from a feeling of petty jealousy, is ready, at the drop of a hat, to regard as his enemy anyone whose task impinges on his own; who insists on his authority because he fears a cur-

tailment of his position; has an altogether discreditable attitude, for it destroys the inner unity of the Movement. Posts have not been created to provide jobs for Party members, but for them to serve the cause of National Socialism. In this service there must be no petty and selfish desires. Only close co-operation in comradely solidarity with all those who serve the Movement will ensure the success and the inner strength of the Party.

17. The Deputy Führer's Staff

After the Assumption of Power by the National Socialist Movement, the Führer, in consequence of the extraordinarily heavy demands made on him by affairs of state, was obliged to appoint a deputy for the leadership of the Party; the head of the Central Political Committee of the N.S.D.A.P. was appointed to this post. This appointment by the Führer has placed an exceptional

△The Führer's personal standard.

degree of responsibility on his Deputy. The Assumption of Power had compelled the Party to second a large proportion of its best men to the State. Although these men did in part continue with their Party duties, they were no longer able to place their entire working capacity at the disposal of the Movement, especially as the re-building of the State demanded tremendous energy and personal effort. The Deputy Führer was thus forced to re-align the Party and to mobilise fresh forces. The organisations and affiliated bodies of the N.S.D.A.P. required a uniform political leadership.

Thus, at any given time, as instructed by the Deputy Leader, it is the main task of the staff, under the direction of the Chief of Staff, to bring the Regional Executives (*Gauleitungen*) of the N.S.D.A.P., as well as its organisations and affiliated bodies, into unified political alignment and to issue political directives to them. By order of the Führer, a further task of the Deputy Führer's staff is to take part decisively in legislative work of State authorities and in staffing them in accordance with National Socialist ideology.

18. The Chief of Chancellery of the Führer

The Führer's Chief of Chancellery heads The Private Chancellery Adolf Hitler, and the Führer's corps of adjutants. Here all Party matters received directly by the Führer are dealt with (provided they do not come under the competence of other offices), especially matters concerning Party members and applications for pardons in respect of sentences passed by courts of justice or Party courts.

19. The National Director of Organisation of the N.S.D.A.P.

The National Director of Organisation has been appointed by the Führer to deal with all organisational questions of the Party, its organisations and affiliated bodies.

In an ordinance dated May 12, 1934, the Deputy Führer has outlined in greater detail the scope of the National Director of Organisation. Accordingly, orders and measures initiated by

Reich Directors as well as by all offices of the Central Executive, which concern Party organisation or which may affect it, must be discussed with and approved by the National Director of Organisation before publication or implementation. Any plan or order of the kind described above requires the counter-signature of the National Director of Organisation. Unless agreement, documented by countersignature, has been reached prior to the measures detailed above coming into force, all orders of the kind described are null and void. Further, by a decree dated October 20, 1934, the Deputy Führer, in order to prevent contradictory comment by Party offices, organisations or affiliated bodies, has given exclusive authority to the National Director of Organisation to issue compulsory directives and orders concerning all questions of organisation. The sovereign rights of Leading Functionaries, and the independence of the S.A., S.S., N.S.K.K., and H.J., in matters concerning their own organisations, are in no way affected by this decree.

In his capacity as National Director of Organisation, this officer is, at the same time, Reich Director of Indoctrination and Reich Director of Personnel. In the execution of his various tasks, he uses the services of his Chief of Staff and Official Adviser who, on his behalf and as instructed by him, will direct the following offices:

  Central Office for Organisation
  Central Office for Indoctrination
  Central Personnel Office.
In addition, Official Advisers will direct the following offices on his behalf:

  Central Staff Office
  Central Office of the N.S.B.O.
  Central Bureau for the Organisation of National Party Rallies
  Central Bureau for Trade and Commerce.
In addition, the following offices which are politically subordinate to the Deputy Führer are in matters of administration, organisation, personnel and discipline, directly subordinate to the National Director of Organisation:

  Central Office for People's Welfare
  Central Office for Public Health
  N.S.D. Students' Association
  N.S.D. University Lecturers' Association

The uniform of a Mann *(Man), the lowest rank, in the* National-sozialistische Betriebszellenorganisation *or* N.S.B.O., *the cell organisation of the* Deutsche Arbeitsfront *(German Labour Front) in commercial and industrial undertakings.*

Central Office for War Victims
Central Office for Civil Servants
Central Office for Education
Central Office for Local Government
Department of Technical Science.

Thus, as shown by the above list, the competence of the National Director of Organisation is not limited to matters of organisation in the narrower sense of the word.

Competence:

The range of duties regarding personnel policy, indoctrination and organisation from an integrated whole. Inclusion and incorporation of Party members in a well-regulated indoctrination system is prerequisite for an efficient personnel policy. Only by adequate indoctrination will Leading Functionaries, and on their behalf personnel departments, be in a position to pursue a successful personnel policy. This in turn is prerequisite for the creation of an efficient organisation.

In the *Ordensburgen* of the N.S.D.A.P. valuable Party members from all Regions undergo two to three years' thorough and exceptionally exacting training under the supervision of the National Director of Organisation.

In order to achieve unity among leading Party members and increased excellence as well as strength of mind especially among Leading Functionaries, the National Director of Organisation will summon District Leaders (and Local Group or Base Leaders) and Regional Administrators to the *Ordensburgen* at regular intervals; this is in addition to regular Regional Leader Conferences. At these conferences, leading figures of Movement and State will speak about their tasks.

The Führer will himself speak at these gatherings, and fellow Party members will have an opportunity of meeting the Führer.

Once every year the three hundred most senior Political Leaders will be invited by the National Director of Organisation to enjoy travelling together through one of Germany's Regions. These journeys serve to strengthen the bonds of comradeship among veteran fighters, and their ties with their fellow citizens. All this results in Political Leaders gaining an increasingly integrated direction and line, in short, it welds them together into an indissoluble community.

The National Director of Organisation provides systematic training to facilitate an efficient personnel policy and the establishment of a suitable organisation. Moreover, he provides for external alignment of Political Officers, and for this purpose he issues basic instructions regarding training facilities.

In the field of personnel policy it is an essential task of the National Director of Organisation continually to supervise the training of potential leaders, particularly of those suitable for higher, specifically political, Party posts.

The National Director of Organisation also bears full responsibility for the organisation of National Party Rallies.

The National Director of Organisation is, at the same time, Director of the German Labour Front (D.A.F.).

The above outlines briefly the National Director of Organisation's range of duties. In detail this establishes the following competences for the National Director of Organisation:

The National Director of Organisation has to guard against over-organisation and must, if necessary, reduce the organisation to its fixed limit. Territorial changes, and changes in office structure must be authorised by the National Director of Organisation. In addition, the National Director of Organisation must ensure that in organisations where men are led, the community spirit should be fully expressed, and that the ideological alignment of fellow citizens in such organisation is safeguarded. Organisations based on economic status must be firmly discouraged; only in exceptional cases will association according to occupational group be permitted.

The task of Directors of Organisation in all areas:

It is necessary above all that Directors of Organisation should possess accurate knowledge of their subject matter. Their work will mostly be done behind the scene of political events, and yet it is among the most important activities of the Party. Just as the chief engineer in a factory, the Director of Organisation must supervise with great precision the organisational apparatus in his care, so that it may satisfy any demands made by the Party. Even small, insignificant mistakes must be stopped. **It must**

never be tolerated that mistakes exist at all.

Precisely because of the tremendous tasks, complicated by an organisation comprising many millions, an organisation without its equal anywhere in the world, perfunctory and careless work does much harm.

The Director of Organisation is the Party member who, in his area, bears full responsibility for implementing all orders and directives issued by superordinate offices, and for all organisational tasks in general.

Orders or directives received from a superordinate office must not be put up for discussion, but must be carried out at once. In this context it must be pointed out, however, that although work must be conscientious and accurate, bureaucratic methods are to be deprecated. The organisation should be lively, flexible, and without rigid arrangements.

If no suitable Party members are available locally, the Office for Organisation must be taken over by the Leading Functionary himself.

It is one of the Director of Organisation's special duties to remain in constant personal contact with subordinate Directors of Organisation. Thus the Regional Director of Organisation should, from time to time, meet the District Director of Organisation, and the District Director of Organisation the Local Group or the Base Director of Organisation, in order to discuss with them any outstanding questions of organisation and keep each other informed, so that official communications between Directors of Organisation may not be confined to written orders and reports. Without personal contact between men in responsible positions, the striking power of any organisation will be ineffectual.

This applies also to co-operation with the Departmental Directors of Organisation of individual sections and affiliated bodies whose work will be supervised by their local Director of Organisation.

It is advisable to call in these Party members for personal discussions or for meetings, as indicated above, to ensure mutual agreement with regard to organisational work. Above all, the Director of Organisation should in every respect be an objective and responsible adviser to his Leading Functionary and relieve him of all technical work relating to

Party organisation.

In cases of friction between offices, or disputes about competences, etc., which may spring up sometimes, he should act in a conciliatory way and eliminate tensions.

Any organisational or territorial change in the Regions may only be made with the approval of the Director of Organisation, to whom a preliminary report must also be sent prior to such changes coming into force.

Directors of Organisation must plan all measures well in advance.

The points below are directives for the work of Directors of Organisation:

(1) On behalf of his Leading Functionary, the Director of Organisation must ensure that all offices, organisations and affiliated bodies co-operate efficiently.

(2) He must ensure that the Party machinery works entirely reliably in all organisations and offices.

(3) It follows that the Director of Organisation must, from time to time, inspect every unit of the Party (Block, Cell, Base, Local Group, etc.).

(4) The Director of Organisation is responsible for the planning of Party Rallies. The internal arrangements are in the hands of the Director of Propaganda.

(5) The holding of membership meetings in Local Groups and Bases is incumbent on the Director of Organisation on behalf of his Leading Functionary, unless the latter wishes to take the meeting himself. The actual arrangements for such meetings are in the hands of the Director of Propaganda.

(6) The Director of Organisation must be exemplary in every respect when dealing with requests. The setting of time limits for the submission of reports is not some bureaucratic request, but necessary for the implementation of tasks for the Movement.

(7) The Director of Organisation must see that the offices of the Movement are not smothered by a paper war or by bureaucratic devices, but that everywhere the life of the Movement should throb vigorously. Thus reports on activities and on the atmosphere among Party members are valuable and useful only if they can be thoroughly dealt with and utilised by the superordinate office.

(8) It is one of a Director of Organisation's special tasks to organise the staff in his area meticulously. As he is his Leading

Functionary's competent Administrator, the establishment of main offices, offices, Cells, Blocks, etc, requires his consent.

(9) The Director of Organisation must supervise the work of Political Officers and make sure

(a) that in their service for the people Political Officers are not overtaxed;

(b) that demands for service by different departments are sensibly distributed;

(c) that in conformity with Party directives the only assignments dealt with are ideological, or tasks which serve to imbue the people with National Socialist ideology;

(d) however, he must also make sure that Party members who do not participate actively are eliminated from the Political Leader Corps in the not too distant future.

(10) The Director of Organisation will keep records of Departments and offices, so that he may at all times be ready to give his Leading Functionary the opportunity of inspection.

(11) The Director of Organisation must take the greatest care to ensure that individual offices do not burden themselves with work outside their competence or outside the ideological tasks of the Party.

(12) On behalf of his Leading Functionary, the Director of Organisation must make sure that the essential activities of Political Leaders are undertaken among the people, by personal contact between man and man, and that the work of political leaders must on no account be restricted to more or less well-organised offices. Our strength will always be in our seeking out our fellow citizens and not in merely giving them the occasional opportunity of attending an appointment graciously accorded.

For this reason the responsible Director of Organisation must watch carefully that the development of Local Group or Base offices is limited to a minimum; at the same time he must ensure the perfect functioning of the Party's Block and Cell system and see that only the best Party members work as Block and Cell Leaders.

If the Party machinery is working efficiently, a wealth of Leader meetings will be necessary; these alone are suitable to align Political Officers and their helpers with each other and, at the same time, indoctrinate them

ideologically.

(13) The Director of Organisation is responsible for the internal and external alignment of the Political Leader Corps. For the implementation of the necessary physical and ideological training, a Training Officer will be at the disposal of the Director of Organisation.

(14) In the pursuit of his activities the Director of Organisation will work in close contact with the responsible N.S.D.A.P. Personnel Administrator and Indoctrination Officer.

(15) The Party rank order for Directors of Organisation is as follows:

Director of Organisation: Central Office for Organisation

Regional Director of Organisation

District Director of Organisation

Local Group Director of Organisation.

(16) The Director of Organisation is authorised to ensure territorial conformity in all fields of action of affiliated bodies, the N.S. Women's League, the N.S. Students' Association, etc. with Party sovereign areas. He is also responsible for all other problems of territorial organisation, such as the demarcation of Regional, District, Local Group, Base, Cell and Block boundaries.

(17) It is one of the duties of the Central Office for Organisation to agree upon and fix service designations for Political Officers, Administrators and Wardens, etc., as well as for affiliated bodies and their offices. The final decision rests with the Führer.

The Training Supervisor and his Tasks

A Political Leader should excel through soldierly bearing and discipline, regardless of whether he is in civilian dress or in uniform. His demeanour, as an individual or in closed formation, at grand ceremonial parades and demonstrations of the Party (the Annual Party Rally, etc.), as well as the handling of his pistol, the weapon of honour bestowed upon him, all these demand appropriate training. His exhausting service as Political Leader demands counterbalancing through sport and physical training.

Thus the tasks of the Training Supervisor, working within the scope of the Director of Organisation, have been determined. They are:

(1) To carry out marching and

shooting training of Political Leaders. Duties will be determined in detail by the Leading Functionary in authority and may not take place more than twice monthly.

In the issuing and carrying out of commands, the Training Supervisor will follow the Regulations for the Training of Political Leaders of the N.S.D.A.P.; in small-arms training, he will follow the special regulation, entitled "The Pistol". An integral part of the training is the familiarisation of the Political Leader with individual commands so that during parades he will, if necessary, be in a position to give these himself.

(2) To carry out parades fixed by the Leading Functionary in authority.

(3) To supervise the observation of regulations when service dress is worn; to check the authority of individuals to wear badges of rank: for this purpose the Training Supervisor will be in charge of the Patrol Service, set up by the Leading Functionary.

(4) To take over (if possible) assignments of the Outdoor Service on behalf of the Director of Organisation.

(5) To supervise or possibly to carry out the sports activities, compulsory within the framework of the training scheme for Political Leaders.

Physical training will generally be carried out. Proper contests are forbidden, unless they are training exercises for the purpose of gaining the S.A. Sports Medal. The Training Supervisor will take part in sports activities. Physical training will be directed by sports instructors, seconded by the N.S. Association "Strength through Joy". The Training Supervisor will make the necessary arrangements. Insofar as arrangements with the "Strength through Joy" Association are not feasible for technical reasons, the Training Supervisor will himself take charge of the physical training of Political Leaders, as directed by the regulations laid down for this purpose. Marching, shooting, and physical training should take place not more often than twice monthly.

Since, for the Political Leader, this training is merely supplementary, in order to mould his exterior demeanour in a soldierly fashion, the Training Supervisor will have to be conscious of his great duty and the complexity of his tasks, namely thoroughly to train Political Leaders in the

comparatively short time available, without tiring them; rather, by means of additional sports activities, to provide compensatory relaxation from their strenuous and responsible activities as Block Leaders, Cell Leaders, Administrators, Local Leaders, etc.

Under no circumstances must the Training Supervisor allow himself to be carried away to the extent of using an insolently peremptory tone, which might incline Political Leaders to lose that capacity for enthusiasm that has always distinguished them. Only then will the Political Leaders regard their training and sports duty as a welcome opportunity for relaxation and recreation from their strenuous work, and comradely association will make their duty pleasurable.

20. The Head Office for Organisation– Central Statistical Bureau

(1) **General remarks**

The Central Statistical Bureau deals with the following matters:

(1) Party member statistics

(2) Political Leader statistics

(3) Sectional statistics

(4) Affiliated Bodies statistics

(5) Statistical research on the subject of Party and People

(6) Population statistics in the Regions of the N.S.D.A.P.

(7) Special statistics.

These statistics are sub-divided into:

(a) National statistics

(b) Regional statistics

(c) District statistics

(d) Local Group and Base statistics

and are composed of:

(i) Statistics relating to mobility

(ii) Statistics relating to strength of establishment

to be compiled:

(A) regularly every two to three years

(B) separately, on request.

(2) **Tasks**

It is the task of the Central Statistical Bureau to determine, by means of investigations made at certain intervals, any deficiencies in the Party organisation; to create the conditions for furthering the tasks of the Party; and to convey to the Führer and his representatives a true picture, in accordance with the facts, of the Party in all its aspects, as far as this is possible through investigations.

For that reason, statistical evaluation of incoming material will be compiled not merely in tabulated form, but will contain, in addition to critical remarks, any suggestions necessary at any given time.

The main purpose of Establishment statistics is to trace and supervise the following:

(1) Party members in relation to population, according to occupation and age

(2) Admissions and withdrawals of Party members according to occupation and age

(3) Exact intelligence of areas (Bases, Local Groups, Districts, Regions) sparsely populated with Party members and thus falling behind in respect of the percentage laid down of the number of Party members per number of general population

(4) Suggestions concerning determination of number of fellow citizens to be admitted, according to occupation and age

(5) Increase or decrease of Local Groups, as required, in a certain relation to households

(6) Activities of Party members

(7) Leadership analysed according to occupation and age

(8) Changes in rank (or promotions) of Political Leaders

(9) Wear and tear on leadership (retirement, admission, and transfer of Political Leaders)

(10) Training and gatherings of Political Leaders

(11) Movement of Leaders and Party members in Party offices and affiliated bodies. The Central Statistical Bureau as well as all Regional and District Statistical Bureaux are in continuous close contact with Government Statistical Departments.

(3) Competence

The Central Statistical Bureau is the sole authorised body to undertake any investigations essential for the Party from an organisational and political standpoint.

Not included in the above investigations are:

(1) Financial statistics and continuous cash reports; these, as administrative matters, are undertaken by the National Treasury Department.

(2) Social and economic statistics; these are undertaken by the statistical sections of the relevant departments. There is, however, liaison with the Central Statistical Bureau.

In order to obtain the necessary material, the Central Statistical Bureau will, in the first place, have at its disposal the Regional head offices for statistics which, moreover, are technically subordinate to it.

Apart from statistical assessments for the Regional Leader, these offices will have to undertake research only as instructed by the Central Statistical Bureau of the N.S.D.A.P. and to create the conditions necessary for such research in Districts and Local Groups.

The Central Statistical Bureau will issue the forms necessary for all statistical research and reports to Regions and Districts and, if required, extend this to Local Groups and Bases. Any questions will be dealt with uniformly and when completed will be reported through official channels.

Existing sub-divisions of Party offices, including organisations and affiliated bodies, engaged in statistical work, are technically subordinate to the Central Statistical Bureau of the N.S.D.A.P. Any investigations by these offices will take place in agreement with the Central Statistical Bureau and in closest co-operation with it.

Within the framework of their competence, any material collected is at the disposal of Party Offices for official purposes only. In order to undertake statistical research within the Party and its affiliated organisations, permission of the Deputy Führer will be required.

21. The National Director of Organisation

Location: Nuremberg.
Tasks: Arrangements and organisation of all National Party Rallies.

The Central Bureau for the Organisation of National Party Rallies works as an office within the scope of the National Director of Organisation. A permanent office is maintained throughout the year, staffed by a Manager, an Assistant Manager, and an Administrative Assistant. Some time prior to the National Party Rally, the following departments will be staffed:

Management
Cashier and Administration
Transport and Parking
Accommodation
Congress and special meetings
Public entertainments and Fireworks

Food and Camp construction
Telecommunications
Guests of Honour
Motor Transport
Sales
Press
Sanitation
Propaganda
Public address system
Road blocks and traffic control
Political Leader Corps Parade Staff
S.A. Parade Staff
S.S. Parade Staff
N.S.K.K. Parade Staff
H.J. Parade Staff
National Labour Service Parade Staff
Armed Forces Parade Staff.

22. The National Socialist Motor Transport Corps

Leadership

The National Socialist Motor Transport Corps (N.S.K.K.), is an independent section of the N.S.D.A.P. and is led by the Corps Leader of the National Socialist Motor Transport Corps.

Organisation and tasks

Next to the S.A. and S.S., the National Socialist Motor Transport Corps stands as an independent section of the N.S.D.A.P., as its motorised unit. Growing out of the Motor-S.A. and the N.S.K.K. as it was in the years of Struggle for Power, reared and tested in the spirit of the S.A., drawing its strength from the eager readiness for action and ideological steadfastness of its men, the Corps is the qualified bearer of banner and will of the idea of motorisation in our New Germany. The higher the level of motorisation, the stronger the nation's defensive power!

It is in the intensification of this realisation and in systematically preparing the way for its practical consequences in a National Socialist fellowship spirit that the N.S.K.K. sees one of its most important tasks. And thus, not only Party members but also young people, growing up in the H.J. and in the Labour Service, who are motoring enthusiasts, will find an eager welcome as new members of the N.S.K.K. The Motoring Schools of the N.S.K.K. all over the country offer six-week courses in which they provide systematic, ideologically-orientated training of prospective members in driving technique and motoring as a sport.

When the time comes for his National Service, any young man trained at one of these schools will be well prepared, physically and spiritually, to don with pride the dress of one of the Nation's arms-bearers – the German Armed Forces – and when he has taken it off once more, to return to the ranks of the Corps, the right sort of man now to be admitted into the great comradeship of its broad organisation which, sub-divided into

4 Senior Motor Corps
3 Motor Divisions
21 Brigades,

comprises German motorists doing voluntary service.

Here, in steadfast concord, with ideologically like-minded men who, after a hard day's work, meet in a National Socialist spirit of fellowship for *Sturm* Evenings and training rides every Sunday, he will not only maintain his flexibility but also retain and enlarge the knowledge he has acquired.

For this purpose, the sport of cross-country driving, an activity carried out by the N.S.K.K., is eminently suitable. To take part in it makes demands on the whole man! Apart from mastery of one's vehicle, courage, perseverance, the ability to make quick decisions, the ability to find one's way, and physical agility, are the most important prerequisites for this sport.

Thus the National Socialist Motor Transport Corps is the fountain of youth and the storehouse of strength of the motorised nation: loyal, self-sacrificing and ready for action!

Notes

N.S.K.K. = *Nationalsozialistisches Kraftfahr-Korps*

Our New Germany: *Das Neue Deutschland*, a Nazi concept, referring to Germany freed from "liberalistic" ideas and wholly immersed in National Socialist thought.

Sturm Evenings: A *Sturm* or Company is the collective word for a group of Brown or Black Shirts.

◁ *An* Oberscharführer *(Colour
Sergeant) of the training
company of Motor Regiment
No. 86 of the N.S.K.K. in
motorcycling kit.*
▷ *An N.S.K.K. Mann in
service dress with crash helmet.*

◁ A Scharführer *(Sergeant) of
the N.S.K.K. Technical
Leaders' School.*
▷ A Sturmführer *(Company
Commander) on the staff of the
1st Squadron* (Staffel) *of Motor-
boat Regiment* (Kraftbootstan-
darte) *No. 1 in service dress.*

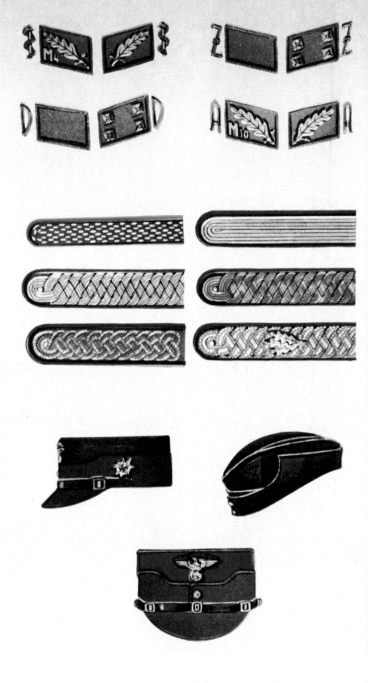

◄ *A* Scharführer *of Motor-boat Regiment No. 1 in service dress with greatcoat.*

Δ *Insignia and headgear of the* Nationalsozialistische Kraftfahrkorps:

Top two lines: *Specialist rank collar patches. These are for the regimental doctor (*Standarten-Arzt*), squadron dental surgeon (*Staffel-Zahnärzt*), squadron dentist (*Staffel-Dentist*), and regimental chemist (*Standarten-Apotheker*).*

Centre three lines: *Epaulettes. These are, from left to right, top to bottom:* Mann *to* Obertruppführer *in the "Saxony" Motor Brigade,* Sturmführer *to* Sturmhauptführer, Staffelführer *to* Standartenführer, Oberführer, Brigadeführer *to* Obergruppenführer, *and* Korpsführer.

Bottom: *Service caps. These are, clockwise from top left:* Mann *to* Obertruppführer, *the field cap, and a* Sturmführer *on the N.S.K.K. high command.*

Opposite page: *N.S.K.K. command flags.*

Corps Leader (Korpsführer)

Corps High Command
(Korpsführung)

Inspector of Technical Training
and Equipment (Inspekteur für
technische Ausbildung u.
Geräte)

Reich Leader School
(Reichsführerschule)

Senior Motor Corps "South"
(Motor-Obergruppe "Sud")

Motor Division "East"
(Motor-Gruppe "Ostland")

Motor Brigade "Saxony"
(Motor-Brigade "Sachsen")

Motor Regiment No. 84
(Motor-Standarte 84)

Motor Squadron No. 2/
Regt. No. 133
(Motor-Staffel 2, Standarte 133)

23. The National Director of Organisation of the N.S.D.A.P.

a. The Central Office for Political Indoctrination

Tasks and Responsibilities of N.S.D.A.P. Indoctrination Offices: A Survey of Activities in its Organisations and Affiliated Bodies:

The National Director of Organisation is at the same time National Director of Indoctrination.

The National Director of Organisation of the N.S.D.A.P. is responsible for ideological alignment and selection of Political Leaders working in the N.S.D.A.P., of Political Leaders seconded to organisations and affiliated bodies, as well as of administrators, wardens, and chairmen of organisations and affiliated bodies.

For the purpose of discharging this task he makes use of the Central Indoctrination Office which comes under his administrative scope. For ideological training purposes the following will be immediately included within the sphere of the Central Indoctrination Office or the Indoctrination offices of the N.S.D.A.P.:

(1) Political Leaders of the N.S.D.A.P. (including all Political Leaders of the N.S.D.A.P. seconded for service to affiliated bodies and organisations under the care of the N.S.D.A.P.);

(2) Members of the N.S.D.A.P. insofar as they take part voluntarily in Indoctrination activities;

(3) Women Leaders and Wardens of the N.S. Women's League and the German Women's Service (N.S.F.S. and D.F.W.);

(4) Chairmen, Administrators, and Wardens of the German Labour Front including those holding leading positions in the N.S. Association "Strength through Joy" and in the Labour Groups;

(5) Chairmen of, or all personnel in leading positions in the N.S. War Victims' Welfare Organisation (N.S.K.O.V.);

(6) Wardens of the N.S. League for Public Welfare (N.S.V.);

(7) Wardens of the Civil Servants' League (R.D.B.);

(8) Chairmen of the N.S. Physicians' League (N.S.A.B.);

(9) Wardens and members of the N.S. Teachers' League (N.S.L.B.);

(10) Leading personnel of the N.S. Lawyers' League (N.S.R.W.B.);
(11) Leading personnel and members of the N.S.D. Students' League (N.S.D.S.B.);
(12) Leading personnel and members of the N.S.D. University Lecturers' League (N.S.D.D.B.); and
(13) Wardens of the N.S.D. Technical League (N.S.B.D.T.).

The Central Office for Political Indoctrination is composed of the following five departments:
(a) Department with Responsibility for Theoretical Indoctrination Tasks: Preparation of teaching material, curriculum, teaching aids, and lists of guest speakers; collaboration with scientific institutions; alignment of instructors; publication of instructions concerning teaching materials for the purpose of indoctrination in the N.S.D.A.P.; and creation of a lecture library. **Sections:** Curriculum Planning; Lecture Arrangements.
(b) Department with Responsibility for Practical Training. Its tasks include: Organisation and supervision of indoctrination activities at the Training Castles (*Ordensburgen*) of the N.S.D.A.P.; organisation and supervision of all other indoctrination arrangements; supervision of instruction at the *Ordensburgen*; supervision of adherence to curriculum; inspection of classes; supervision of technical training in affiliated associations; appointment, recall, and transfer of skeleton staff at the *Ordensburgen*; compilation and evaluation of reports; evaluation of assessment papers; and preparation of progress reports. **Sections:** Indoctrination Activities; Reports.
(c) Recruiting Office. Tasks: Collaboration with enlistment for the *Ordensburgen*; calling up of Political Officers for annual manoeuvres at District or Regional training establishments; close co-operation with Central Staff Office; and issue of cheap travel vouchers. **Sections:** Special and Refresher Courses; Selection.
(d) Administrative Office (Commissariat). Tasks: Control of establishment at Schools and *Ordensburgen*, and supervision of technical matters in connection with all indoctrination operations and activities.
(e) Department with Responsibility for Indoctrination Circulars. Task: Publication of N.S.D.A.P. Indoctrination Circulars and supervision of editorial training work in the Party. (The editor may be given the title of Head Office Director.)
Sections: Editor's Office; Management and Records; Inspection of Distribution.

b. The Regional Office for Political Indoctrination

Regional Indoctrination Supervisors will be appointed by the Regional Leader in agreement with, and under the supervision of, the National Director of Organisation.

The structure of the N.S.D.A.O. Regional Office for Political Indoctrination corresponds with the structure of the Central Office for Political Indoctrination. In place of individual departments of the Central Office for Political Indoctrination, there are at the Regional Office for Political Indoctrination corresponding sections having the same tasks, of which the following may be specially mentioned:
(a) Management of Regional Schools; organisation and execution of political indoctrination at N.S.D.A.P. Regional Schools; and supervision of Technical Schools run by affiliated bodies and organisations;
(b) Selection of participants in Regional school indoctrination courses;
(c) Co-operation with training staffs of organisations and affiliated bodies within the framework of tasks and responsibilities laid down;
(d) Supervision of District Indoctrination Supervisors' work;
(e) Distribution of Indoctrination Circulars; and
(f) Formation and care of the necessary politico-ideological nucleus of Political Indoctrination Lecturers.

c. The District Indoctrination Supervisor

District Indoctrination Supervisors will be appointed by the District Leader in agreement with the Regional Indoctrination Supervisor.

Generally, the tasks of the District Indoctrination Supervisor correspond to those of the Regional Indoctrination Supervisor. The following are the duties incumbent upon him and his regional office:
(a) To suggest participants for Indoctrination courses at the Regional school;
(b) organisation and execution of politico-ideological training in the District area;
(c) supervision of District school; arrangement of Indoctrination courses or week-end courses;
(d) distribution of Indoctrination Circulars;
(e) supervision of technical training of association; and
(f) formation and continuous alignment of all politico-ideological Indoctrination lecturers (Indoctrination Speakers).

The organisational structure of the Central Office for Political Indoctrination applies, by analogy, to all District Offices for Political Indoctrination.

With the District Office for Political Indoctrination there will be three Main Offices:
(1) Main Office with responsibility for practical indoctrination Tasks: Creation and constant control of Indoctrination establishment;
(2) Main Office with responsibility for theoretical indoctrination Tasks: Formation and constant control of staff of speakers; and
(3) Main Recruiting Office Tasks: Inclusion of all Political Leaders, Administrators, and Wardens in Local Group Indoctrination; calling-up for Indoctrination course at District schools.

d. The Local Group (or Base) Indoctrination Supervisor

The Local Group Political Indoctrination Supervisor will be appointed by the Local Group Leader in agreement with the District Indoctrination Supervisor.

The Local Group Indoctrination Supervisor has the following duties:
(a) organisational preparation of Indoctrination Evenings;
(b) placing of Indoctrination Speakers, particularly for the political indoctrination of Block and Cell Leaders and all leading members of the Party (including those of organisations and affiliated bodies) within the Local Group area, as well as Party members participating voluntarily;
(c) suggestions for participants at District schools from among participants in Local Group or Base indoctrination;
(d) distribution of Indoctrination Circulars; and
(e) supervision of technical training of associations within the Local Group or Base area.

The Local Group Indoctrination Supervisor (or Base Indoctrination Supervisor) must see to the uniform execution of political indoctrination work within the area of his Local Group (or Base).

He has not been appointed to undertake indoctrination work himself, but his task is the preparation and organisation of indoctrination functions. at which Regional or District Indoctrination Speakers will be made use of as lecturers.

As far as all indoctrination work is concerned, the principle, in direct contrast with propaganda work, that it addresses itself exclusively to a select circle of people must be borne in mind, and it is for that reason that it refrains from the usual forms of propaganda at its functions.

The task of indoctrination must be one of selection. This process of selection takes place, first of all, by dint of the fact that fundamentally participation in indoctrination functions is on a voluntary basis for all Party members, and that Political Leaders only will be called in compulsorily for indoctrination.

From among this circle, selection for attendance at District and Regional schools will be made at the suggestion of the Leading Functionary, according to the candidate's participation and aptitude record during Local Group or Base Indoctrination functions.

Speakers will be put at the disposal of Indoctrination Evenings from the staff of Indoctrination Speakers of the Regional Office for Political Indoctrination or the District Office for Political Indoctrination. The Local Group (or Base) Indoctrination Supervisor will be responsible for the fixing of dates and for notification of the Indoctrination Speaker, just like the Local Group Propaganda Supervisor. In addition, he has to take care that indoctrination topics arranged monthly by the Central Office for Political Indoctrination are discussed exhaustively and in good time.

Thus, within his area, the Local Group (or Base) Indoctrination Supervisor bears the responsibility for all indoctrination activities of the N.S.D.A.P.

Notes

German Women's Service = *Deutsches Frauenwerk* (Organisation for the social and educational concerns of women)
N.S.K.O.V. = N.S. *Kriegsopferversorgung* (care of war victims)
N.S.V. = N.S. *Volkswohlfahrt* (League for Public Welfare)
R.D.B. = *Reichsbund Deutscher Beamter* (Civil Service Organisation)
N.S.B.D.T. = *Nationalsozialistischer Bund Deutscher Technik* (German Technical League)

e. The Central Office for Political Indoctrination

(1) *a.* Appointments of Political Leaders, and the allocation of rank will take place according to existing staff regulations for all fellow workers in Indoctrination Offices.

b. All politico-ideological Indoctrination Speakers belong to the staff of their local N.S.D.A.P. Office for Political Indoctrination. They will be made available for N.S.D.A.P. Indoctrination Evenings at Local Groups, etc. by the Supervisor of the Indoctrination Office.

(2) Among others, the following topics are part of the whole subject of politico-ideological alignment: the delineation of the fundamental National Socialist attitude *vis-à-vis* internal politics, foreign affairs, racial and hereditary science, economic and social politics, history, geopolitics, cultural and educational politics, etc.

(3) **Indoctrination of the S.A., S.S., H.J. and N.S.K.K.**
Ideological indoctrination of the leaders of the above formations will be undertaken in those formations on the part of their local offices in mutual agreement with the National Director of Organisation, the Central Office for Political Indoctrination or the N.S.D.A.P. Offices for Political Indoctrination.

(4) All Political Leaders, seconded to affiliated bodies on the part of the N.S.D.A.P., since, in their capacity as Political Directors, they belong directly to the staff of the Leading Functionary in their area, will, notwithstanding their activities as Administrators, Wardens and Chairmen in the affiliated bodies, be ideologically aligned solely and directly by their local Supervisor of Indoctrination.

(5) **Indoctrination Departments in Affiliated Bodies** are concerned with the technical training of their Administrators, Wardens, etc. on an ideological basis.

This technical training is independent; it will be supervised by the Indoctrination Offices of the N.S.D.A.P.

Insofar as purely ideological indoctrination is provided, (i.e. for teachers, students, and lecturers), this will be undertaken according to instructions by the competent Supervisor of Indoctrination.

Speakers on the subject of technical training in organisations and affiliated bodies will join the staff of the competent Administrator of Indoctrination of their affiliated body in Reich, Region, or District. They will have to be approved by their local N.S.D.A.P. Supervisor of Indoctrination.

Administrators of Indoctrination in affiliated bodies will have their seat of office at the offices of their affiliated body; they are attached to the staff of the leading Administrator of the affiliated body.

(6) Politico-ideological propaganda *vis-à-vis* members of organisations and affiliated bodies is incumbent upon the National Directorate for Propaganda, as well as upon N.S.D.A.P. Regional and District Directors of Propaganda and, on their behalf, upon Propaganda departments of affiliated bodies.

The Central Office for Political Indoctrination works in closest co-operation with the National Directorate for Propaganda.

f. N.S.D.A.P. Indoctrination Castles and Technical Schools of Organisations and Affiliated Bodies

(1) The N.S.D.A.P. Indoctrination Castles serve for politico-ideological alignment of N.S.D.A.P. Political Leaders and Administrators of affiliated bodies. They are under the sole supervision of the Regional, or District, Supervisor for Indoctrination. Insofar as he does not reserve for himself the direction of the school, he may detail a fellow Party member to act as director of the school.

(2) All schools of affiliated bodies are technical schools. They work independently. Technically they are supervised by the Administrator of Indoctrination of the body in question.

The number of schools will be determined in agreement with the National Director of Organisation in his capacity as Director of the Central Office for Political Indoctrination. Directors of technical schools must be Party members.

(3) **Staffing of N.S.D.A.P. Schools and Ordensburgen** The above will be staffed by the following:
A. Administrative Staff (Chief Financial Officer, Administrator, etc.); and
B. Teaching Staff (Castle Commandant or School Director, leading and teaching staff). Teaching staffs as a body will come under the auspices of the Central Office for Political Indoctrination. As far as skeleton staff in *Ordensburgen* is concerned, we must distinguish the following:
(*a*) The solely responsible leader in the *Ordensburg* is the Castle Commandant.

The Castle Commandant will remain at the same *Ordensburg* during his entire term of office. The Castle Commandant is supported by
(*b*) one adjutant, and
(*c*) the staff (drill sergeant, chief administrator, etc.). In this connection, the following subdivision should be noted:
(*d*) senior teachers for physical hardening and alignment of students (drill sergeant, sports coach, etc.);
(*e*) senior teachers for ideological and spiritual education of students.
(*f*) In addition, there will be a senior teacher, on whom it will be incumbent to impart knowledge of deportment.

Immediately subordinate to the Castle Commandant are
(*g*) three stand-to leaders (for 300–400 men).

Each stand-to leader also has an adjutant at his disposal. The most senior stand-to leader will lead the first stand-to squad. At the same time, he will act as deputy to the Castle Commandant, should the latter be prevented from being present.

The maximum age on appointment for stand-to leaders is 40. A stand-to leader will remain at the same *Ordensburg* during his entire term of office.

The following are subordinate to stand-to leaders:
(*h*) Leaders of Centuries:
All ten leaders of Centuries must have passed their sports coach's examinations.

Leaders of Centuries remain at *Ordensburg* for six years' service. In future, they will be withdrawn successively from the *Ordensburgen* as and when their term of office expires. In due course, leaders of Centuries will be accepted for senior Party service. Maximum age on appointment for leaders of Centuries is 35.

The following are subordinate to leaders of Centuries:
(*i*) Squad (*Kameradschaft*) leaders (for 50 men).

The Squad represents simultaneously the seminar of spiritual and ideological education.

The Squad leader must be physically well trained, through and through. Squad leaders are changed every three years. In future, they will be withdrawn successively from the *Ordensburgen*, as and when their term of office expires.

If he is considered suitable, any Squad Leader, having completed his course of instruction, will be accepted into active Party service; only at a later point in time will he be ordered to return to do service as Squad leader. In due course, Squad leaders will be accepted for senior Party service. Maximum age will be 30.

The appointment of teaching staffs will take place on the strength of a muster, for which Regional Administrators, District Leaders, District Administrators, and Local Group Leaders will be considered.

For a muster of Skeleton Staff the regulations are similar to those for a muster of students at *Ordensburgen.*
C. Guest Instructors
(*a*) Full-time scientists, directly subordinate to the Central Office for Political Indoctrination and
(*b*) N.S.D.A.P. National, Regional and Central Administrators.
(*c*) There are, however, Instructors (called Indoctrination Specialists), who are attached to the teaching staff of an *Ordensburg*, and who may, at the same time, should this prove expedient, work as guest instructors at other *Ordensburgen* or Party schools.
D. The following subjects will be taught:
(1) Racial theory (to be taught by a biologist and a philosopher);
(2) History (to be taught by an instructor each for ancient, mediaeval, and modern history);
(3) Ideology and Philosophy;
(4) Art and Culture;
(5) Economics and Sociology; and

(6) Military science.

If instructors for the above-mentioned subjects are civilians, they will teach at any *Ordensburg* for three months in a year.

E. Regulations concerning Recruitment for Prospective Participants in Ordensburg Courses

Recruitment will be carried out by a commission consisting of the National Director of Organisation, the Regional Leader, the District Leader, the competent Staff Administrator, and the confidential medical officer of the Department for Public Health. Application will be made voluntarily to the Local Group Leader.

Conditions for admission to an Ordensburg:

(*a*) Applicant must have worked actively in the N.S.D.A.P.;

(*b*) Perfect health and freedom from defects;

(*c*) Aryan origin and freedom from hereditary disease;

(*d*) Favourable opinion of Leading Functionary after receipt of report from Staff Administrator;

(*e*) Age 23 to 30; in exceptional cases, applicants below and above the age limits may be considered.

After the age of 26, celibacy is undesirable.

24. The German Labour Front and N.S. Association "Strength through Joy"

Extracts from Regulations issued by the Führer on October 24, 1934, concerning the nature and aims of the German Labour Front.

"**Nature and aims:** The German Labour Front is the organisation for all Germans who labour with hands and brains.

"It includes particularly members of the former trade unions, the former Unions of Salaried Employees, and the former Employers' Association, as members enjoying equal rights.

"Membership of professional, socio-political, economic, or ideological organisations does *not* serve as substitute for membership of the German Labour Front.

"The Reich Chancellor may order legally recognised professional organisations to belong as a body to the German Labour Front. The aim of the German Labour Front is the creation of a genuine all-German fellowship of people and production.

"**Tasks:** The German Labour

Front must safeguard industrial peace by creating among management understanding for the justified claims of their employees, and, conversely, among employees, for the situation and potential of their place of employment.

"It is the task of the German Labour Front to establish between the justified interests of all parties a balance which corresponds with National Socialist principles, and which limits the number of cases which, according to the law of January 20, 1934, will have to be transferred to the competent State authorities for their decision.

"The representation of all parties involved, necessary for the achievement of that balance, is exclusively the concern of the German Labour Front. The formation of other organisations and activities of such organisations in this connection are prohibited.
(signed) Adolf Hitler
Führer and Reich Chancellor"

(1) Introduction

An end having been put by National Socialism to the many political parties and their seditious activities, it was necessary for group egotism and the class struggle caused by it, and manifesting itself in the shape of fighting units and trade unions, to disappear from among German workers.

A new organisation has been

created according to the National Socialist principle of "Public Need Before Private Greed", namely the National Socialist Co-operative Organisation known as

"The German Labour Front". Fellowship of the people has taken the place of class struggle. In the German Labour Front, this fellowship of the people is given tangible expression through the incorporation of all Germans earning their living by the labour of their hands and brains.

The aim of the German Labour Front is the creation of a true all-German fellowship of people and production. The German Labour Front must take care to see that every individual takes his place in the economic life of the Nation in a spiritual and physical disposition which will enable him to achieve the highest possible output and thus ensure the greatest benefit for the fellowship of the people.

The N.S.D.A.P. retains the leadership of the German Labour Front. The National Director of Organisation is Director of the German Labour Front. He is appointed by the Führer and is responsible to him only. The Director of the German Labour Front appoints and dismisses all office holders of the German Labour Front. Party members only should be appointed to such a post, in the first place.

The following are office holders of the German Labour Front:
(1) D.A.F. Foremen
(2) D.A.F. Stewards; and
(3) K.d.F. Wardens.

The geographical structure of the German Labour Front corresponds to that of the N.S.D.A.P.

For the purpose of organisation of the German Labour Front, the target of organic order, as laid down in the programme of the N.S.D.A.P., is decisive.

The geographical and technical organisation of the German Labour Front will be determined by the National Director of Organisation of the N.S.D.A.P.

The financial administration of the German Labour Front will be under the control of the National Treasurer of the N.S.D.A.P., in accordance with the first Regulation for the Implementation of the Law for Safeguarding the Unity of Party and State, of March 23, 1934.

With the incorporation into the German Labour Front of the organisations of commercial economy, transport economy, and agrarian economy, the foun-

△ *The uniform of a D.A.F.* Werkschar-Mann, *a D.A.F. Steward (*Walter*), and a "Strength through Joy" Warden (*Wart*). The* Werkschar *was a political organisation of factory employees.*
Opposite page: *Flags of the* Deutsche Arbeitsfront. *From top to bottom these are: the standard of the Aalen branch; the service pennant of a D.A.F.* Gauwalter *(Regional Steward), a Department Leader of the D.A.F. Central Bureau, and an Administrator in a Reich manufacturing industry; and a D.A.F. Leader's standard.*

dations have been laid for the creation of **social self-consciousness** which the Führer confirmed in his edict of March 21, 1935.

The German Labour Front is the holding organisation of the National Socialist association "Strength through Joy".

(2) The Tasks of the German Labour Front
In fulfilment of the Regulations issued by the Führer and Reich Chancellor on October 24, 1934, and of the Law concerning the Regulation of National Labour, dated January 20, 1934, the tasks of the German Labour Front are as follows:

(*a*) the ideological education of all members of the D.A.F. so that they may become National Socialists;

(*b*) care of all members in safeguarding their labour and social rights;

(*c*) their professional education and training;

(*d*) in its capacity as National Socialist Fellowship and according to the principle of "Public Need Before Private Greed", to maintain within the scope of their potential the livelihood of its members in case of need, or to offer able persons the possibility of advancement;

(*e*) care of members' staff-management relations by creating a social balance in co-operation with the organisation of the economic sector as well as the Labour Trustee;

(*f*) organisation of leisure time through the N.S. Association "Strength through Joy" in the D.A.F.;

(*g*) social care of all German nationals abroad within the scope of the host country's laws; and

(*h*) any other tasks set the D.A.F. by Adolf Hitler, Führer and Reich Chancellor.

Tasks of the N.S. Association "Strength through Joy"
It is the task of the N.S. Association "Strength through Joy" to gather together labouring German fellow citizens of all classes and occupations, in order to mould German working life in a uniformly National Socialist way.

Those contrasts which existed formerly in the assessment of workers, made possible by contrasting and discriminatory assessment of their work, must be overcome through the experience of human values, which have their roots in that very work.

D.A.F. uniforms:
◁ *A member in field dress with greatcoat.*
▷ *An Administrator or Warden in field dress, with the D.A.F. emblem on his left sleeve.*

It is therefore the special historic task of the N.S. Association "Strength through Joy" to do away with the former exclusively materialistic assessment of technical-mechanical working life by ascertaining and putting forward the ideal values of that work, and of work as such.

For that reason, the leisure movement organised by the N.S. Association "Strength through Joy" must always take care to carry out the organisation of leisure time in the closest relationship to working life.

National Socialist leisure time organising does not mean: Let's do away with work! but: Up and at it!

It is in work experienced mentally and spiritually that the N.S. Association "Strength through Joy" sees life's most lofty purpose fulfilled. For that reason, all cultural activities organised by the N.S. Association "Strength through Joy" must always maintain their close relation to working life, artistically as well as spiritually. Participation of the German working class in artistic life must always be aligned on the basis of working-class fellow citizens' natural relationship to art, and with special consideration being given to possible understanding and increasing interest on the part of the workers.

The N.S. Association "Strength through Joy" must strengthen the German worker's belief in himself and in his abilities, not only in the mechanical work processes he carries out, not only in his manual work, but beyond that, in his mental and spiritual powers and abilities.

In this belief, the N.S. Association "Strength through Joy" must be in a position to convince the German worker of his ability one day to give suitable artistic expression to his mental and spiritual experiences. However, the German worker will be able to tackle such tasks only when this belief in himself will be confirmed by the experience of general ideals of beauty which compel him towards creative activity. The path thither leads through the experiencing of nature, of man, and of scenery. To clear this path for the German worker is the aim of all organisational endeavours and measures of the N.S. Association "Strength through Joy". All cultural and social activities must be channelled in this direction.

To awaken and strengthen communal life, as demanded by National Socialist ideology, the N.S. Association "Strength through Joy" will have to include the German worker in the lofty world of ideals, treading ever new paths and using ever new means, so as to enable him to believe with all his might in the sense and in the greatness of that German life which he helped to fashion.

That is why the N.S. Association "Strength through Joy" is not only the organisation for spare time and leisure time arrangements, but wants to create a totally

new conception of life

It is the most vigorous expression of the life-affirming National Socialist Idea.

Notes

former: The Nazis had, of course, abolished all parties, trade unions, and other organisations which might have represented an opposition.

does not serve as substitute: an insidious way of pointing out that membership of the German Labour Front was compulsory.

employees: The German word used here is *Gefolgschaft*. Only in the Nazi period was this used to describe employees. Its correct meaning is "vassals", "followers", "partisans".

25. The N.S. Women's League

The N.S. Women's League, being an organisation of the N.S.D.A.P., is found in every area, down to the Block.

German girls or women, of unblemished character, having completed their twenty-first year and belonging neither to any Freemasons' Lodge nor to any other Secret Society, may become members of the N.S. Women's League. If they are married, their husbands must also be of Aryan origin.

Tasks: It is the task of the N.S. Women's League to educate politically and ideologically reliable women leaders for the Führer, to lead German women in the important spheres of work of the N.S. Women's League; these comprise all areas where the co-operation of a nation's womenfolk is required.

This takes place

(1) through the exercise of total ideological alignment within women's work by the N.S. Women's League;

(2) through the supervision of ideological or political alignment and attitude of all women's work in places of education or on any other occasions; and

(3) through the creation of establishments necessary for the execution of this work.

Organisation: Geographically the structure of the N.S. Women's League coincides without exception with the structure of the areas of the N.S.D.A.P. Within each Local Group area, there exists a Local Group Women's League. Cells and Blocks of the N.S. Women's League correspond in every way to Cells and Blocks of the N.S.D.A.P.

German Women's Service

The N.S. Women's League looks after its affiliated body, the German Women's Service.

Department with responsibility for National and Domestic Economy

The task of the Department with responsibility for Political and Domestic Economy consists in guiding the German woman, as regards National Economy, in her peculiar position as main consumer of the national income. Work carried out by women's guilds up to now has been devoted to this work. The housewife as main consumer has to be guided towards adapting her domestic tasks to the requirements of German National Economy. By thoughtful housekeeping, by careful shopping, by wise management of her store cupboard, she must contribute to the safeguarding of the German people's nutrition and to a recovery of the National diet.

With the aid of lectures, courses in domestic science, leaflets, exhibitions, films, practical cookery demonstrations, as well as through the Department's organ, the periodical *German Domestic Economy*, an attempt is made to guide housekeeping in its entirety from the point of view of political economy. The younger generation, too, being the housewives of the future, must be trained in the same way as the housewives of today.

There is a Regional Woman Official responsible for this department in every Region, who is subordinate to the Regional Leader of the N.S. Women's League. This applies also to Districts and Local Groups.

In co-operation with the Central Employment Exchange and Unemployment Insurance, and the B.D.M., the Department for Political and Domestic Science organises the "Domestic Year" during which a minimum of domestic skill is imparted in a family household to young girls who have left school. The two-year domestic apprenticeship is the focal point for the training of future housewives; it imparts thorough training in domestic science, together with a final examination. With the institution of two-year courses for the training of home economists, the Department contributes towards raising the status of housekeeping in its entirety and, at the same time, it creates a nucleus of housewives, always ready for action, to do instruction and information work in connection with the subjects of National and Domestic Economy.

The National Motherhood Service

Training courses arranged by the National Motherhood Service, the purpose of which is to help create the preconditions for healthy families, provide training and drill for German women in the following subjects:

(a) Housekeeping (cookery and sewing);

(b) Health and hygiene (baby care, domestic nursing, including population policy as well as genetic and race hygiene); and

(c) Education (with instruction in handicrafts).

A Regional Woman Official will be responsible for the organisation of this training work for mothers within a Region. She will be a specialist who must be specially equipped with administrative skills.

The actual training courses will be carried out by full-time and part-time ideologically reliable specialists. Part-time teaching staff will be drawn from the ranks of District Women Welfare Officers, women doctors, women youth leaders, etc.

There are training courses for mothers in town and country. In town there are permanent Schools for Mothers; in the country there are mobile courses. Work has been organised in such a way that each political District in the Reich is allocated a full-time Supervisor of the School for Mothers (District Woman Specialist Officer), possessing the necessary specialist qualifications, and who, working under the District N.S. Women's League Supervisor, will be responsible for putting into practice all relevant work in the District with the help of part-time specialist instructresses. Courses will be run according to the skeleton syllabus worked out by the National Women's Executive. Work is most important in areas with a high infant mortality rate, or where there is still unemployment, or which require special attention because they are distressed or border areas.

The National Motherhood Service comprises German women from all walks of life, the housewife and the domestic help, the university woman and the working woman; but, above all, it is the woman worker who will be extensively enlisted in training courses for mothers, by dint of the happy co-operation which exists between the D.A.F. Women's Bureau and the N.S. Women's League.

The work of the National Motherhood Service is effectively promoted because of the close connection with Party and State Offices, especially the Ministry of the Interior and the N.S. Public Welfare, both of which give far-reaching and much valued support to the National Motherhood Service.

Foreign Department
It is the task of the Foreign Department to give information in response to the many enquiries from abroad concerning the position and the work of women in our New Germany; to maintain connections with organisations abroad; to give to correspondents of important foreign newspapers insight into women's work; to report to journalists, professors, teachers, etc., about women's work in New Germany and to give them the opportunity of getting to know German women's work on the spot (by means of conducted tours of Women's Labour Service Camps, training courses for mothers, N.S.V. work). For the purpose of disseminating information about the position of women in the New Germany, the following should be used:
Short-wave radio (Woman's Hour);
the despatch abroad of publications of all kinds;
regular supply to news agencies representing foreign papers, and papers for German nationals abroad, of short articles about German women's work; as well as:
lectures to groups of foreigners temporarily in Germany as students.

Notes
National economy: The German expression used here is *Volkswirtschaft*, the correct translation of which is "national economy". However, the text which follows clearly shows that what is meant is simply "management of domestic matters" or *Wirtschaft*. Tongue in cheek, the correct translation has been used throughout to illustrate the fact that the Nazi predilection for long words was not always backed by knowledge of their meaning.

26. The Reich Director of Propaganda of the N.S.D.A.P.

The responsibility for propaganda activities of the N.S.D.A.P., its organisations and affiliated bodies, is in the hands of the Reich Director of Propaganda.

Tasks:
(1) He determines the entire propagandistic demeanour of the Movement, including its organisations and affiliated bodies.
(2) He issues guide lines to the Party including organisations and affiliated bodies, concerning the realisation of the Führer's cultural commands.
(3) He exercises control over the entire German radio network with regard to its internal organisational, cultural, and economic development.
(4) By using his initiative, he is concerned about the penetration of the entire German people with National Socialist ideology.
(5) He informs the people about the accomplishments of the leadership of Party and State.

For the purpose of propaganda, use will be made of press, radio and film.

The following are subordinate to the Reich Director of Propaganda: the Chief-of-Staff and the Adjutant.

The fields of duty of the Reich Propaganda Executive are divided into five parts, each of which is dealt with by a separate office administration:
(1) Active Propaganda
(2) Film
(3) Radio
(4) Culture
(5) Liaison.

The Chief-of-Staff:
The following come under the immediate control of the Chief-of-Staff:

(1) The Reich Ring for National Socialist Propaganda and National Enlightenment;
(2) the "Reich Motor Column Germany" with the auxiliary "Motor Column Bavaria";
(3) the office of the Reich Propaganda Executive;
(4) the section for Press Propaganda; and
(5) the section for Exhibitions and Trade Fairs.
It is the task of **the Reich Ring for National Socialist Propaganda and National Enlightenment** to safeguard the unified leadership through the Party of propaganda activities in all organisations and associated bodies. The competent Leading Functionary will detail one representative from the Propaganda Offices of each of the organisations and affiliated bodies to serve with the Reich Ring. In addition, there will be further representatives of certain offices of the National Executive, etc.

The Reich Motor Column Germany is designated to supply the latest technical aids necessary to the Party, its organisations, and affiliated bodies at all important rallies. Moreover, the Reich Motor Column Germany will look after demonstrations which, outside the Party, are of political importance to the state.

The Office: The Office is responsible to the Chief-of-Staff of the Reich Propaganda Executive for all questions in connection with financial and administrative problems of the Reich Propaganda Executive.

The Section for Press Propaganda: It is the task of the Section for Press Propaganda to deal with all propagandistic measures arising from the general activities of all Offices of the Reich Propaganda Executive; to edit them for publication; and to direct them via the competent channels to the National Socialist Party as well as the remaining Press.

The Section for Exhibitions and Trade Fairs: It is the task of the Section for Exhibitions and Trade Fairs to supervise from a propaganda point of view all exhibitions in which the Party proposes taking part.

(1) Office for Active Propaganda
It is the task of Active Propaganda to organise the execution of all propaganda campaigns devolving upon it, from large-scale functions of gigantic proportions with their architectural arrange-

ment to functions of Local Groups or Bases.

This necessitates the entire organisation of propaganda speakers of Movement, organisations, and affiliated bodies being concentrated in Active Propaganda.

Parallel with the continuous analysis of topical political questions goes the penetration of the entire speaking staff with items of information and the despatch to all propagandists in the Reich of the monthly journal *Our Will and our Way*.

Furthermore, the use of speakers requires the design and distribution of suitable posters and leaflets, as well as careful examination of reports of meetings on the part of speakers and the immediately relevant propaganda executives.

An overall picture of propaganda activities will emerge through statistical analysis of all reports from Districts and Regions (with reference to propaganda).

The Section for Public Speaking: The Section for Public Speaking, in its subordinate office "Organisation of Speakers", includes all N.S.D.A.P. Reich, Regional, and District speakers and, in addition, all specialist speakers of organisations and affiliated bodies. This speaking staff of the overall Movement will be continuously supplied with material by the Speakers' Information Bureau, and this will be the only speakers' and information material of the Party.

The supply of Reich speakers, Mobile Squad speakers of the Reich Propaganda Executive, and trainees for the Mobile Squad, will be in the hands of the Speakers' Bureau.

The Speakers' Training Bureau, subordinate to the Section, will take care not only of prospective political and specialist speakers, but also of the continuous extension of the knowledge of all active speakers. For this purpose a special "Reich Speakers' School" has been created.

The Party Speaker
Speakers are registered under the following titles:
(1) Reich speakers
(2) Mobile Squad speakers
    Trainee Mobile Squad speakers
(3) Regional speakers
(4) District speakers
(5) Specialist speakers.
When advertising meetings,

speakers' titles, as listed above, must be strictly adhered to.

Employment of speakers will be guided
(a) by performance
(b) by a veteran Party fighter's merits.

In principle, a distinction will be made between political speakers and specialist speakers.

It is the task of the political speaker, by means of the spoken word at public demonstrations and meetings, to make the German people familiar with National Socialist ideology, as well as with the measures of the National Socialist Government.

At present, only those Party members will be confirmed as political speakers who were members of the N.S.D.A.P. before the Assumption of Power, and who, at that time, had worked actively as speakers, as Political Leaders, or in the S.A., the S.S., or the H.J.

In future, only those Party members will be used as Reich speakers or Mobile Squad speakers who have spent a probationary period as Trainee Mobile Squad speakers.

(2) Film Office

It is the task of the Film Office to arrange regular film shows which will serve to enlighten and educate the public and which are suitable for spreading National Socialist ideology.

(3) Radio Office

It is the duty of the Radio Organisation of the N.S.D.A.P. to exercise constant control over the entire German broadcasting network, in order to weld the development of the broadcasting network, as far as internal organisation, culture, technical know-how, and economics are concerned, to National Socialist principles.

(4) Bureau for Culture

It is the task of the Bureau for Culture to stimulate, further, and supervise all artistic activities in accordance with the formative expression of National Socialist ideology, and to make use of them in the propaganda work of the Party, its organisations, and affiliated bodies.

The following departments will serve that purpose:

Department for Architecture: This office will issue directives and instructions concerning questions of architectural design of monuments and edifices which serve the official activities of the National Socialist Movement.

Department for Artistic Design: This office will issue directives and instructions concerning all remaining questions of artistic design for symbols, artefacts, etc., which are used in the official activities of the National Socialist Movement.

It will also issue directives and instructions for the artistic setting of demonstrations and for the design, through the use of cultural means, of the content of National Socialist ceremonies.

Department for Selection: Among the tasks of this office are the examination and selection of musical and poetic works from the point of view of their suitability for demonstrations and functions of the National Socialist Movement.

Department for Programme Design: It is the purpose of this office to prepare specimen programmes for functions of the National Socialist Movement and for designing the setting of National Socialist demonstrations on the basis of the design tradition which has grown up during the Time of Struggle.

Its tasks include: the exclusion of unsuitable designs which unauthorised elements may attempt to introduce; the struggle against *Kitsch*; the preservation of National Socialist lucidity in the design of functions; the prevention of mystical and pseudo-religious falsifications of ideology through the tortuous constructions of cranky cult-apostles; the commissioning of qualified artists according to the directives above-mentioned; suitable personalities will be called in by the Reich Propaganda Director to be regular contributors to the Bureau for Culture, for instance, in order to deal with special areas; and the organisation of practical courses for the encouragement of singing, in order to recruit suitable personnel for artistic planning work in all units of the Movement.

The monthly publication of the Bureau for Culture, *Suggestions for Planning of National Socialist Functions*, will furnish Directors of Propaganda and Directors of Bureaux for Culture with the material required for their work. In this publication will also be found instructions commensurate with our attitude of mind and excluding the danger of intellectual shallowness, for the organisation of lecture evenings, Party meetings, Social evenings of the H.J., Social gatherings of the S.A. and S.S., etc. The unity of Party and official bodies within the realm of culture has been safeguarded by means of liaison between the decision-making departments.

27. The Reich Press Director

Tasks: Incumbent upon the Reich Press Director are tasks connected with editorial policies. He has been charged with creating for the German people a Press which is committed and responsible to him, and which reflects life and events in the German community. Moreover, the Reich Press Director's functions include the necessary arrangements for the realisation of the demands concerning editorial policies made in Article 23 of the Programme of the N.S.D.A.P., and to supervise their execution. The latter is particularly relevant to the decree of April 25, 1935 "for the protection of the independence of newspaper publishing" and concerning "the closure of newspaper concerns for the purpose of elimination of unhealthy competition". Finally, he has been charged with the publishing of all writings of significance to the National Socialist Movement.

Competence

The Reich Press Director has been authorised by the Führer to take all measures necessary for the execution of his task. In detail, his competence comprises the following:
(1) the acknowledgement of periodical printed publications as official Party organs;
(2) decisions concerning the establishment of periodical printed publications, published by Party members, even insofar as they do not aspire to acknowledgement as official Party organs;
(3) (a) the issuing of general regulations for the entire publishing business to the whole press owned by Party members (unless, in individual cases, special instructions are issued by the Reich Press Director, his regulations are orders);
(b) decisions concerning all publishing problems of fundamental importance beyond the individual publishing concerns, insofar as he wishes to make the decision himself (in this case, publishing houses are obliged to submit these problems to the Reich Press Director before a final decision is made); and

(c) insight, at all times, into all official Party publishing firms and their entire economic organisation and management, as well as the right of exercising whatever influence he wishes.

This does not in any way affect the responsibility of individual publishers for the management of their business.
(4) All publishers and responsible editors of official Party publications are subordinate to the Reich Press Director. The appointment of a responsible editor may only take place with his approval. Should the Reich Press Director demand the dismissal of a responsible editor, this will have to be granted, if necessary, by means of immediate leave of absence.

△ *The armband of the Party Press Office's Chief Editor* (Hauptschriftleiter).

The N.S.D.A.P. Foreign Office

(1) The Office for Foreign Affairs of the N.S.D.A.P. (A.P.A.) comprises two spheres of activity: one is internal, the other external.
(2) Internally, it is the task of the A.P.A. to carry the aims and aspirations of the National Socialist State, as far as foreign policies are concerned, into all offices and organisations of the Party.
(3) Externally, it is the task of the A.P.A. to spread information about the aims and essence of National Socialism, both abroad and among foreigners visiting Germany or staying in Germany as representatives of foreign newspapers, and in this way to awaken the understanding of other peoples for the vital necessities of the German people and to convince those foreign peoples that National Socialism wants peace for constructive development in Germany, as well as peace with all nations without, however, relinquishing the defence of its vital rights.

Notes
Kitsch: "worthless pretentiousness"
A.P.A. = *Aussenpolitisches Amt*

28. The N.S. Parliamentary Group

(1) Tasks

Just as the N.S.D.A.P. embodies and moulds the political will of the German people, the National Socialist Parliamentary Party Group must embody and mould the political will of the people's representatives (the *Reichstag*). By means of the Parliamentary Party Group it is intended to ensure that, at all times, the *Reichstag* is guided by the overall interests of the nation; that it does not become subservient to special interests; and that it renders responsible and disciplined allegiance to National Socialist government. It is also the task of the Party Group to pass on to competent Party or Government departments applications and suggestions received from members of the public.

(2) Responsibilities

The Parliamentary Party Group is represented and led by the Group Leader. The Group Leader is responsible for Group discipline. He must see to it that in their entire conduct members of the Parliamentary Party Group show themselves worthy of the honour of being members of the *Reichstag* and of the Parliamentary Party Group, and, in case of misdemeanours, he must take the necessary measures. According to Paragraph 35 of the Reich Electoral Law of July 3, 1934, the Group Leader has authority to exclude members of the *Reichstag* from the Parliamentary Party Group with the effect that, at the same time, they lose their seat in the *Reichstag*. The same law authorises him, on the occasion of a member retiring (through death, resignation, or expulsion), to appoint a replacement from among applicants officially nominated at the last election but not yet called up for service in the *Reichstag*. By virtue of Party Group discipline, the Group Leader may prohibit a member exercising his parliamentary mandate until further notice (e.g. if there should be Party Court proceedings pending against the member). It is incumbent upon the Group Leader to evaluate applications for the withdrawal of a member's Parliamentary immunity. As far as is necessary, he makes his decision in agreement with other Party Departments (e.g. the Deputy Führer, the Supreme Party Court) and Government Departments

(e.g. when the member holds an official post at the same time). During sessions of the *Reichstag*, the Leader of the Parliamentary Party Group is responsible for the introduction of bills in the *Reichstag*.

29. The Office for Racial Policy of the N.S.D.A.P.

(1) The Office for Racial Policy has the task of unifying and supervising all indoctrination and propaganda work in the field of population and racial policies. By the Deputy Führer's decree of November 17, 1933, this task has been assigned to the head of the Office for Racial Politics, for the N.S.D.A.P. and its organisations.

(2) Only the Office for Racial Policy is authorised to make arrangements about indoctrination and propaganda in connection with problems of racial and population policies, and to issue press releases.

In consequence, all press releases in the field of racial or population policies require, without exception, the prior approval of the Office for Racial Policy of the N.S.D.A.P.

(3) On the part of the N.S.D.A.P., the Office for Racial Policy deals with all measures concerning the field of population and racial policies, in co-operation with the competent authorities. Consequently, the office for Racial Policy will continuously take part in Government legislative measures in this field.

30. The National Association of German Families with Four or more Children

The National Association of German Families with Four or more Children includes families with at least four (three in the case of widows) legitimate children; families must be German, free from hereditary disease, Aryan, and living in respectable circumstances. Admission will take place upon application by persons wishing to join if the above conditions are fulfilled.

The National Association of German Families with Four or

more Children is a militant association, population-politically orientated, whose aim it is to take National Socialist population-political thinking to the people.

Its purpose is the preservation and encouragement of the healthy German Aryan family. Its public-spirited activities do not extend to welfare work nor do they include the conducting of a business organisation.

31. The Bureau for Kinship Research

(Established on October 15, 1934, as directed by the Deputy Führer)

(1) Tasks

The Bureau for Kinship Research is responsible for the following:

(a) during proceedings before a Party Court, it will have to decide whether or not a person is of German origin and free from the taint of Jewish blood, in accordance with conditions for admission to the N.S.D.A.P. (i.e. by delivering an expert opinion). On the basis of these findings the Party Courts will decide what conclusions are to be drawn.

(b) It will have to issue character references for Political Directors in connection with their proof of origin *vis-à-vis* Party offices.

(c) It will issue certificates about German origin, confirming an applicant's German origin and freedom from the taint of Jewish or Negro blood, in accordance with conditions for admission to the N.S.D.A.P.

(2) Organisation and Classification

The head of the Bureau for Kinship Research is a member of the Deputy Führer's staff. He is at the same time Director of the Reich Office for Kinship Research at the Reich, as well as the Prussian, Ministry of the Interior, where all matters connected with origin are dealt with on behalf of the Party.

The organisation of the Reich Office for Kinship Research is as follows:

Sub-divisions:

(1) Research Department "A" (preparation of expert opinions concerning pure-blooded origin)

(2) Research Department "B" (auxiliary expert opinions concerning racial and genetic factors, naturalisations, half-breeds)

(3) Protection of literary monuments

(4) Drafting of law for Kinship Office

(5) Records of persons of alien races

(6) Ancestral Register

(7) Library

(8) Photographic service

(9) Finance, cashier, personnel

(10) Record office, administration, etc.

The special tasks of the Reich Office have been determined by the stipulations of several laws (such as the Reich Civil Service Law, the Reich Civil Law, Conditions for admission to the N.S.D.A.P., and others), and they consist in the establishment of purity of blood in the Aryan sense, the safeguarding of those sources which are most vital for proof of origin, by means of photographic reproduction of parochial registers in danger, and in co-operation with the protection of literary monuments. In addition, by going through personal records in existence (Register Office records, parochial registers, Residents' Records, Citizens' Registers, court records, etc.), it will be in a position to show genealogical connections.

Moreover, it will be responsible for awakening and encouraging the appreciation of the population for the significance of family and kinship connections within the re-organisation of the German people.

32. The Party Investigation Committee for the Protection of N.S. Literature

I. The Investigation Committee is no censorship office, but an office for protection against and resistance to pseudo-National Socialist literature; it guards against the adulteration of National Socialist ideas by unauthorised persons, and their commercial exploitation in a manner which may mislead the general public.

II. The Investigation Committee evaluates:

(1) N.S. literature in the strictest sense
This includes N.S. literature which was created under the immediate influence of the Movement. In accordance with National Socialist ideology, this literature is exclusively political;

(2) literature which is essentially related to National Socialism
Chronologically this extends over a considerable period and includes literature about political thought and demands within the growth of National Socialism.

III. A reliable staff of lecturers assists the Party Investigation Committee as advisers.
Writings against which no objections have been raised during investigation will be included in the N.S. bibliography (N.S.B.). The chairman of the Party Investigation Board will communicate the final decision to the publisher, on the basis of evaluation by the lecturers. This decision will include the following statements:
(1) From the point of view of the political intentions represented by the Party, this publication is unobjectionable. In that case, the publication in question will receive an endorsement to that effect, that is to say, the following sentence may be printed in it: "There are no objections on the part of the N.S.D.A.P. against the publication of this book."

(2) There are no objections against the contents of a publication. However, it cannot be counted among National Socialist literature in the strictest sense.
In this case, however, there is the possibility of the publication being listed in the N.S.B. under literature essentially related to National Socialism. Such a publication will contain no endorsement in the text.

(3) The publication in its statements is not in accordance with the principles of the N.S.D.A.P.; it is therefore rejected. In such cases there are the following possibilities:
(*a*) the sale of the publication is permitted, but not in connection with National Socialism; and
(*b*) the publication may not be distributed. The formal ruling is issued by the President of the Reich Chamber of Literature.

33. The Central Archives of the N.S.D.A.P.

All documents, printed publications, reports etc., which may be of interest to future historians, will be collected, examined and dealt with scientifically by the Central Archives.

The Central Archives are divided into the following departments:

A. Historical Archives
The Historical Archives deal with the historical material of the N.S.D.A.P., its organisations, and affiliated bodies: Forerunners, foundation, early years, different phases in the Struggle, symbols; compilation of the entire history of the Party. Moreover, the questions of Judaism, of Freemasonry, of Political Catholicism, and of Racialism from the historical point of view.

B. Newspaper and Periodical Archives
A collection of newspapers and periodicals of all former parties and organisations and of the N.S. press, particularly the press during the Time of the Struggle.
Linked up with those archives are the Archives of the Reich Press Director as well as the Foreign Press Director. Combined with the archives is an information service for all Party offices.

C. Library
The Library collects all N.S. literature, the literature of Marxism, the Trade Unions, and other organisations of the old régime. The Library is available for the use of all Party offices.

D. German People and Culture Abroad
A collection of all events concerning German people and culture abroad, as well as the National Socialist Movement abroad.

E. Department for Cultural History and Cultural and Educational Policy
The preparation of historically sound pictorial and textual material for cultural purposes of the Party and for propaganda purposes; card-indexing of all areas of working activities, with particular reference to the Nordic-Indo-European culture group.

F. Collections
Collection of pictures, documents etc., of famous men of the Party and of men of the Movement fallen in action; the preservation of mementoes of parties and organisations of the old régime as well as of gramophone records of political personalities.

Notes
Parliamentary Party Group = *Reichstagsfraktion.*
Residents' Records: Every resident in Germany had to register with the *Einwohnermeldeamt,* where he had to report any change of address.
Indo-European: This used to be "Indo-Germanic", and is actually called *indogermanisch* in the text. However, today, the linguistically correct expression is "Indo-European".
fallen in action: This does *not* refer to war service, but to the many street battles fought against Socialists, Communists, and the Police.

34. Party Jurisdiction

Its nature and tasks:
While during the Time of Struggle the hatred of all others made sure that no one joined the N.S.D.A.P. who was not infused with honest belief in the Führer's aims; while in those days a declaration of loyalty to the Party had as a result nothing but disadvantages of every kind; after the Assumption of Power, individual place hunters and climbers believed that membership of the Party would be of advantage to them, and for that reason they allowed themselves to become members of the Party. That natural process of selection, as we knew it particularly during the Time of Struggle of the Party before the Assumption of Power, will now have to be complemented by an artificial one.

To be a Party member means to have greater duties

To watch over this field of duty, extended beyond general civic limits, in severe cases to remove the guilty person from the Party; in addition, to keep obviously unsuitable fellow citizens away from the Party; that is the task which has been entrusted to the Party Jurisdiction.

Thus the Party Jurisdiction is essentially in part responsible for the continued existence of the pure idea of National Socialism. It does not only see to it that an obviously unsuitable Party member is swiftly removed from the Party, but it is equally important that everybody who endeavours to co-operate with an honest will and a believing heart should be preserved for the Party. Every incorrect assessment does not only wrong the individual affected by it, but to a much greater degree the Party which could not survive the loss of genuine old National Socialists while place hunters were being encouraged. Thus a sum total of wrong decisions would create an inverse selection in the Party, on account of which it would be bound to perish.

Structure
The Party Jurisdiction has been entrusted to:
(1) District Courts
(2) Regional Courts
(3) the Supreme Party Court.
Organisationally, individual Party Courts belong to the area of their Leading Functionary. In matters of proceedings only, Party Courts are independent and not tied to orders by the Leading Functionary for their decisions.

Internal Organisation:
According to its size, each Party Court has one or more divisions. Each division is manned by a chairman and two or more assessors. One of the assessors must belong to the S.A. or another organisation, and if the accused is a leader in the S.A., he must hold a service rank not lower than that of the accused. The same goes for all other organisations. District Courts are almost exclusively manned by laymen. As far as Regional Courts and the Supreme Party Court are concerned, professional judges predominate. They are there to ensure that the facts of the case in which judgement will have to be given in collaboration with Party members who are proven National Socialists, are elicited incontestably. For judgement corresponding to justice can only be based upon correctly established facts.

A Party Judge must therefore spare no effort in order to fulfil the first part of his task, namely the ascertainment of the true facts; only after he has done so, he may venture upon the second part, the critical examination of the facts he has ascertained.

Different types of proceeding:
The following five types of proceedings are provided for in the

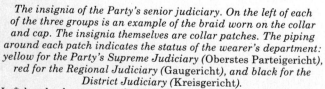

The insignia of the Party's senior judiciary. On the left of each of the three groups is an example of the braid worn on the collar and cap. The insignia themselves are collar patches. The piping around each patch indicates the status of the wearer's department: yellow for the Party's Supreme Judiciary (Oberstes Parteigericht), red for the Regional Judiciary (Gaugericht), and black for the District Judiciary (Kreisgericht).
Left-hand column, top to bottom: Senior Judge and Reich Leader; Court President; two different patches for a Judge; Assistant Judge, Department Leader; and Department Assistant. [All in the Party Supreme Judiciary.]
Right-hand column, top to bottom: President; Court President; Judge; Department Leader; and Department Assistant [all in the Regional Judiciary]; and President; Court President; Judge; and Department Assistant [all in the District Judiciary]. The last two were both Department Leaders in the Kreisgericht.

Directives for Party Courts.
(1) Disciplinary proceedings
(2) Litigious proceedings
(3) Protection of Honour proceedings
(4) Rejection proceedings (in connection with applications for admission to the Party)
(5) Proceedings in connection with race and Freemasonry matters.

Disciplinary proceedings:

If a Leading Functionary should consider necessary the punishment of a Party member whom previously he had attempted to reprimand by means of kind or severe words, he will apply to his competent Party Court for permission to start proceedings against that Party member in order to bring about his punishment or, should the man have proved altogether unsuitable, his expulsion from the Party. The Party Court will consider whether the attitude of the Party Member in the particular case cited by the Leading Functionary calls for punishment. If, on the other hand, an incident of that kind should come to the ears of the Party Court or a Party member, then the Party Court or the Party member will ask the Leading Functionary to make an application for sentence to be passed. If he refuses, an appeal to his superordinate Leading Functionary will be indicated. In all cases, the ultimate decision rests with the Supreme Party Court.

Litigious proceedings:

The second kind of proceeding is one the purpose of which is to bring about an amicable settlement of personal disputes and disagreements among Party members. With these proceedings it is possible for both the accused and the plaintiff to be punished, should the Party Court consider them both to be guilty. Here, in particular, it is the foremost task of the Party Judge to intervene as soon as squabbles come to his notice, and to nip these in the bud. Rather than by punishment, it is through successful arbitration that the close fellowship of the Party may be restored, especially in its smallest groups. Exactly as in the Time of Struggle before the Assumption of Power, the Party will have to rely even today upon appearing to the outside world as a close-knit unit. For that reason, there is no room in the N.S.D.A.P. for personal wrangling and squabbling between members.

Protection of Honour proceedings:

The third kind of proceeding is one which any Party member may initiate against himself, in order to restore his own honour and thus the common honour of the Party, should it have been injured through an assertion against or an attack upon him. Here the co-operation of the Leading Functionary is not called for. In these proceedings, a Party member has the possibility of knocking the bottom out of rumours spread about him, without knowing their author. It is therefore the most effective protection of his honour imaginable for every Party member to apply for proceedings to be taken against himself.

Rejection proceedings:

Even though Party Courts are competent for Party members only, and do not deal with outsiders other than in their capacity as witnesses, there exists an essential exception to this rule. Party courts participate in the rejection of applications for admission to the Party. A Leading Functionary may not reject any application for admission without the approval of the Party Court. In every case, the rejection of new applicants will take place without explanation through the competent Local Group Leader in agreement with the competent Local or District Court. In this way, any unreasonable rejections of fellow citizens who are valuable to the Party will have been obviated.

Proceedings in connection with Race and Freemasonry matters:

One of the Party Judiciary's special tasks is the removal of those Party members who, because of their non-Aryan origin or kinship, or because of membership of Lodges, should never have been admitted in the first place. In these cases, the Party Court will act without an application by the Leading Functionary. These proceedings which almost always appear to be deceptively simple on the surface, frequently conceal great hardships for those affected, which, however, will have to be borne for the sake of the purity of the Party in its capacity as a fighting nucleus of National Socialism within the German people. Because the Party is a sworn racial fellowship, it cannot tolerate that its members maintain links with international organisations, such as Masonic Lodges. Because the Party preaches purity of blood to the people, it cannot itself tolerate members within its ranks who do not comply with these standards.

Proceedings before State courts of law:

In every walk of life, a Party member must put the interests of the Party community before his own. Personal friction among Party members should not take place, and even when it cannot be avoided, it must be dealt with within the Party. That is why it is a part of maintaining Party discipline for a Party member not unnecessarily to drag internal Party matters before State law courts by instituting civil actions. The same is valid for all other legal proceedings.

Not every trifle is suitable to be inflated into legal proceedings. Often a warning or a simple hint suffices to draw the attention of a Party member to his duties *vis-à-vis* the Party. Besides, a comradely hint of that nature will not leave the person affected with a bitter feeling of condemnation.

It is the task not only of Court, chairman, and assessors, but also of all parties concerned, of the accused as well as of the responsible S.A. or S.S. Leader, of the witnesses as well as of the Leading Functionary, to contribute their share towards establishing the true facts and, in so doing, towards arriving at true justice in the interest of the Movement.

The course of proceedings:

A summons for the main hearing will be made under safeguard of an eight-day time limit upon proof of delivery of writ. The chief difference between the main hearing and proceedings at State courts of law is that proceedings at Party Courts are not conducted in public. This is necessary so as not to draw the attention of wide circles inside or even outside the Party to the investigation by means of public proceedings. The Party is itself deeply interested in the pureness of its own ranks. It is, however, not interested in carrying out the purification in public. A record will be kept of the main hearing. The guide lines determining the course of the proceedings, approved by the Führer, have been issued not because of the Party's delight in legal subtleties, but in order to provide, by adhering to prescribed proceedings, a guarantee for the justice of a verdict which is based on the proceedings and on the investigations made during the proceedings. A just verdict, the be-all and end-all of all proceedings, can only be arrived at if, first of all, the facts are established correctly and afterwards the verdict is given correctly. The course of proceedings prescribed in the guide lines, during and after the main hearing, is devised solely to this end.

The main hearing:

After the calling of all concerned, they will be cautioned to be silent, the witnesses, in addition, being reminded of the need to be truthful, after which the latter will be given leave. There will follow the reading of the opening statement, and subsequently the examination of the accused. In contrast to proceedings at regular courts of law, the accused, too, is obliged to tell the truth. Thus, to lie before a Party Court represents a punishable offence for the accused also. Not included, however, under this head is the obvious freedom for every accused to present the established facts in a light most favourable for himself.

Following the examination of the accused, the hearing of evidence will begin. Witnesses and experts will be called individually, one after the other, and examined. Non-appearance and unwarranted refusal to give evidence before the Party Court will be punished as lack of discipline.

After the hearing of evidence, permission to speak will be given first to the Leading Functionary and subsequently to the Leader responsible for the organisation in question, for the purpose of putting their point of view. Finally, the accused will make his concluding remarks.

The decision:

The Party Court will take its decision in secret session. This decision requires delivery in writing, even if it is announced publicly.

Whereas a State court of law is obliged to apply a number of legally defined factors to the individual case, Party Courts are not bound in this way. For them, the essential law is represented by the relevant regulations contained in the Articles of the Party, as well as by general commands and orders of the Führer. The absence of concise rules as to what actions will be considered dishonourable, and damaging to the Party, although it gives greater freedom—in comparison with State judges—to the Party judge in his assessment of each individual case, places upon him, at the same time, much greater responsibility to examine whether the case before him might not be a private matter, not in the least affecting the good of the Party, or a matter which might be dealt with disciplinarily by the organisation concerned. Only an action which is culpable, whether committed negligently or deliberately, is punishable. Incapacity alone, therefore, can never furnish grounds for prosecution by a Party Court.

Party Courts, with the exception of the Supreme Party Court in cases of complaints, do not impose punishment themselves, but make application for punishment by the competent Leading Functionary. Once it has become valid, he will have to act on the decision, that is to say, if he has not made use of his right of appeal in time. In matters of complaints, the Supreme Party Court will itself enact whatever measures it has decided upon. The fact that, in general, Party Courts lack executive power is accounted for, just as in Courts Martial, by the military organisation of the Party. The Leading Functionary is the supreme judicial authority of his competent Party Court.

Penalties:

The following penalties have been laid down:

(1) Expulsion from the Party, if the Party Court is convinced that the accused, by his behaviour, has forfeited the right to remain in the N.S.D.A.P.

(2) Caution, if the Party Court is convinced that the accused, because of the behaviour laid to his charge, has not become unworthy of remaining in the Party. Over and above the caution, the Party Court may inflict the following additional penalties:

(*a*) Loss of ability to hold Party Office for not more than three years.

(*b*) Loss of right to carry a weapon for not more than 12 months.

(*c*) Loss of right to appear as a public speaker.

(3) Reprimand, if the Party Court is convinced that the misdemeanour of the accused and the significance of the action laid to his charge, are trivial.

(4) Fines, or Imprisonment have been statutorily provided; however, up to now, the Party Juris-

diction has not made use of this means of punishment.

The Party membership book which, during the course of proceedings, must be filed in the dossier, will be impounded on expulsion. Any caution or additional penalties will be entered in the membership book.

When meting out punishment, the personality of the accused in relation to the Party must be taken into consideration in addition to the circumstances of the individual case. As a rule, services to the Party during the Time of Struggle justify the granting of extenuating circumstances and thus preclude expulsion which on consideration of nothing but the facts of the case in question, might have appeared necessary. On the other hand, services to the Party, however great, are not sufficient exoneration if the individual case to be dealt with should obviously be not a single lapse but the product of a character defect.

Future development of Party Jurisdiction:

Party Jurisdiction has grown together with the Party. Its precursors, the Committees for Investigation and Arbitration date back to the time of the foundation of the Party. In the same way, the future development of Party Jurisdiction will take place consciously from within the Party. Never will it be possible for an impression to be created that something alien is to be implanted into the Party. In their capacity as conscience of the Movement, Party Courts, in preserving the increased spheres of duty of Party members, will take care to see that the old fighting spirit will never be lost and that the Party will increasingly become the Order of the Best of the German People.

Notes

a number of legally defined factors: In Britain and the United States, the law is administered by precedent, whereas in Germany it is laid down in sets of rules.

35. The S.A.

Whereas the Political Organisation of the N.S.D.A.P. must carry out the practical political leadership, the S.A., on the other hand, is the Party's instrument of training and education.

According to the Führer's directions at the Reich Party Rally of

Standarte (München)

Flags of the S.A. or Sturmabteilung:
△ △ *The standard of the Munich Regiment.*
△ *The flag of the 1st Sturm (Company) of the Leibstandarte, Hitler's personal bodyguard.*

Freedom, the S.A., in its capacity as a volunteer political soldierhood, is the guarantor of the National Socialist Movement, of the National Socialist Revolution and of the rise of the German people.

Consequently, in the S.A., a young German will, first and foremost, be fortified by ideological and character training and moulded into a disseminator of National Socialist thought. In addition, it is incumbent upon the S.A. to strengthen its militant spirit by cultivating soldierly virtues and, by systematic training according to the principles of the S.A. Sports Badge to further the physical toughening of the individual and, in that way, prepare him for service with the Armed Forces.

Just as significant, however, is a corresponding task of education and training which the S.A. must tackle among those age groups who have completed their compulsory military service. It is essential that, up to old age, these men should be kept ready for action with all their mental, spiritual, and physical powers alert, to serve Movement, People, and State. In the S.A., they are to find their home from home. Anything at all which might set them apart economically, culturally, professionally, or because of their origin, will be overcome in the S.A. through the spirit of comradeship and manly discipline.

In this way, the S.A. represents a decisive factor on the road to the community of the people. Its spirit must radiate soldierly tradition and potential usefulness to all organisations outside the Movement. Thus, to look after them is an essential task of the S.A.

A leader corps, exemplary through continually increasing education and training, ensures the efficiency of the S.A. Such a leader corps will be qualified to provide from among S.A. units suitable personnel for the group of leaders in the Party's Political Organisation. Furthermore, the S.A. will have to school its units for action as an internal political fighting force and to train them for practical service to people and state.

Membership of the S.A. is voluntary.

The nature and scope of the S.A. are peculiarly its own. For that reason, the S.A. is an organisation built up on soldierly principles and under the direct command of the Führer. The Führer

prescribes its codes of action; it is he who orders it into action. On the Führer's behalf, a Chief-of-Staff represents the S.A. as a whole.

Membership of the S.A.:
In principle, membership of the S.A. is voluntary. However, it is the Führer's will that every German, from early childhood to old age, should receive continuous education in a National Socialist spirit.

In a National Socialist State it is required, therefore, that once a young German has joined the S.A., he should devote himself, body and soul, to it and to the fulfilment of its tasks.

Admission to the S.A.:
In principle, recruitment for the S.A. will generally be made from the H.J., and insofar as requirements cannot be supplied by the H.J., by admission of other volunteers of German extraction who fulfil the following conditions:

They must be:
(1) of irreproachable character and willing, by dint of their idealism and selflessness, to identify themselves to the utmost with the ideas of the Führer and the tasks of the S.A.;
(2) able to prove Aryan descent up to and including great-grandparents;
(3) worthy to be admitted to the N.S.D.A.P.;
(4) physically suited to all demands by S.A. service (i.e. route marches, physical training, action in emergency service); and
(5) of unexceptionable reputation, with no previous conviction.

The procedure during admission is as follows:
To begin with, a volunteer will report to the leader of the S.A.-*Sturm* (Company) with headquarters in the volunteer's quarter, his town, or his District. Facing the *Sturm* Leader, he will make the voluntary declaration that he wishes to join the S.A. The volunteer will then be registered for examination by a selection committee. This will establish the applicant's physical fitness; it will examine him from a genetic point of view; it will examine his *curriculum vitae* and his personal documents, such as military and work records, certificate of political conduct etc.; and evaluate his

▷ *An S.A. member of the Gruppe "Hochland" (Upper Bavaria and Schwabia) in sports kit with a javelin.*

appearance from a racial aspect.

On the decision of the Selection Committee depends the volunteer's admission as an S.A. trainee. After completion of a period of six months as a trainee (in exceptional cases a shorter period will be accepted) and after successful completion of a trainee examination, final admission as S.A. Man will take place. (In the case of men who are only conditionally suitable, the recruiting office will decide, in conjunction with the S.A. Doctor, whether there is a possibility of transfer to an S.A. Reserve Unit, or whether rejection will have to follow.

Principles for promotion:
S.A. Men who, according to their achievements and personality, have proved themselves as above average, may be promoted to Lance-Corporal after six months' service, and to Corporal after another six months. Further promotion to Troop Leader, Senior Troop Leader, Section Leader, and Senior Section Leader will only be possible when, in the course of time, the S.A. Man has shown distinct qualities of leadership.

In particular, he must be able, according to the service rank in question, to weld together men of a Troop or a Section, to indoctrinate and train them to becoming excellent ideological (political) soldiers of the Führer, and to lead them, not only during peaceful parades and ceremonies, but also in action, in mortal combat. The demands made upon middle-ranking S.A. Leaders, *Sturm* Leaders, Senior *Sturm* Leaders, Chief *Sturm* Leaders, *Sturm* Unit Leaders, and Senior *Sturm* Unit Leaders, are based on the same principle as the demands which will have to be made on Troop Leaders and Section Leaders.

However, in all areas correspondingly higher and more demanding standards will, of course, have to be applied. Whoever would be appointed leader of a *Sturm*, or leader of a *Sturm* Unit, and accordingly promoted to a corresponding service rank, must, above all, have proved himself most convincingly at the front.

Training courses for leaders will take care of the appropriate extension of knowledge and of practical ability. An examination for *Sturm* Leaders or *Sturm* Unit Leaders will have to be taken which will cover all areas of S.A. service. Last but not least, a man's overall demeanour and the general merits of his personality will carry considerable weight in his evaluation.

After prolonged activity as a leader of units and on staffs, as well as after completion of the appropriate examinations, it will be possible for a middle ranking S.A. Leader to move up into the higher S.A. Leader Corps, which comprises the service ranks of Standard Leader, Senior Leader, Brigade Leader, Group Leader, and Senior Group Leader.

It is a matter of principle that, after the present state of transition, every S.A. Leader will once again have to be a Party member, just as during the Time of Struggle.

The enhanced standing and the extended scope which are concomitant with promotion or transfer to a higher service office are meant to benefit not the person thus distinguished, but the S.A. and the Party.

Notes
S.A. *Sturm:* a *Sturm* is the collective term for a company of Brown Shirts.
Lance-Corporal = *Rottenführer*
Troop Leader = *Scharführer*
Section Leader = *Truppführer*
Sturm Unit Leaders = *Sturmbannführer*. (A *Bann*, in the military sense, is a "unit"; it is likely that the Nazis derived the word from *Heerbann*, signifying "a body of vassals".)

Resignation from the S.A.:
Service in the S.A. is, and will always be, voluntary. Just as, when recruiting for the S.A., there must be neither prospects of advantages nor pressure of any kind in order to persuade a man to join, the S.A. Man must have the opportunity of leaving the S.A. if he believes that he is no longer able to agree with the line taken by the S.A., or if he is no longer in a position to discharge fully the duties laid upon him by dint of his being a member of the S.A. If there are honourable grounds, the S.A. Man may, at his own request, be "honourably discharged from the S.A.". Should he show lack of interest, or prove to be only a fellow traveller, driven into the S.A. by capricious or opportunist motives, "discharge from the S.A." will take place as an official measure.

Should he have become guilty of any disciplinary, political, or possibly criminal, misdemeanours, his competent disciplinary superior may bring in a verdict of "permanent and penal discharge from the S.A.". Should there be serious misdemeanours, the verdict may be for "expulsion from the S.A.".

Insofar as the S.A. Man is, at the same time, a Party member, permanent and penal discharge from the S.A., as well as expulsion, will be reported forthwith to the competent Party Court for a decision as to whether a man thus dismissed from the S.A. is still worthy to remain a member of the Party.

Training of the S.A.:

National Socialism is governed by two ideas, the idea of community and the idea of individuality. Particularly in the S.A., the relationship of individual and community to one another must take a form which is commensurate with its task as instrument of ethnic reinforcement within the population. It is the aim of its training activities to enable S.A. Leaders and S.A. Men to educate the widest circles possible in National Socialist ideology and in the physical hardening connected with it.

In order to achieve uniform training, division into the following three main groups has been arranged:

(a) ideological training
(b) general training
(c) operational service.

In the main, these groups comprise the following individual areas:

(a) (1) education and training based on the aims and teachings of the Führer, as formulated for all aspects of our life and National Socialist philosophy of life in *Mein Kampf* and the Party Programme.
(2) the teaching of the history of the Germanic peoples and its relevance to the tasks of our time.
(3) practice of the National Socialist doctrine of duty.
(b) (1) Formation duty
(2) Physical culture
(3) Drill
(4) Field training
(5) Rifle practice
(6) Anti-gas and air raid defence
(7) Service in special units (naval, intelligence, engineering, and cavalry units).
(c) (1) Parades and demonstrations
(2) Contests and proficiency tests

for the S.A. Sports Badge
(3) Security Service
(4) Home defence (emergency service, etc.).

The S.A. Sports Badge:

The new state demands a hard race with great powers of resistance. In addition to ideological indoctrination, we must demand combative training of the body by means of simple, useful and natural physical exercises.

In order to provide increased incentive and direction to youth's endeavours, I herewith renew the foundation for the entire S.A. and all its former formations of the

S.A. SPORTS BADGE
which may be acquired, after completion of a training period conscientiously carried out, by taking a proficiency test.

In order to give conscious expression to the cultivation of a militant spirit in all parts of the German people, I furthermore decree that this S.A. Sports Badge may also be acquired and worn by those not belonging to the Movement, as long as racially and ideologically they conform to National Socialist requirements. The Chief-of-Staff will issue directives for the implementation of the above decree.
The Supreme S.A. Leader
(signed) Adolf Hitler

In the National Socialist State, the focus for every thought and every action is the Nation; within it, and in connection with it alone, the "I" and the "We" are decided. The National Socialist revolution comprises life in its entirety, giving us the lofty ethos of our idea of State, the brotherhood of the people, and the community of the people. And thus it consciously determines the Nation's new life. As for all areas of cultural life of the people, the motto of "Public Need Before Private Greed" holds good for sports too, and for physical culture in general. To do physical exercises is a serious obligation which the citizen has *vis-à-vis* the people.

It was reserved for our time, returning as it is to everything natural and, in so doing, to the purest sources of human life, to demand physical exercises for all fellow citizens. Today it is a matter of course that from his early days a child receives physical training and, in this way, is

◀ *A* Rottenführer *(Corporal) of the 100th Regiment of* Gruppe *"Sachsen" in service greatcoat.*

moulded to command greater vitality and efficiency. However, the Nation further demands a race which is hard, tough and strong. This vital demand has created a form of physical education which comprises not only the training of the body to fighting pitch, but also the ideological indoctrination of the mind. The tangible acknowledgement which may be gained in this connection is the

S.A. SPORTS BADGE.

It is called the S.A. Sports Badge—but that by no means signifies that only the S.A. may gain it; on the contrary, it is only because the thought of and the demand for physical and mental education of the body stems from the S.A.; because it was the S.A. which first carried out this kind of training, the spirit of which was created out of comradeship and the readiness to help each other, a spirit which must continue to live as such; that today the symbol of manly fighting-fitness still carries the honourable name of the S.A. And yet it is dedicated to the entire German youth, nay, over and above, to the entire German people.

The S.A. Sports Badge, in its clear and characteristic structure, embodies political education in a comradely spirit, and readiness for action in National Socialist Germany. It symbolises political indoctrination through the body, putting the Community before the Self. In addition to ideological training, all areas of sport and physical exercise have been utilised to help mould the National Socialist fighter. It is precisely here, in doing the exercises for the S.A. Sports Badge, in doing scouting exercises and nowhere else, that a German, whatever his age, may demonstrate to what degree he is capable of risking body and soul for any task set by the Führer; and what manly virtues, namely, discipline, courage, determination and a spirit of comradeship, he possesses. Any German, as long as he has completed his seventeenth year and complies with the general requirements laid down, may acquire the S.A. Sports Badge. The following are the general requirements: The would-be acquirer must be

(1) eligible, that is he must conform, racially and idelogically, to S.A. requirements;

(2) able-bodied, i.e. he must have been declared "capable of sports and marching activities" after a medical examination;

◀ *An* Obertruppführer *(Senior Section Leader) of the 1st Company of S.A. Regiment No. 1 in ceremonial service dress.*

(3) fully trained, i.e. he must be able to prove, according to regulations, his training by recognised teachers of scouting exercises (who must be holders of teachers' certificates); and

(4) fully examined, i.e. his training and proficiency test require authentication by recognised examiners. The acquisition of the S.A. Sports Badge necessitates the passing of a proficiency test as termination of preparatory training. This comprises three groups of exercises: physical exercises, ground exercises, and scouting exercises.

Notes

the history of the Germanic peoples = *deutsch-völkische Geschichte*: a free rendering of the untranslatable concept of both the National Socialists and the German National Party (*Deutsch-Nationale Partei*).

scouting exercises = *Geländesport*: Harrap's Standard Dictionary remarks that this applies "especially in the Nazi period as para-military training".

The physical exercises included the 100 metres, long jump, shot putting, and 3,000 metres. The ground exercises included a forced march, small bore rifle shooting, and dummy grenade throwing. Scouting exercises included map-reading, reconnaissance, use of terrain, and signalling, etc.

36. The S.A. Uniform

I. General remarks

(1) The service uniform is a dress of honour. Whoever wears it, represents the Movement in public. Therefore, his uniform must be neat and tidy, according to regulations. If service uniform is worn, it must always be full service uniform. The wearing of individual items of S.A. service uniform together with civilian dress, and conversely, the wearing of individual items of civilian dress (e.g. an overcoat) together with S.A. service uniform, is prohibited. It is not fitting for an S.A. Man, for instance, to appear in public without head covering, without his leather belt or in an open-necked shirt without a necktie.

(2) S.A. Leaders and S.A. Men in S.A. service uniform must avoid acting in any way which may be

△ A Marinesturmführer *(Naval Company Commander) of the 4th Company of S.A. Naval Regiment (Marinestandarte) No. 9 in service dress.*

△ A Marinescharführer *(Naval Sergeant) of the 3rd Company of S.A. Naval Regiment No. 52 in Naval S.A. greatcoat.*

Standartenführer *(Colonel) in charge of Regiment No. 16's medical services.*

Standartenführer *on the veterinary staff of the* Gruppe *"Hochland" group staff*

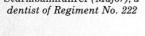

Standartenführer, *a chemist on the group staff of* Gruppe *"Franken" (in Bavaria)*

Sturmbannführer *(Major), a dentist of Regiment No. 222*

This page, left-hand columns: *S.A. specialist collar rank patches.*
This page, right-hand column: *S.A. epaulettes.*
Opposite page: *S.A. service collar rank patches.*

S.A. Mann *(Private) of the 2nd Company of Cavalry Regiment No. 25 of Gruppe "Berlin-Brandenburg"*

S.A. Mann *of the Signals Company of Regiment No. 32 of Gruppe "Thüringen"*

S.A. Mann *of the 15th (Pioneer) Company of Regiment No. 69 of Gruppe "Westmark" (on the Rhine)*

S.A. Mann *of the 5th Company of Naval Regiment No. 27*

Sturmführer *(Company Commander) on the staff of the* Reichsführerschule

Musikzugführer *(Bandmaster) of Regiment No. 100 of Gruppe "Sachsen" (Saxony)*

detrimental to the standing of the S.A. in public, such as eating and smoking in public places, lounging about with hands in trousers pockets, idly hanging about at street corners, especially at main thoroughfares, sitting about on park benches, walking in the street arm in arm with one's female companion, carrying a cane or an umbrella, pushing a perambulator, carrying a child on one's arm, etc.

(3) Every member of the S.A. *must* wear his service uniform on duty, and he *may* wear it off duty. Men applying for admission into the S.A. must be in possession of an S.A. service uniform by the time they are admitted, at the latest. Whoever wears his service uniform off duty is subject to S.A. regulations and to S.A. senior personnel, even though they may be in civilian dress themselves, as long as they are known to the S.A. Leader or S.A. Man in question, or prove their identity as senior personnel.

It is forbidden to wear S.A. service uniform in exercising one's civilian occupation as commercial traveller, street trader, newspaper vendor, etc., if in so doing the impression may be created that the S.A. service uniform was being worn for the purpose of obtaining personal gain.

Similarly, S.A. service uniform must not be worn in the exercise of occupations where the work process may result in soiling the service uniform, thus possibly affecting unfavourably the wearer's standing; or in the exercise of occupations which require the rendering of personal services to customers. The entire service uniform may be worn at all times in the exercise of one's occupation in public offices, schools, banks, etc.

(4) It is forbidden to appear in court wearing S.A. service uniform, or the S.A. Civilian Badge, whether as plaintiff, accused, witness, juryman, expert, assessor, etc.

(5) S.A. Leaders and S.A. Men in service uniform are, in principle, forbidden to frequent public restaurants after midnight. In the event of functions at public restaurants, at which members of the S.A. in S.A. service uniform take part, and which are planned to extend beyond midnight, exceptions are permissible. However, it is forbidden for members of the S.A. in S.A. service uniform to visit other restaurants after the function. The S.A. service

S.A. Mann *to* Obertruppführer *(Senior Section Leader)*

Sturmführer *(Company Commander) to* Sturmhauptführer *(Captain)*

Sturmbannführer *(Major) to* Standartenführer *(Colonel)*

Oberführer *(Brigadier-General) to* Obergruppenführer *(General)*

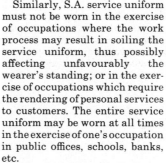

Stabschef *(Chief-of-Staff)*

uniform demands the keeping of the midnight curfew.

(6) It is forbidden to collect money, or sell post-cards or badges while wearing S.A. service uniform, either in the street or in public restaurants. The Chief-of-Staff is the sole person authorised to grant exceptions to this rule.

(7) Unless exceptions are specifically granted, clothing for all members of the S.A. must be uniform in cut as well as in colour.

(8) The following are forbidden: visibly displayed watch chains, fobs, handkerchiefs in breast pockets, etc.

(9) Only persons possessing valid S.A. passes, i.e. bearing authentication for the current month, are permitted to wear S.A. service uniform, or the S.A. Civilian Badge with their civilian suits. Applicants waiting to join the S.A. will wear the S.A. Civilian Badge with their civilian suits.

Any S.A. Man unable to identify himself must be prepared to have his service uniform or his S.A. Civilian Badge taken away from him. In case of doubt, S.A. Leaders holding the rank of *Sturm* Leader and above are authorised to ask men wearing

S.A. service uniform or the S.A. Civilian Badge for proof of identity. Any unauthorised person wearing service uniform or the S.A. Civilian Badge must be handed over at once to the nearest S.A. Office. There the S.A. service uniform and/or the S.A. Civilian Badge will be seized and the matter reported to the super-ordinate office.

(10) The service uniform of any closed unit must be uniform. The wearing of overcoats, uniform jackets, or gloves by individual S.A. Leaders or S.A. Men in closed units is prohibited.

II. Description of different uniforms

There are four kinds of service uniform:
(a) Full Dress uniform
(b) Battle dress
(c) Sports dress
(d) Evening dress.

(a) Full Dress Uniform consists of:

(1) Service cap with coloured band
(2) Brown shirt
(3) Epaulettes
(4) Collar flash
(5) Service rank badge
(6) Service station badge
(7) Necktie
(8) Party badge (for Party members only)
(9) Armband
(10) Breeches
(11) Footwear
(12) Leather belt with shoulder strap
(13) Dagger with adjustable strap.

General remarks concerning full dress uniform:

(1) full dress uniform will be worn on solemn occasions, such as parades in the presence of the Führer, inspections by the Chief-of-Staff, swearing-in ceremonies, consecration of colours, funeral ceremonies, tattoos, etc.
(2) Decoration clasp with decorations as well as any other decorations, worn at the neck or on the chest, are part of regulation full dress uniform.
(3) In principle, the leather belt with shoulder strap must always be worn with full dress uniform. At the office or in closed society the dagger may be taken off.

(b) Battle Dress consists of:

(1) Uniform cap with coloured band
(2) Uniform jacket
(3) Epaulettes
(4) Collar flash

Mann *of the 32nd Company of the* Leibstandarte *of* Gruppe "Hochland"

Sturmmann *(Lance-Corporal) of the 33rd Company of Regiment No. 1 of* Gruppe "Nordsee" *(Oldenburg)*

Rottenführer *(Corporal) of the 13th Company of Regiment No. 2 of* Gruppe "Pommern" *(Pomerania)*

Scharführer *(Sergeant) of the 1st Company of* Jäger Regiment No. 15 of Gruppe "Ostmark"

Oberscharführer *(Colour-Sergeant) of the 21st Company of Reserve Regiment No. 76 of* Gruppe "Hansa"

Truppführer *(Sergeant-Major) of the 24th Company of Regiment No. 21 of* Gruppe "Franken"

Obertruppführer *(Warrant Officer) of the 2nd Company of Regiment No. 4 of* Gruppe "Kurpfalz"

Sturmführer *(2nd Lieutenant) of the 3rd Company of* Jäger Regiment No. 3 *("Ostmark")*

Obersturmführer *(1st Lieutenant) of the 4th Company of Regiment No. 25 of* Gruppe "Niederrhein"

Sturmhauptführer *(Captain) of the 5th Company of Regiment No. 5 of* Gruppe "Ostland"

Sturmbannführer *(Major) of the 4th Battalion of Regiment No. 8 of* Gruppe "Westfalen"

Obersturmbannführer *(Lt.-Col.) of the 3rd Battalion of Regiment No. 9 ("Berlin-Brandenburg")*

Standartenführer *(Colonel) of Regiment No. 7 of* Gruppe "Schlesien" *(Silesia)*

Oberführer *(Bdr.-Gen.) on the staff of the S.A. high command*

Brigadeführer *(Major-General) in command of the 56th Brigade of* Gruppe "Südwest"

Gruppenführer *(Lt.-Gen.) in command of* Gruppe "Sachsen"

Obergruppenführer *(General) in command of* Gruppe "Berlin-Brandenburg"

Stabschef *(Chief-of-Staff)*

(5) Service rank badge
(6) Service station badge
(7) Armband
(8) Brown shirt with turn-down collar and tie
(9) Party badge (for Party members only)
(10) Breeches
(11) Footwear
(12) Leather belt with shoulder strap
(13) Dagger with strap.

General remarks concerning Battle Dress:
(1) Battle dress will be worn on

(c) **Sports Dress consists of:**
(1) White sleeveless sports vest with badge
(2) Brown twill sports trousers
(3) Light-weight heelless sports shoes.

General remarks concerning Sports Dress:
Care must be taken to ensure uniform sports dress for any unit lined up for sports activities.

(d) **Evening Dress consists of:**
(1) Uniform cap with coloured band

Der Stabschef

all official and non-official occasions which do not require the wearing of full-dress uniform.
(2) Unless otherwise instructed, a small decoration clasp will be worn with battle dress.
(3) On as well as off duty, the leather belt with shoulder strap must always be worn in public with battle dress. In public places, theatres, and restaurants, the leather belt will be taken off. The dagger is retained by the wearer and will be fastened on the ring of the left-hand jacket pocket. In closed society and at the office the dagger may be taken off.
(4) The wearing of white shorts with battle dress is not permitted.

(2) Uniform jacket
(3) Epaulettes
(4) Collar flash
(5) Service rank badge
(6) Service station badge
(7) Armband
(8) Light-coloured shirt with brown tie
(9) Party badge (for Party members only)
(10) Long black trousers
(11) Black boots
(12) Dagger.

General remarks concerning evening dress:
(1) Unless special orders are issued in exceptional cases, evening dress is worn off-duty only.

Hochland

S.A. flags:
◄◄ *The standard of Motor Regiment No. 86.*
△◄ *The Chief-of-Staff (Stabschef).*
◄ *The High Command (Oberste S.A.-Führung).*
▽◄ Gruppe "Hochland".
▽▽◄ *The 12th Brigade.*
△△▷ *Regiment (Standarte) No. 231 and the 3rd Battalion (Sturmbann) of Regiment No. 134.*
△▷ *The 1st Naval Brigade (Marine-Brigade).*
▷ *Naval Regiment (Marine-Standarte) No. 130 and the 1st Naval Battalion (Marine-Sturmbann) of Naval Regiment No. 112.*
▽▷ *Cavalry Regiment (Reiter Standarte) No. 133.*
▽▽▷ *The pennant of the 4th Cavalry Company (Reitersturm) of Cavalry Regiment No. 41.*

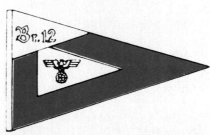

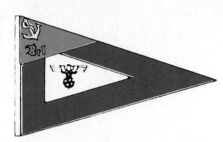

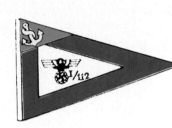

(2) Unless otherwise ordered, a small decoration clasp will be worn with evening dress.

(3) With evening dress, the dagger will be worn on the ring of the left-hand jacket pocket. In closed society and for dancing the dagger may be taken off.

(4) If an overcoat is worn with evening dress, the leather belt will be omitted. The dagger will be fastened on the ring of the left-hand overcoat pocket.

(*e*) Members of the *Hochland* Group may wear leather shorts, white stockings, and black or brown lace-up shoes with their brown shirts. In closed units, dress must be uniform.

(*f*) For the rifle Regiments One and Three of the *Hochland* Group, battle dress consists of mountain and ski cap, mountain and ski jacket, climbing and ski trousers, climbing boots. For full-dress uniform, brown shirt will replace mountain and ski jacket, and S.A. uniform cap the mountain and ski cap.

In summer, the above standards may wear shorts, white knee stockings, or *Wadenstutzen*, and black or brown shoes.

In closed formations, dress must be uniform.

In future, the phrase "S.A. brown" will describe the brown-green colour introduced in Ordinance I No. 1648, of November 3, 1933. The word "brown" will describe the colour prescribed before the above Ordinance came into force.

Notes

fobs: the German word *Bierzipfel* describes "a ribbon worn on watch chain displaying the colours of a student club".

Wadenstutzen: These are the traditional knee stockings without feet, worn by Bavarians with their national dress.

37. The Hitler Youth

The leader of the entire H.J. is the Reich Youth Leader of the N.S.D.A.P. who is also Youth Leader of the German Reich.

Created during the Years of Struggle of the National Socialist Movement, and enlarged during the years of rebuilding of a new Reich, the Hitler Youth symbolises the expression of purpose and development of the new rising generation.

While that small handful of former Hitler Youths had fought

for the realisation of the aims of National Socialism shoulder to shoulder with the fighters of the Movement, not conscious of any task other than that of holding their own in that struggle, the Hitler Youth, since the Assumption of Power, has accepted the great responsibility and the important task given to it by the Führer of introducing Germany's youth to National Socialist ideology. Once they are in the Hitler Youth, these young people, through constant political indoctrination, will be trained to become true and keen National Socialists. In addition to the work of political education which the Hitler Youth must carry out, there is also the task of the physical training of Germany's youth. On the one hand, they must be taught obedience and discipline; on the other hand, through the educational work of the H.J., the foundations of true leadership must be laid. Later on, when arrangements will be made for German boys and girls to join the Party, they must already be staunch National Socialists. The Hitler Youth must solve its tasks in close co-operation with home and school. Lofty and sacred is the trust left behind by those who fell in the struggle for this Reich, and likewise the obligation which the Hitler Youth bears because it bears the Führer's name.

The Hitler Youth is aware of its obligation; it realises its task, and it is going to carry it out because of its belief in the Führer and for the sake of the future of his Reich.

The Hitler Youth is responsible for all matters concerning youth. In co-operation with the respective Party Offices, it deals with all questions concerning youths aged between ten and eighteen, and girls between ten and twenty-one. However, it is not allowed to develop its own education policy.

Any German boy and any German girl who is Aryan and free from hereditary disease may join the H.J., the D.J., the B.D.M., or the J.M.

In general, new members will be enrolled only on the Führer's birthday, April 20 of each year. Similarly, the transfer of German *Jungvolk* (or of *Jungmädel*) to the Hitler Youth (or to the League of German Girls) will take place annually on April 20 for those who have reached the age of 14.

A solemn symbolical transfer of members of the H.J. or the B.D.M. to the Party and its organisations will take place an-

Gefolgschaftsfahne

Bannfahne

nually on November 9.

Members of the Hitler Youth who have completed their 18th year will be admitted into the Party, as will members of the League of German Girls who have completed their 21st year, on the following conditions:
Boys must have been members of the Hitler Youth for four consecutive years before admission into the N.S.D.A.P.
Girls must have been members of the B.D.M. for four consecutive years before admission into the N.S.D.A.P.
It is a further condition for admission of boys and girls into the N.S.D.A.P. that they should have proved themselves reliable National Socialists by enthusiastically carrying out their service duties and by impeccable conduct on as well as off duty, so that there will be no doubt of their becoming valuable members of the N.S.D.A.P. after admission.

Enrolment of individual boys and girls will have to take place by means of the usual correctly completed enrolment forms. Applications for admission will have to be sent to the Central Executive through official channels—that is to say via Local Groups, Bases, or Regions.

Together with the application for admission, a certificate issued by the competent Hitler Youth Unit Leader or the Junior Woman Regional Leader, confirming membership of the relevant organisations as well as satisfactory conduct to date, must be submitted. No admission fees will have to be paid by members of either the Hitler Youth or the League of German Girls.

It is the duty of all offices to submit only application forms of boys and girls who have al-

ready completed their 18th or 21st year.

Applications for admission may be submitted to the Central Executive throughout the year, as long as the member of the Hitler Youth or the League of German Girls has completed his or her 18th or 21st year, and as long as the conditions outlined above apply.

According to regulations, the day of admission will be determined exclusively by the Central Executive. The day of admission will be the first day of the month in which the application has been received by the Central Executive. Thus the day of application is not the day of admission. Similarly, November 9 is not the day of admission. What happens on November 9 is simply a solemn symbolic act in which all those members of the Hitler Youth and of the German Girls' Organisation who have, up to that time, reached the age of 18 or 21, take part.

Lawful admission into the N.S.D.A.P. will be implemented according to an administrative decree of the Central Executive and will have taken legal effect only after the handing over of the membership card issued by the Central Executive.

From the point of view of organisation and discipline the Hitler Youth is independent. However, it is a matter of course that Leading Functionaries may exercise the right of supervision.

Personnel Office:
The activities of the Personnel Office comprise two major tasks:
(1) selection of the most able comrades, and
(2) elimination of harmful elements.

(1) Selection of the most able comrades:
The selection of the best members of the Hitler Youth for the purpose of forming the leadership of the future is of vital importance for the development both of Hitler Youth and Party. The principles of selection are guided by the following criteria:

A member of the Hitler Youth must display qualities of leadership which will enable him to lead not only during his limited time of activity in the Hitler Youth, but which, over and above this, destine him in years to come for greater responsibilities in Party and State. Hence follows the necessity of carrying out the selection of leaders with the greatest possible care. With the increased responsibility of the Hitler Youth towards the future of our people, the standard applied to the young leader with regard to his ideological reliability, his character as well as his physical and mental alertness, has become steadily more demanding. Appointments of *Sturm* Unit Leaders and Junior *Sturm* Unit Leaders will take place only after careful examination by the Reich Youth Executive. In addition, lower-ranking leaders are subject to strict control through the Personnel Department of the Reich Youth Executive. Only he whose bearing reflects an impeccable character, who has proved himself as a National Socialist, who, on duty, during hiking expeditions, and in camp, has shown himself the best among his comrades, and who fulfills certain mental and physical demands, only he may be confirmed as a leader.

These severe conditions for selection are effective for lower-

ranking leaders up to Troop Leaders who are confirmed by the Area Personnel Department. For Unit Leaders, the following conditions have been laid down:
(1) Successful activity as leader of smaller units for a number of years
(2) Completion of compulsory labour and national service
(3) Successful attendance at Reich School for Youth Leaders or the Leaders' Academy of the Hitler Youth
(4) Fulfilment of conditions for the H.J. Proficiency Badge
(5) Successfully completed school or vocational education
(6) Proof of Aryan origin
(7) Proof of freedom from hereditary disease.

By analogy, these conditions are valid for all other male and female leaders. The aim of this selection is the formation of a leader corps composed of the most outstanding young Germans from all walks of life, and which, one day, will take over smoothly the leadership of Party and State.

(2) Elimination of harmful elements:
Any member harmful to the community will be expelled from the Hitler Youth through regular expulsion proceedings. At the same time, care will be taken to see that this fellow citizen will be kept away from all Youth leader and Youth education work, and, in severe cases, from any greater responsibilities in Party and State.

In addition to this most severe punishment there exist several punishments intended to give the young comrade an opportunity of showing his earnest endeavour to fulfil the conditions expected from a member of the

Fähnleinfahne

Jungbannfahne

Opposite page: *Flags of the Hitlerjugend or Hitler Youth. On the left is that of the 33rd Regiment or Bann, a unit some 3,000 strong, and on the right that of the 2nd Company of the 86th Gefolgschaft.*
This page: *Flags of the Deutsches Jungvolk or German Youth. On the left is that of the 1st Company of the 1st Regiment or Jungbann, and on the right that of the 1st Squad or Fähnlein of the 150th Regiment. The Fähnlein was 150-boys strong.*

Hitler Youth.

Hitler Youth jurisdiction is based upon the terms of reference of the Supreme Party Court. However, taking into account the character of a youth organisation, it must, in its assessment of misdemeanours, look upon punishment as a corrective measure to a far greater degree than would be possible in an adult organisation.

Notes

H.J. = *Hitler-Jugend* (Hitler Youth)
B.D.M. = *Bund Deutscher Mädel* (League of German Girls)
D.J. = *Deutsches Jungvolk*
J.M. = *Jungmädel*

Office for Ideological Indoctrination:

In agreement with, and according to instructions from the representative of the Führer for the supervision of all spiritual and ideological education in the N.S.D.A.P., this office directs and supervises the entire work of indoctrination in the Hitler Youth and its junior section, the "Young Folk" (*Jungvolk*), of the League of German Girls and

its junior section, the "Young Girls" (*Jungmädel*). The work of this office is sub-divided, as follows:
(1) Indoctrination of leaders
(2) Indoctrination of units
(3) Schools for leaders
(4) Department responsible for literature
(5) Ideological supervision
(6) Direction of seminar for H.J. Leaders at the College for Political Studies.

Special Indoctrination Departments working according to instructions from the Reich Youth Executive have been assigned to the staffs of all areas. Indoctrination work in the smallest units will be carried out by Formation Leaders.

All indoctrination material will be distributed free to all units in the Reich.

Office for Physical Training:

It is the aim of Hitler Youth Physical Training that every German boy should acquire a basic knowledge of physical exercises, air rifle and small-bore shooting, and of scouting exercises. These activities go side by side with systematic training of every German girl by means of physical culture. To include every boy and every girl in this scheme of physical training, and to lead German youth in its entirety towards a systematic and steady increase in their physical proficiency, is a vital task of the Hitler Youth's physical training. Another important task consists in creating for all young people in town and country opportunities for and forms of exercise which will ensure the systematic physical training of all young Germans. Moreover, the Hitler Youth must create healthy and

efficient future soldiers for the army. For that reason, one of its tasks is the training of prospective personnel for the special weapons unit of the armed forces. This training takes place in the special units of the Hitler Youth.

The entire implementation of this work is in the hands of the Office for Physical Training of the Reich Youth Executive. This office is sub-divided into three main columns:
(1) General training
(2) Special training
(3) B.D.M. physical training.

Office for Cultural Activities:

Early attempts by the Hitler Youth to organise cultural activities have developed into the steadily increasing readiness of German youth to come face to face with all cultural values. What is most essential for the Hitler Youth is

Vitality.

And thus it is not surprising to learn that it is song, as well as musical activities altogether, that is most popular and most assiduously practised among members of the Hitler Youth. In the foreground of our cultural work can be found activities such as the organising of ceremonial occasions, morning assemblies, parents' evenings, producing plays, handicrafts, the making of posters, book jackets, pictures for the hostels, and building and furnishing hostels.

We realise that only by daily uninterrupted detailed work in all cultural matters will we be in a position one day to produce an achievement which will seize the imagination of German youth and imprint upon it the stamp of a coherent cultural purpose. Out of the radio work of the Hitler

Youth numerous works and, at the same time, ideas have emerged which have become trend-setting for the continuation of our cultural work. Out of that work was created the "workshop of young Hitler Youth artists", which is not a new and self-sufficient organisation, but which, on the contrary, joins together and commits all creative forces in order to bring to German youth new works and values as their heritage.

The Hitler Youth knows that it will be able to solve these cultural problems only if, on the one hand it includes German youth as a whole, and, on the other hand, it works together with all organisations of the Movement. For that reason, it strives particularly hard to keep in constant touch and work hand in hand with the S.A., the S.S., the N.S.K.K., the Labour Service, the N.S. Association "Strength through Joy", the Reich Propaganda Executive, the Reich Agricultural Board, and others.

The Legal Office:

It is the task of the Legal Office of the Reich Youth Executive to deal uniformly with all legal interests of the Hitler Youth (including the B.D.M., D.J., and J.M.).

Thus it is incumbent upon the Legal Office to conduct a legal advisory service for the leadership and also to deal with the legal aspects of a large variety of matters concerning all offices of the Reich Youth Executive. Particular mention should be made of legal actions which take place in close consultation with the Reich Legal Department of the N.S.D.A.P.

Further tasks arise out of the great demands made upon the

H.J. If the H.J. is to include youth as a whole and, at the same time, take charge of each individual member and of all his actions, then, in special cases, the young person must be afforded legal protection. In more important cases, this will be arranged directly through the Legal Office, whereas in cases of minor importance the legal expert of the unit in question will be called in.

Out of the character of the H.J. as an élite organisation arises its duty to pay close attention to the strictest purity among its ranks. In this connection, the Legal Office will help by putting at the disposal of the Personnel Office its legal experts for the purpose of interrogations, and for supervision in the case of court proceedings.

To this extent, the sphere of activities of the Legal Office does not differ materially from that of similar offices of other organisations. But as the significance and the tasks of the H.J. as such are unique and cannot be compared to those of any other organisation, the activities of the Legal Office must not be limited to such laborious details. In the Third Reich, youth has been given an area of tasks and responsibilities of its own. The Legal Office must co-operate in the development of a whole series of new laws concerning different aspects of youth care.

The Broadcasting Department:

The Broadcasting Department of the Reich Youth Executive has been established as the centre for all German youth broadcasting activities.

In May 1933 the H.J. began its work in various German broadcasting centres and was in a position, during that year, to install specialists in charge of Hitler Youth broadcasting at all stations. Within the Reich Broadcasting Executive the post of a representative of the Reich Youth Leader was created, and the direction of all H.J. broadcasting activities is incumbent upon him. Today, at every broadcasting station, there are radio drama groups whose task is not only the creation of broadcasts, but also the organisation of active borderland work which receives the greatest possible radio support.

H.J. broadcasting is, in addition, responsible for spreading among the German people the treasury of folk songs accumulated by the H.J. Moreover,

Kameradschafts-
führer *(250th* Bann,
Gefolgschaft *1)*

Bannführer *of the
22nd* Bann

Gebietsführer

Obergebietsführer
*(Department Leader
in the Reich Youth
Leadership)*

Stabsführer *(highest
rank in the H.J.)*

Scharführer *(on the
staff of* Gebiet 4)

Unterbannführer
*(on the staff of the
Reich Youth
Leadership)*

Oberbannführer
*(on the staff of
a Gebiet)*

Oberbannführer
*(on the staff of
the Reich Youth
Leadership)*

broadcasting has become an active cultural source.

In closest co-operation with the Office for Ideological Indoctrination within the R.J.F., the Broadcasting Department creates the weekly "Hour of the Young Nation", which is the centrepiece of Social Evenings arranged by the Hitler Youth. In particular, the Broadcasting Office takes part in all major campaigns organised by the H.J., as, for instance, the Reich Vocational Competition, the Drive for New Hostels, or the H.J. Summer Camp.

With regard to listeners, the Broadcasting Department of the R.J.F. carries out preliminary work for the safeguarding of communal reception, by means of an organisation specially created for this particular purpose, namely the H.J. Broadcasting Wardens Organisation. Radio receivers obtained through the Radio Set Supply Campaign will be installed and serviced by H.J. Radio Wardens. They receive their training and education at the Reich Radio School at Göttingen, where there are workshops and laboratories supplying every device necessary for first-class technical training. Young amateur radio operators who are also members of the H.J. Broadcasting Organisation are trained in special courses. After taking an examination set by the D.A.S.D. and the German Postal Authority, they will receive an operator's licence which permits the operation of a short-wave transmitter. There are radio engineering groups attached to many area headquarters which are employed in tackling a large variety of radio engineering tasks.

The Youth Hostelling Office:

The Youth Hostelling Office, which is connected with the Executive of the Reich Association of German Youth Hostels by sharing some of its staff, has the task of acting in an educational capacity by propagating the idea of hiking as well as youth hostelling among young Germans.

The Office organises hikes which bring together boys and girls from all parts of the Reich and contribute towards levelling regional differences by bringing together people from different regions. The activities of the Office support the work of the German Youth Hostels Association which has established altogether 2,000 youth hostels all over Germany. These youth hostels serve as quarters for the H.J. and in addition are used by wider circles of the Party for the purpose of holding training courses. Through international agreements with 20 Youth Hostels Associations all over the world, our youth hostels are open to foreigners and may be used by them, just as youth hostels abroad are at the disposal of young Germans. By this means a beginning has been made towards a fellowship of young people and also towards the understanding of youth beyond the frontiers of their own countries.

Office for Youth Organisations:

The J.V. includes two major fields of activity.

First: in collaboration with the official departments in existence for this purpose, all manifestations of opposition in the field of youth work will be observed and suitably interpreted. Similarly, any incidents between the H.J. and other youth groups will be dealt with.

Second: the Office acts as Police Liaison Office. With the help of official Police organs, all misdemeanours of a criminal character which, after all, are unavoidable in an organisation as large as the H.J., will be dealt with. Individual units of the Hitler Youth will be watched to ascertain whether they are, in fact, removing all criminal elements from their ranks, and whether they are taking the measures necessary for reducing to a minimum misdemeanours of a criminal nature.

In the Police Liaison Office, central records will be kept about certain misdemeanours, and these will not only provide a survey, but also render impossible the emergence of certain criminal elements in different districts. The causes of crimes which young people are most likely to commit will be especially investigated, and general guide-lines for their prevention will be sought.

In addition, the Office for Youth Organisations is responsible for the supervision of the Hitler Youth Patrol Service which is being built up throughout the Reich and which is to supervise the behaviour in public of the Hitler Youth.

All tasks of the Office for Youth Organisations will be carried out in co-operation with Party and State offices, such as the Secret

For Landjahr *service (The* Landjahr *was a year's compulsory service on the land)*

Gefolgschaftsführer *of a Flying* Gefolgschaft *in the 250th* Bann

Bannführer *(as Financial Administrator in a Gebiet)*

Hauptarzt *(Senior Doctor)*

Hilfsapotheker *(Assistant Chemist)*

Epaulettes of the Hitlerjugend. *This was run on military lines, and before the war its organisation was as follows: the smallest unit was the* Kameradschaft *of 15 boys, under a* Kameradschaftsführer; *two to four of these made up a* Schar, *under a* Scharführer; *two to four* Scharen *made up a* Gefolgschaft, *under a* Gefolgschaftsführer; *three to five* Gefolgschaften *made up an* Unterbann, *under an* Unterbannführer; *four to eight* Unterbanne *made up a* Bann, *under a* Bannführer; *and 10 to 30* Banne *made up a* Gebiet, *under a* Gebietsführer. *This was the highest level at which H.J. activities took place, but on the administrative level there was the* Obergebiet, *led by an* Obergebietsführer, *to co-ordinate the activities of four to six* Gebiete.

State Police, the S.D., the Reich Leader of the S.S., the Reich Minister for Church Affairs, and other relevant bodies.

The Frontier and Foreign Office:

The tasks of the Frontier and Foreign Office are as follows:
(1) to deal with all immediate youth problems in the area of frontier and foreign work, in co-operation with the Party and State political offices working in this field;
(2) to indoctrinate all young people in the spirit of National Socialist work for and knowledge of our national heritage and the foreign policies of the Third Reich. It is the aim of this indoctrination one day to bring about the awakening of our people to the sensitivity and instinct required for these matters;
(3) to look after the borderlands and to take care of frontier and foreign travel.

Out of these tasks and within this wide framework arises the organisation of work in the Reich Youth Executive's Frontier and Foreign Office.

It consists of four main political sections:
(1) Ethnical German Section;
(2) Foreign Section;
(3) Area 26: Abroad of the Hitler Youth;
(4) Colonial work.

The activities of these main political sections are supported by two further sections:
(5) Hiking Office;
(6) Foreign Press Office; in addition, from the point of view of indoctrination, they are carried down to the most subordinate units of the Hitler Youth, the Young Folk and the League of German Girls through Section 7: G.A. Indoctrination.

The following aspects of the G.A.'s practical work should be mentioned: The holding of ethnical-German indoctrination conferences; work in the borderlands through cultural and social development of borderland youth; camps of German and French or English young people; German/Polish exchange radio programmes; socio-political discussions with foreign youth leaders; and, above all, constant care of foreign visitors in Germany.

The Langemarck Section:

On November 11, 1934, the day on which, 20 years earlier, Germany's youth from all sectors of the people had charged and

A Stammführer of the D.J. or Deutsches Jungvolk in winter service dress.

A Jungzugführer (Youth Troop Leader) in summer service dress with drum.

A Jungbannführer (Youth Deutsches Jungvolk in winter service dress.

An Untergauführerin *(Deputy*
Gau *Leader) of the B.D.M. in*
winter costume.

A Jungmädel *(Young Girl) of*
the B.D.M. in standard summer
costume.

An Untergauführerin *of the*
B.D.M. in standard summer
costume.

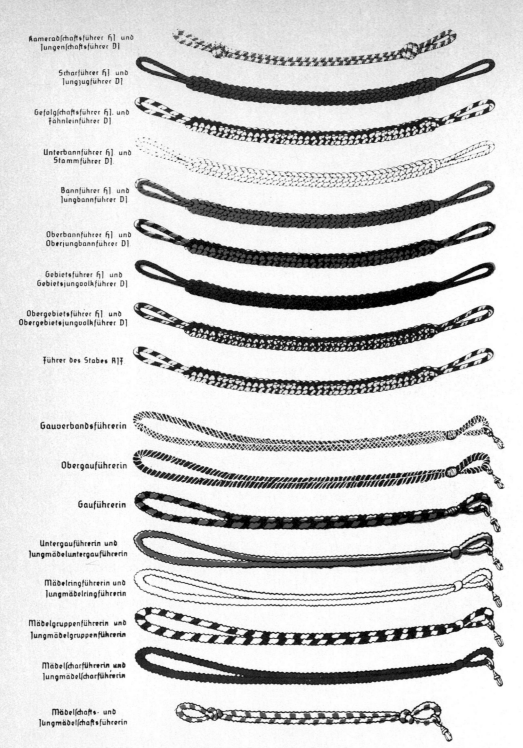

Kameradschaftsführer HJ. und
Jungenschaftsführer DJ.

Scharführer HJ. und
Jungzugführer DJ.

Gefolgschaftsführer HJ. und
Fähnleinführer DJ.

Unterbannführer HJ. und
Stammführer DJ.

Bannführer HJ. und
Jungbannführer DJ.

Oberbannführer HJ. und
Oberjungbannführer DJ.

Gebietsführer HJ. und
Gebietsjungvolkführer DJ.

Obergebietsführer HJ. und
Obergebietsjungvolkführer DJ.

Führer des Stabes RJF.

Gauverbandsführerin

Obergauführerin

Gauführerin

Untergauführerin und
Jungmädeluntergauführerin

Mädelringführerin und
Jungmädelringführerin

Mädelgruppenführerin und
Jungmädelgruppenführerin

Mädelscharführerin und
Jungmädelscharführerin

Mädelschafts- und
Jungmädelschaftsführerin

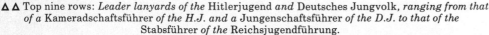

△△ Top nine rows: *Leader lanyards of the* Hitlerjugend *and* Deutsches Jungvolk, *ranging from that of a* Kameradschaftsführer *of the* H.J. *and a* Jungenschaftsführer *of the* D.J. *to that of the* Stabsführer *of the* Reichsjugendführung.

△ Bottom eight rows: *Leader lanyards of the* Bund Deutscher Mädel *and* Jungmädel, *ranging from that of the* Gauverbandsführerin *to that of a* Mädelschaftsführerin *of the* B.D.M. *and a* Jungmädelschaftsführerin *of the* J.M.

▷ *Car pennants of the* H.J. *From top to bottom these are the pennants of the* Stabsführer *of the* Reichsjugendführung (R.J.F.), *an* Amtsleiter (Department Leader) *of the* R.J.F., *the* Gebietsführer *of* Gebiet *No. 20 "*Württemberg*", and the* Bannführer *of the 193rd* Bann *"*Neustettin*".*
Opposite page, top to bottom: *the obverse* (Vorderseite) *and reverse* (Rückseite) *of the* D.J. Leader *of* Gebiet *No. 20, the* B.D.M. Leader *of* Obergau *No. 25 "Pfalz-Saar", the obverse and reverse of a* J.M. Leader *in the same* Obergau, *and the* Reichsjugendführung *and* Gebiet *staff car pennant.*

Kraftwagenstander
für Stabsführer RJF.

Kraftwagenstander
für Amtsleiter der RJF.

Kraftwagenstander
für Führer der Gebiete

Bann 193

Neustettin

Kraftwagenstander
für Führer eines Bannes

3200

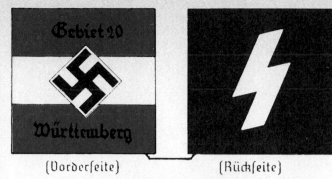

(Vorderſeite)   (Rückſeite)

Kraftwagenſtander für Führer des DJ. im Gebiet

**Kraftwagenſtander
für die Führerin
eines Obergaues**

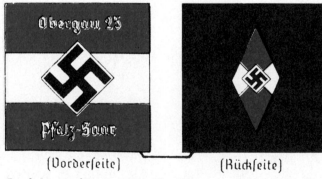

(Vorderſeite)   (Rückſeite)

**Kraftwagenſtander für die Führerin der Jungmädel
im Obergau**

**Wimpel für den Stab
der RJF. und die Gebietsſtäbe**

died at Langemarck, the Reich Youth Leader took charge of Langemarck work for German youth in its entirety and established the "Langemarck Section".

Its work comprises the following tasks:

(1) to honour our heroes by showing respect and reverence for their sacrifices;

(2) for the heritage of our front line soldiers to be received and faithfully administered by Germany's youth who, standing shoulder to shoulder with living front-line soldiers, inspired as were those who died before them, must in turn be inspired to perform similar deeds and achievements for Germany.

(3) In serving the community, the will to emulate the spirit of our Langemarck comrades must be placed first and foremost as the loftiest fulfilment of genuine and true National Socialism.

Notes

R.J.F.: *Reichsjugendführung* = Reich Youth Executive

D.A.S.D.: I have been unable to ascertain the exact meaning of this abbreviation, but it probably stands for: *Deutscher Amateur-Sender Dienst* = German Amateur Radio Operators' Service.

J.V.: *Jugendverbände* = Youth Organisations

Secret State Police = *Geheime Staatspolizei* or Gestapo

S.D.: *Sicherheitsdienst* = Security Service

Area 26: Abroad: It must be assumed that areas 1–25 represent the German Reich.

G.A.: *Grenz- und Auslandsamt* = Frontier and Foreign Office

Langemarck: On the Ypres front in 1914 a unit of German students advanced against the British with arms linked and singing, and was cut to pieces by British rifle and machine gun fire.

38. The S.S.

Leadership:

The *Schutzstaffel*, an independent unit of the Party, is led by the *Reichsführer*-S.S.

Tasks:

The first and foremost task of the S.S. is to take care of the protection of the Führer.

By order of the Führer, the scope of the S.S. has been enlarged to include the country's internal security.

Selection of Members:

In order to carry out these tasks,

a fighting force, uniform, closely-knit, and ideologically dedicated to one another, has been created whose fighters are selected from among the best of Aryan stock.

The realisation of the importance of *Blut und Boden* is a directive in the selection for the *Schutzstaffel*. Every member of the S.S. has got to be permeated with sense and essence of the National Socialist Movement. Ideologically and physically he will receive exemplary training so that individually or with his unit he may be sent into action successfully in the determined fight for National Socialist ideology. Only racially outstanding Germans are suitable for this combat. Therefore it is necessary for a continuous process of selection to be carried out among members of the *Schutzstaffel*, first roughly and then with ever increasing care.

However, this selection is not only confined to the men, for its purpose is the preservation of a pure-bred race. Therefore every S.S. Man is required to marry only a racially compatible woman. From year to year, demands for keeping the S.S. untainted are becoming more exacting.

Loyalty and honour, obedience and valour determine the S.S. Man's actions. His weapon bears the inscription awarded by the Führer: "Loyalty is my Honour!" Both those virtues are inextricably joined together. Whoever transgresses against them is no longer worthy of being a member of the S.S.

Unconditional obedience is demanded. It arises out of the conviction that National Socialist ideology has got to rule. Whoever possesses it and supports it passionately will, of his own free will, submit to compulsory obedience. For that reason, an S.S. Man is ready to execute blindly every order coming from the Führer or given by one of his own superiors, even if it demands of him the greatest sacrifice.

To an S.S. Man, valour is the highest manly virtue in the struggle for his ideology.

Openly and mercilessly he fights the Reich's most dangerous enemies: Jews, Freemasons, Jesuits, and Political Clergy.

At the same time, by his example he will woo and convince those who are weak and wavering and who have not yet been able to fight their way through to a National Socialist philosophy of life.

Whoever is fighting, like the

S.S. Man, for lofty ideals will have to be able to accomplish extraordinary feats, physically and mentally. The S.S. engages in every sport. Wherever the S.S. Man enters into competition publicly, he is conscious that he has to give his best, his utmost, for the honour of his S.S. Squad.

One of his most outstanding publicity aids is the magazine *The Black Corps*. It is published on Wednesdays. Every S.S. Man is obliged to read this fighting and propaganda paper of the S.S. and to do his utmost to see that it is distributed among the entire German people.

Organisation and Scope:
The organisation of the S.S. arises from the variety of its tasks.

The following are directly responsible to the Reichsführer S.S.: The chiefs of: the three main Offices, the Adjutant's Office, the Staff Chancellery, the S.S. Tribunal, the Administration, the Board of Health, and the Office for Population Policy.

The Central Office of the S.S.,
being the highest command post of the *Reichsführer*-S.S., has been assigned the job of forming, training for their allotted tasks and sending into action the three sections into which the S.S. has been sub-divided: the General S.S.; the S.S. Stand-by Troops; and the S.S. Guard Troops.

Hence follows the necessity for establishing the offices mentioned. These have the following tasks:

Central Chancellery:
The Chief of the Central Chancellery, together with his staff of Assistants, directs the command post of the Chief of S.S. Head Office. He is in charge of registering and sorting the entire incoming mail. He reports immediately to the Chief of the S.S. Head Office concerning any important occurrences. He carries out decisions and receives instructions and orders from the Chief of S.S. Head Office. He looks after liaison with all offices under the authority of the Chief of S.S. Head Office. He supervises and checks the entire business administration within S.S. Head Office.

(1) Operations Section:
The Operations Section deals with all matters in connection with training and organisation of the three sections of the *Schutzstaffel*.

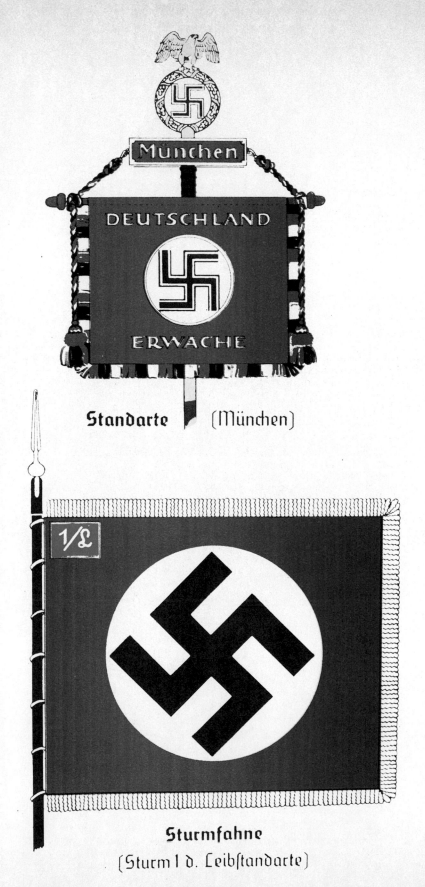

Standarte (München)

Sturmfahne
(Sturm 1 d. Leibstandarte)

(2) Staff Office:

As Chief of the Staff Chancellery, the Chief of the Staff Office is a member of the Personal Staff of the *Reichsführer*-S.S. The three Staff Offices of the S.S. Head Office, the Race and Settlement Head Office and the S.D. Head Office work under the authority of the Staff Chancellery. The Staff Chancellery is responsible for dealing with all staff matters of S.S. Leaders and of Junior Leaders of the entire Squadron who have been commissioned with Leaders' posts.

Within the scope of the Staff Chancellery falls the drafting of trainees for training courses for prospective leaders, as well as the care of standard bearers, discharged from S.S. Leader training schools.

(3) Administrative Office:

The Chief of the Administrative Office is simultaneously Chief of S.S. Administration (on the personal staff of the *Reichsführer*-S.S.). He is responsible for all administrative and domestic affairs of the three Head Offices.

As sole representative of the Reichsführer S.S. he is also in charge of negotiations concerning these matters with all offices outside the S.S.

He is sole authorised representative of the National Treasurer for the entire S.S.

For the purpose of strengthening the means for expansion and routine work of the S.S., an establishment has been created in the Administrative Office, where the names of Aryans not belonging to the S.S. are kept as Supporting Members, as long as they undertake to pay a monthly contribution, the amount to be stipulated by themselves.

(4) Medical Office

The Chief of the S.S. Medical Office deals with all areas concerning the medical service of the S.S. In his capacity as "National Medical Officer of the S.S." he is, at the same time, responsible to the *Reichsführer*-S.S. for the entire medical service of the S.S.

(5) Recruitment Office:

The Recruitment Office deals with all admissions of Junior Leaders and Men, as well as with re-admissions, appointments, transfers and removals, secondments and dismissals. Among its tasks are also the inclusion in a card-index with intelligence about their particulars of all members of the S.S., as well as computation and statistics regarding the total force of the S.S.

(6) Office for Security Matters:

Its scope corresponds with the title of the office.

Of the three sections of the S.S., S.S. Stand-by Troops and S.S. Guard Troops are equipped with light and heavy infantry weapons, the General S.S. only with daggers.

The two **S.S. Leader (Training) Schools** are meant to train prospective leaders.

At the Riding School, S.S. riders and drivers are perfected in their riding and driving training.

The School of Motoring trains members of the S.S. Motor Unit and the Motorised Convoys to become exemplary drivers and teachers.

The Race and Settlement Office (R.u.S.) provides the equipment for the S.S., being a kinship community selected according to Nordic-racial principles, to enable it to realise among itself, by living in a way characteristic for the species, the idea of *Blut und Boden*, to serve as an example to the entire people. The R.u.S. is divided into the following six offices:

(1) Office for Organisation and Administration:

It creates the organisation, personnel, and material basis for the remaining offices in order to facilitate their work.

(2) Race Office:

It is the task of this Office to prove and exploit the fact that blood alone determines history, morality, law, and industry.

(3) Office for Indoctrination:

The purpose of the Office for Indoctrination is the ideological education of the S.S. Its aim is to bring every S.S. Man to accept, in its totality, the National Socialist ideological point of view and thus to create a self-contained ideological block within the population.

(4) Kinship Office:

Incumbent upon the Kinship Office is the examination, from the point of view of race, parentage, and freedom from hereditary disease, of S.S. Men, Junior Leaders, and leaders already in the S.S., as well as those about to be admitted.

Opposite page: S.S. standards. Above is that of the Munich Regiment, and below that of the 3/1st S.S. Regiment.
Δ *An S.S.* Unterscharführer *(Senior Corporal) of the cordoning detail at Nuremberg in service dress.*

Dienstanzug der SS.-Verfüg.-Truppe
Sturmmann

3204

Feldmütze

Sportanzug

Uniforms of the Schutzstaffel:
◁◁ An Unterscharführer of the Allgemeine S.S. (General S.S.)
in parade dress.
◁ A Sturmmann (Lance-Corporal) of the S.S. Verfügungstruppen
(the S.S. military arm) in Dienstanzug or service dress.
△△ The S.S. field cap (Feldmütze).
△ S.S. sports kit (Sportanzug).
▷ A Scharführer of the S.S. Verfügungstruppen in Paradeanzug
(parade dress).

The examination and selection takes place according to the directions of the *Reichsführer*-S.S., according to his principle that the S.S. is to be the élite of the best German Nordically-determined blood; through the extension of the S.S. to become a kinship community and by recording the best pedigrees in the Kinship Book it is intended that this valuable heritage of blood should be preserved for the German people and increased for future generations.

(5) Settlement Office:
It puts into practice the thought of *Blut und Boden* by settling racially valuable S.S. families in connection with the re-creation of German peasantry and "homestead" settlement.

(6) Records and Newspaper Office:
This Office has been given the task of putting at the disposal of all offices items of literature, the daily press and pictorial material for the purpose of adaptation and utilisation. In addition, this Office is to propagate the attitude of the S.S. in questions affecting the Head Office for Race and Settlement beyond the limits of the S.S. and, if necessary, to influence the General Press, Radio, Film, and Exhibitions in our favour.

(7) Office for Population Policy:
This Office deals with all questions of population policy within the S.S. It has been appointed by the *Reichsführer*-S.S. as Chief Assessment Office for Freedom from Hereditary Disease.

In collaboration with offices run by the State (Advice Bureau for Heredity and Race Affairs attached to State Health Offices) it exploits scientifically the genetic stock-taking of the S.S. In short-term training courses it instructs all S.S. medical officers in the subjects of genetics, hereditary health hygiene, and marriage counselling.

S.D. Head Office
The Security Service of the *Reichsführer*-S.S. is the source of political intelligence of the Movement and Reich.

This Head Office supervises and assesses all political events. As quickly as possible it transmits to the leadership of Movement and Reich its evaluation of the political situation at any

given time, to serve as basis for their decisions.

The organisation of the Security Service corresponds to these tasks. Its directorate makes use of three offices. The most subordinate offices of the Security Service are branches working either for a division of a subordinate Government Board or for a District Office of the N.S.D.A.P.

S.S. Tribunal
On behalf of the *Reichsführer*-S.S., the S.S. Tribunal carries out investigations into matters of discipline, complaints, and affairs of honour. Taking into consideration the instructions, orders, and directions issued by the *Reichsführer*-S.S., it judges all cases exclusively according to National Socialist ideological soldierly principles.

The Relationship of the S.S. within the Party, and with Government Offices
Within the framework of the tasks set by the Führer to the *Reichsführer*-S.S., all S.S. Leaders are urged by the *Reichsführer*-S.S. to create harmony in co-operation with Leading Functionaries of the Party, and to see to it that National Socialist authority is preserved.

Supporting Members of the S.S.
Service with the S.S., making as it does exceptional demands especially at meetings of Leaders is economically a great deal harder because individual units of the S.S. are geographically more widely distributed than units of the S.A. As a result, the S.S. has considerably higher transport costs in the execution of their duties.

For that reason, the Führer has consented to the establishment by the S.S. of the F.M. Organisation. Supporting Members, who need not be party Members, pay fixed amounts monthly. Only those S.S. Offices which have been specifically appointed for this purpose by the R.F.S. (Administrative Office S.S.) are authorised to collect these contributions. The F.M. Organisation is of the greatest importance for the existence of the S.S., and it must not be impeded in its work by any other office.

Notes
Schutzstaffel = "Defence Squadron" (S.S.)
Reichsführer: Reich Leader
Blut und Boden = "Blood and Soil"
S.D. = *Sicherheitsdienst* (Security Service).
National Treasurer: of the Party, not of the Reich.
Supporting Members: *Fördernde Mitglieder.*

39. Tasks and Organisation of the Reich Labour Service

As a sub-division of the N.S.D.A.P., the N.S. Labour Service has provided the basis for the law relating to compulsory labour service (issued on June 26, 1935).

The N.S. Labour Service has become the Reich Labour Service.

The Reich Labour Service is subordinate to the Reich Minister of the Interior.

The Reich Labour Service represents an honorary obligation *vis-à-vis* the German people: all young Germans of both sexes are liable to Labour Service (Reich Labour Service Law).

Young men will be called up for compulsory labour service for a period determined by the Leader of the Reich Labour Service. The same goes for young women within the framework of possibilities given at present. (The eventual expansion of the Women's Labour Service is a matter of course).

Tasks:
As its name conveys, the Labour Service is a service which, in contrast to military service, is carried out, not with the help of arms, but through labour.

The R.A.D. has an educational as well as an economic task.

(1) The education takes place in a soldierly manner in closed camps outside towns. Its chief aim is to provide an education towards a National-Socialist outlook on labour and towards the Fellowship of the People.

Because he labours for Germany in a community and without pay, the worker will be brought to realise that the intrinsic meaning of labour lies not in wages earned, but in the spirit in which it is performed. The elevation of labour to a service will teach him that labour is not a curse but an honour. And

Abteilungsfahne

◄ *The standard of the "Andreas Bauriedl" Detachment* (Abteilung) *of the R.A.D. or* Reichsarbeitsdienst *(Reich Labour Service).*
▽ *The flag of an R.A.D. Camp or House* (Lager *or* Haus).

Lager- u. Hausfahne

3207

3208

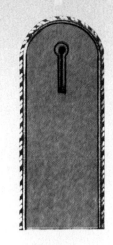

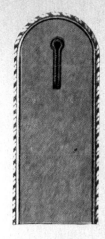

Arbeitsmann　　　　**Vormann**　　　　**Obervormann**

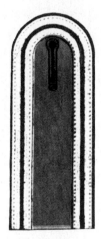

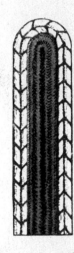

Truppführer　　　**Obertruppführer**　　　**Unterfeldmeister**

Uniforms and insignia of the
Reichsarbeitsdienst:
◁◁ *An* Arbeitsführer *(Leader).*
◁ *An* Arbeitsmann *(Worker).*
△ *Collar rank patches, from
that of an* Arbeitsmann *(top),
via* Vormann, Obervormann,
Truppführer *and*
Obertruppführer, *and*
Unterfeldmeister *to*
Oberstfeldmeister *(bottom).*
▷ *R.A.D. epaulettes.*

Feldmeister　　　**Ober-
feldmeister**　　　**Oberst-
feldmeister**

3209

Heilgehilfe
im Range eines Truppführers

Arzte
hier Arbeitsarzt

Musikzugführer

Ober-
musikzugführer

R.A.D. specialist collar patches and epaulettes:
△ △ ◁ *Medical Assistant* (Heilgehilfe) *with the rank of*
Truppführer.
△ △ ▷ *Doctor* (Arzt).
△ ◁ *Bandmaster* (Musikzugführer).
△ ▷ *Senior Bandmaster* (Obermusikzugführer).

thus he will realise that there is no difference between manual and white-collar workers, but rather that the value of any labour will be determined by the attitude of mind with which it is carried out. Therefore, the main characteristics of Labour Service education are soldierly bearing, closeness to the soil, a National Socialist outlook on labour, and a community spirit.

(2) The Reich Labour Service labours for the reclamation and amelioration of German soil. Germany is obliged to utilise her land to the uttermost, and for that reason she must transform fallow plains, waste land and fens into fertile soil. The productivity of German agriculture may be significantly increased by processes of amelioration. The R.A.D. serves this important task of safeguarding the people's food supplies from their own soil.

Regulations concerning careers as leaders:

There exists in the Labour Service a junior career as leader, comprising the ranks of Troop Leader, Senior Troop Leader, Second Lieutenant; as well as an intermediate and a higher career as leader, which includes leaders from Lieutenant upwards. There is no rigid and final separation between these careers.

Conditions for the acceptance of applications for places as trainee leaders are:

(1) the applicant must have completed his seventeenth year and produce evidence of permission of parents or guardian;

(2) the applicant must provide proof of Aryan origin;

(3) the applicant must produce proof of unblemished character by means of a certificate of conduct issued by the Police, and by extracts from the penal records.

Applications for enrolment as trainee leader must be made to the Regional Labour Leader by means of a written request. General suitability having been proved, final acceptance as trainee leader will take place only after a period of six months as a Private. There follows a probationary period, including two years' National Service, for all trainee leaders. During this training period, no difference exists between trainees for the lower, the intermediate, or the higher career levels.

At the end of the probationary period those trainees who are most suitable will be selected for the intermediate career, while the

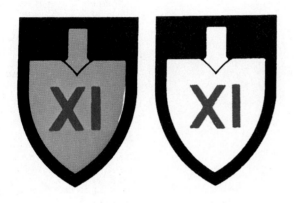

Shoulder patches of the Reichsarbeitsdienst:
Top row, left to right: Reichsarbeitsführer *(Reich Labour Leader),* Obergeneralarbeitsführer, *and* Generalarbeitsführer *of the Reich Labour Executive;* Generalarbeitsführer *as* Gauarbeitsführer (Gau *Labour Leader) of* Gau *No. 9; and two patches for the* Reichsleitung *(Central Executive) up to the rank of* Oberstarbeitsführer.

Centre row, left to right: *Two patches for the* Arbeitsgauleitung (Gau *Labour Executive) of* Gau *No. 11, up to the rank of* Oberstarbeitsführer; *and two patches for the* Gruppenstab *(Group Staff) of* Gruppe *No. 120.*
Bottom row, left to right: *Two patches for* Abteilung *(Detachment) No. 6 of* Gruppe *(Group) No. 120; and two patches for the* Reichsschule *(Reich School).*

3211

Verwalter bei Abteilungen   **Verwaltung** Reichs- u. Gauleitung. Gruppenstab   **Planung**

Heildienst   **Rechtshof**   **Mufikzug- und Obermufikzug-führer**

Ringkragen für Streifendienst

Brustschild des Fahnenträgers

remaining men will, if suitable and having signed a ten-year agreement, continue with the lower career, and as vacancies occur, they will be finally accepted into the Reich Labour Service as regular Troop Leaders.

At a later stage, able leaders will have an opportunity to gain promotion to the intermediate career after taking an examination.

Commensurate with the great demands made upon intermediate career leaders, severe standards will have to be applied during the process of selecting applicants for the intermediate career, after completion of their probationary period. In addition to personality, what must be expected from trainee leaders for the intermediate—

and thus possibly for the higher—leader career is an appropriate mental aptitude as well as a level of education corresponding to the average level of a person having completed their grammar school education. Proof may be provided not only by means of a leaving certificate from a Grammar School, but also by passing a special examination.

Gifted trainee leaders who do not possess a leaving certificate from a Grammar School, but who, according to their personality, are suitable for the intermediate leader career, will be given an opportunity of preparing for this examination.

Trainees for the intermediate career will have to undergo a further year of training, on com-

pletion of which, that is to say, after successful attendance of the *Feldmeister* School as well as having proved their mettle in field work, they will receive their appointment as lieutenant.

Further training of Labour Service leaders will be carried out at District Schools and at the Reich Labour Service School, as well as, under certain circumstances, in special technical courses.

Retiring leaders and their surviving dependents are entitled to maintenance, according to Article 24 of the Reich Labour Service Law.

In addition to the above-mentioned leader careers, there exists the possibility of entry as "Long Service Volunteer". There

Top row, left to right: R.A.D. specialist shoulder patches. From left to right these are for an Abteilung Verwalter *(Detachment Administrator), the Administrative Branch in the Reich or Regional Executive* (Reichs- *or* Gauleitung)*; the Reich or Regional Planning Department (*Planung*).*
*Centre row, left to right: the Reich or Regional Health Service (*Heildienst*); the Reich or Regional Judicial Branch (*Rechtshof*); and a Bandmaster and Senior Bandmaster.*
*Bottom row, left: The gorget (*Ringkragen*) for R.A.D. patrols.*
*Bottom row, right: The breast-plate (*Brustschild*) for R.A.D. standard bearers.*

are special regulations for their service promotion.

The flag of the Reich Labour Service:

The symbol of the Reich Labour Service is the union of spade and ear of corn. The spade indicates the closeness to the soil of the Reich Labour Service which, with the help of that implement, is creating new land for the German people; the ear of corn signifies the fruits of labour, the crop which grows in the newly created field.

Between two crossed and stylised ears of corn stands the blade of the spade: black, on a round, white field, on red cloth. Thus the symbol of the Reich Labour Service is repeated on all its flags, banners and standards.

No further ornament and no symbol other than this appears on the house flag, while on the divisional flag the symbol rests on a swastika, angled at 45 degrees. In addition, the standard of the Reich Labour Leader displays the embellishment of a wreath of golden ears of corn. Black surrounds or black diagonal bars designate individual offices which obtain further identification by means of a system of different combinations of figures.

Notes

R.A.D. = *Reichsarbeitsdienst* (Reich Labour Service)
Second Lieutenant = *Unterfeldmeister:* the rank of *Feldmeister* was created specifically for the Labour Service.
Private = *Arbeitsmann*: another rank created for the Nazi Labour Service.

40. The Party and the State

(1) The State

The State has been created out of the necessity to regulate the community of a people according to certain laws. Its distinguishing mark is its power *vis-à-vis* every member of the community. The State has the right to demand that every fellow citizen should obey the law. Whoever acts contrary to the laws of the State will be punished. To supervise its laws and regulations the State has its civil servants. The constitution of the State is the basis of its legislation. The State is the embodiment of power! In a State, people holding differing con-

victions and different views may live side by side. The State may not demand that all men should hold the same convictions. However, it may demand that all men should respect its laws.

(2) The Party

In contrast to the State, the Party is a community of like-minded men. It was born out of the struggle for ideology. In order to come out of this struggle victoriously, the Party rallied all those who were ready to fight for this ideology. And it is this ideology that is the foundation of the order according to which men live within the Party. While in the State many citizens consider its laws to be oppressive, hindering and difficult, the laws of the Party are no burden, but represent the will of the community. The characteristic of the State is the "I must", that of the Party is the "I will".

(3) The tasks of Party and State

(a) It is conceivable that Party and State might be one and the same thing. That will be the case if all fellow citizens are convinced of the Party's ideology and if, at the same time, the laws of the State are the clear expression of that ideology. Then it is the State that will be the great community of like-minded people. This ideal State will but rarely be achieved in history. Altogether, it is conceivable only if that ideology is the sole basis of an attitude of mind which has completely penetrated all men.
(b) If the ruling Party possesses no ideology at all, but is merely an artificial organisation for the purpose of achieving temporal aims, then Party and State will decline into a technical institution, where no spiritual values are given to the people, and which, acting merely as watchman and police state, maintains peace and quiet. This is the state of affairs which prevailed in the past few decades.
(c) If the people are not totally penetrated by the Party and its ideology, then Party and State must remain separate. In that case, the Party will represent an Order where a selection of leaders and fighters takes place. It is by these fighters that the ideology will be taken to the people. The Party must prepare the state of receptiveness and the will of the people for legislation, so that the spiritual disposition of the people will correspond to the

actual legislation of the State.

It is therefore not enough that the Party is uniformly held together as an élite, as a minority. Rather, it is the task of the Party to carry out the political education and the political union of German people. That is why it has a right to the leadership of what are known as affiliated bodies. Through them the Party is accomplishing its most vital task: the ideological conquest of the German people and the creation of "the people's organisation". The State then becomes a technical aid for this community of the people: it is the instrument for implementing the ideology.

The Party, thus, is the intrinsically vital body which, again and again, gives life and the will to live to defunct matter. The State apparatus functioned before the war, and it also functioned after the war. Nevertheless, the whole German people experienced Black November 9, 1918; nevertheless it experienced the terrible collapse of the post-war years in all spheres of political, cultural, and economic life. Only the spirit, the will and the readiness for action of the German Freedom Movement were able to save Germany from drowning in a Communist chaos. Only the German Freedom Movement's volitional and spiritual strength have made possible the country's reconstruction. It is the right and the task of the Party again and again to pump the stream of its spiritual and volitional strength into the State machinery.

The Party must reserve this function to itself, and it must also take care that it does not become too closely connected with the administrative machinery of the State; for, unless it takes care, it runs the risk of being devoured by the bureaucracy of the State and of becoming itself petrified as a Party bureaucracy.

All over the world we observe this struggle for new forms of government. Gone are those soulless days when parties represented merely a pragmatic programme, and when the State was a dead machine. We call it the age of materialism. In the 20th Century, nations struggle for their souls and for a new life style which must necessarily find expression in forms of government. We have seen these struggles in Italy, in Hungary, in Germany, and in other countries, such as Spain.

After each revolution, bureau-

cracy fights for its position, and in most cases it is victorious. In the National Socialist revolution it may already be clearly observed that the struggle between bureaucracy and Party has been decided in favour of the Party. Not even a few rearguard actions can alter that fact.

According to the Führer's will, the connection between Party and State in Germany will take the following form:

The link at the summit between Party and State has been forged by the appointment of the Deputy Führer as Party-Minister and, of course, through the Führer as Leader of the Party and Reich Chancellor. It is not necessary for the remaining National Executive of the Party to be merged with the State.

A further connection at the summit of Party and State will be the Great Senate, the creation of which has been planned for a later date. The Great Senate is purely a Party institution, while, at the same time, it will also be the highest national State authority.

The third link between Party and State in National Socialist Germany may be found in the person of the Regional Leader who is, at the same time, Reich Governor.

This intention of the Führer will be taken into account in the reforms of the Reich.

There is a further connection of Party and State in the establishment, through the German Communities Regulation, of a Party Representative within every community, who has been given certain rights of participation in the shaping of community life.

In any form, the State is bound to be somewhat rigid; the Party, however, must at all times stay alive and flexible. If it wishes to be the conscience of the people, it must take its impulse from its ideology alone.

41. The Law to Safeguard the Unity of Party and State (December 1, 1933)

The Government of the Reich has decreed the following law which is promulgated herewith:

Article 1

(1) After the victory of the National Socialist revolution, the National Socialist German

Workers' Party has become the carrier of the principles of the German State and is indissolubly linked to the State.

(2) It is a body incorporated under public law. Its statutes will be determined by the Führer.

Article 2

For the purpose of safeguarding closest co-operation between Party offices, the S.A., and official authorities, the Deputy Führer and the Chief-of-Staff of the S.A. will become members of the Government of the Reich.

Article 3

(1) As the leading and motive power in the National Socialist State, increased duties *vis-à-vis* Führer, people, and State are incumbent upon members of the National Socialist German Workers' Party and the S.A. (including its subordinate formations).

(2) In case of failing in these duties they are subject to a special Party and S.A. judiciary.

(3) The Führer may extend these regulations to include members of other organisations.

Article 4

Any action or omission will be regarded as violation of duty which attacks or jeopardises the existence, organisation, activities, or standing of the National Socialist German Workers' Party, and, in the case of the S.A. (including its subordinate formations) especially any contravention against discipline.

Article 5

In addition to the usual penalties, arrest and detention may be imposed.

Article 6

Within the framework of their competence, authorities will have to render legal and administrative assistance to Party and S.A. offices, entrusted with Party and S.A. jurisdiction.

Article 7

The law concerning official penal power over members of the S.A. and the S.S. of April 28, 1933, is repealed herewith.

Article 8

The Reich Chancellor as Führer of the National Socialist German Workers' Party and as Supreme Leader of the S.A. will decree the regulations required to execute and complement this law, in particular concerning development

and proceedings of Party and S.A. jurisdiction. He will determine the date of coming into force of the regulations concerning the said jurisdiction.

Berlin, December 1, 1933

(signed) Adolf Hitler
Reich Chancellor
Frick
Reich Minister of the Interior

Notes

Black November 9, 1918: the day of Germany's internal collapse in World War I. That, and the "shameful treaty" (*Schandvertrag*) of Versailles were among the stock phrases in Nazi demagogics.

42. The Law for the Protection of German Blood and German Honour (September 15, 1935)

Imbued with the realisation that the purity of German blood is presuppositional for the continued existence of the German people, and inspired by the unswerving will to safeguard the German Nation for all times, the Reichstag has unanimously decreed the following law, which is promulgated herewith:

Article 1

(1) Marriages between Jews and German nationals of German or kindred blood are forbidden.

(2) Only the Public Prosecutor is authorised to institute nullity proceedings.

Article 2

Extra-marital intercourse between Jews and German nationals of German or kindred blood is forbidden.

Article 3

Jews are not permitted to employ female German nationals of German or kindred blood.

Article 4

(1) Jews are forbidden to hoist the Reich national flag or to display the national colours.

(2) However, they are permitted to display Jewish colours. The exercise of this right is protected by law.

Article 5

(1) The contravention of the prohibition of Article 1 carries a punishment of penal servitude.

(2) Contravention of the regu-

lations of Articles 3 and 4 carries a penalty of up to 12 months' imprisonment and an additional fine, or either.

Article 6

In agreement with the Deputy Führer and the Reich Minister of Justice, the Reich Minister of the Interior will issue the legal and administrative regulations for executing and complementing this law.

This law will come into force one day after promulgation; Article 3, however, will come into force on January 1, 1936.

Nuremberg, September 15, 1935, at the Reich Party Rally of Freedom

(signed) Adolf Hitler
Führer and Reich Chancellor
Frick
Minister of the Interior
Dr. Gürtner
Reich Minister of Justice
R. Hess
Deputy Führer
Reich Minister without Portfolio

43. The Reich Citizenship Law (September 15, 1935)

The Reichstag has unanimously decreed the following law which is promulgated herewith:

Article 1

(1) A person is a German national if he lives under the protection of the German Reich and so is indebted to it.

(2) Nationality may be acquired according to the regulations of the Reich Citizenship and Nationality Law.

Article 2

(1) Only a German national of German or kindred blood who by his demeanour proves his willingness and suitability faithfully to serve the German people and the German Reich may become a Citizen of the Reich.

(2) Citizenship of the Reich will be acquired by means of granting of the Patent of Citizenship.

(3) A Citizen of the Reich is the sole possessor of full political rights, according to the law.

Article 3

In agreement with the Deputy Führer, the Reich Minister of the Interior will issue the legal and administrative regulations required for the execution and implementation of this law. Nur-

emberg, September 15, 1935, at the Reich Party Rally of Freedom

(signed) Adolf Hitler
Führer and Reich Chancellor
Frick
Reich Minister of the Interior

44. The First Directive for the Implementation of the Reich Citizenship Law (November 14, 1935)

On the basis of Article 3 of the Reich Citizenship Law of September 15, 1935, the following is decreed herewith:

Article 1

(1) For the time being, and until further regulations concerning the Patent of Citizenship are issued, Citizens of the Reich will be all persons who are German Nationals of German or kindred blood and who, at the time of the coming into force of the Reich Citizenship Law, were entitled to vote in Reichstag elections, or to whom the Reich Minister of the Interior, in agreement with the Deputy Führer, has granted temporary Reich Citizenship.

(2) The Reich Minister of the Interior may, in agreement with the Deputy Führer, withdraw temporary Reich Citizenship.

Article 2

(1) The regulations of Article 1 apply also to Jewish mixed-parentage German nationals.

(2) A Jew of mixed parentage is a person who is descended from one or two racially wholly Jewish grandparents, unless he is a Jew according to the definition in Article 5/2. A grandparent is immediately considered to be wholly Jewish if he was a member of the Jewish religious community.

Article 3

As possessor of full political rights a Citizen of the Reich is the sole person entitled to exercise his voting rights in political affairs and only he is entitled to hold public office. During the period of transition, the Minister of the Interior, or the office authorised by him, may allow exceptions for the admission to public offices. The affairs of religious societies are not affected.

Article 4

(1) A Jew may not be a Citizen of the Reich. He is not entitled to

vote in political affairs: he may not hold public office.

(2) After December 31, 1935, all Jewish civil servants will retire. Any Jewish civil servant who, in the Great War, fought at the front for Germany or her Allies, will, up to retirement age, continue to receive the full emoluments he received upon retirement; however these emoluments will no longer increase according to scale of seniority. On reaching retirement age, the pension will be newly calculated according to the last full pension-related emoluments received.

(3) The affairs of religious societies are not affected by this regulation.

(4) Until fresh arrangements for the management of Jewish schools have been made, the contract of employment of teachers at Jewish state schools will remain unaffected.

Article 5

(1) A person is a Jew if he is descended from at least three racially wholly Jewish grandparents. Article 2/2, Sentence 2, applies.

(2) A Jewish mixed-parentage German national who is descended from two wholly Jewish grandparents will also be held to be a Jew,

(a) if at the time of issue of this law he was a member of a Jewish religious community, or is subsequently admitted as a member,

(b) if at the time of issue of this law he was married to a Jew, or subsequently marries a Jew,

(c) if he is the child of a marriage with a person who is a Jew according to the definition of paragraph (1), which has been contracted after the Law for the Protection of German Blood and German Honour of September 15, 1935, came into force,

(d) if he is the child of extra-marital intercourse with a person who is a Jew according to the definition of Paragraph (1), and is born after July 31, 1936.

Article 6

(1) Insofar as requirements concerning the purity of blood are demanded in laws of the Reich or in regulations of the National Socialist German Workers' Party and its organisations, which exceed Article 5, they are deemed to be unaffected.

(2) Other requirements concerning the purity of blood exceeding Article 5 may only be stipulated in agreement with the Reich Minister of the Interior and the Deputy Führer. Insofar as requirements of this kind already exist, they will become void on January 1, 1936, unless they are approved by the Reich Minister of the Interior in agreement with the Deputy Führer. Application for approval must be made to the Reich Minister of the Interior.

Article 7

The Führer and Reich Chancellor may grant exemption from the regulations of this directive.
Berlin, November 14, 1934

(signed) Adolf Hitler
Führer and Reich Chancellor
Frick
Reich Minister of the Interior
R. Hess
Deputy Führer
Reich Minister without Portfolio

45. The First Directive for the Implementation of the Law for the Protection of German Blood and German Honour (November 14, 1935)

On the basis of Article 6 of the Law for the Protection of German Blood and German Honour of September 15, 1935, the following is decreed herewith:

Article 1

(1) German nationals according to the definition of the Reich Citizenship Law will be deemed to possess German nationality.

(2) Article 2/2 of the First Directive of November 14, 1935, to the Reich Citizenship Law defines a Jewish mixed-parentage person.

(3) Article 5 of the same Directive defines a Jew.

Article 2

Included in marriages prohibited according to Article 1 of the law are marriages between Jews and Jewish mixed-parentage German nationals with only one wholly Jewish grandparent.

Article 3

(1) Jewish mixed-parentage German nationals with two wholly Jewish grandparents, wishing to marry either German nationals of German or kindred blood, or Jewish mixed-parentage German nationals with only one wholly Jewish grandparent, require the permission of the Reich Minister of the Interior and the Deputy Führer, or of the office appointed by them for that purpose.

(2) In making the decision, allowance must be made for the physical and mental qualities as well as the personality of the applicant; for length of residence in Germany of his family; or for his father's participation in World War I, as well as for the rest of his family history.

(3) Applications for permission to marry must be made to the higher administrative authority of the district where the applicant is domiciled or where he normally resides.

(4) The Reich Minister of the Interior in agreement with the Deputy Führer will regularise the procedure.

Article 4

Marriages between Jewish mixed-parentage German nationals with only one wholly Jewish grandparent must not take place.

Article 5

The impediments to marriage due to the infusion of Jewish blood have been exhaustively regulated through Article 1 of the law, and through Articles 2–4 of this Directive.

Article 6

In addition, a marriage should not be contracted if it is to be anticipated that the offspring of such a marriage may jeopardise the continued purity of German blood.

Article 7

Before contracting a marriage, each partner must prove, by means of a certificate of qualification (as per Article 2 of the Law for the Preservation and Safeguard of Racially Healthy Stock of October 18, 1935) that there is no impediment to the marriage according to Article 6 of this Directive.

The following are points from the Law for the Preservation and Safeguard of a Racially Healthy Stock which may apply:

Article 1

(1) A marriage must not be contracted

(a) if one of the partners suffers from a contagious disease which it is to be feared may result in considerable damage to the health of the other partner or their descendants;

(b) if one of the partners has either been declared incapable of managing his, or her, affairs, or has been temporarily placed under the care of a guardian;

(c) if one of the partners, although not declared incapable of managing his, or her, affairs, suffers from a mental disorder which appears to render the marriage undesirable for the community;

(d) if one of the partners suffers from a hereditary disease, in accordance with the Law for the Prevention of Hereditarily Diseased Offspring.

(2) The regulations of paragraph (1)(d) do not stand in the way of a marriage if the other partner is sterile.

Article 2

Before contracting a marriage, the partners must prove by means of a certificate from the Public Health Department (certificate of qualification) that there is no impediment according to Article 1.

Article 8

(1) The nullity of a marriage contracted in contravention of Article 1 of the law or Article 2 of this Directive may only be enforced by way of plea of nullity.

(2) For marriages contracted in contravention of Articles 3, 4, and 6, the consequences of Article 1 and Article 5/1 of the law do not apply.

Article 9

If one of the partners holds foreign nationality, the decision of the Reich Minister for the Interior must be obtained prior to refusal to publish the banns because of an impediment according to Article 1 of the law or Articles 2–4 of this Directive, as well as prior to refusal of a certificate of qualification in cases relating to Article 6.

Article 10

A marriage contracted before a German Consular authority is held to have been contracted in Germany.

Article 11

Extra-marital intercourse in accordance with Article 2 of the law is understood to refer to sexual intercourse only. In addition punishable according to Article 5/2 of the law is extra-marital intercourse between Jews and Jewish mixed-parentage German nationals with only one wholly Jewish grandparent.

Article 12

(1) A household is Jewish (Article 3 of the law) if a Jewish male is

head of the household or a member of it.

(2) Any person who has been accepted into the household within the framework of a contractual relationship or alternatively who performs diurnal household tasks or other diurnal tasks in connection with the household, is deemed to be working in the household.

(3) Female German nationals of German or kindred blood who were working in a Jewish household when the law came into force, may remain in that household in their former contractual employment, if they have completed their thirty-fifth year by December 31, 1935.

(4) Foreign nationals who are neither domiciled nor normally resident in the country are not affected by these regulations.

Article 13

Any person contravening the prohibition of Article 3 of the law in conjunction with Article 12 of this Directive will be punishable according to Article 5/3 of the law, even if he is not a Jew.

Article 14

For offences against Article 5/1–2 of the law, the Central Criminal Court is the competent Court of primary jurisdiction.

Article 15

Insofar as the regulations of the law and its ordinance refer to German nationals, they must be applied to stateless persons who are domiciled or normally resident in this country. Stateless persons who are domiciled or normally resident abroad will only be affected by these regulations if previously they held German nationality.

(1) The Führer and Reich Chancellor may grant exemption from the regulations of the law and its directives.

(2) Prosecution of a foreign national requires the approval of the Reich Ministers of Justice and of the Interior.

Article 17

This directive comes into force on the day following its promulgation. The Minister of the Interior will determine the date of the coming into force of the law; up to that date, certificates of qualification need to be submitted in cases of doubt.
Berlin, November 14, 1935

(signed) Adolf Hitler
Führer and Reich Chancellor

Frick
Reich Minister of the Interior
R. Hess
Deputy Führer
Reich Minister without Portfolio
Dr. Gürtner
Reich Minister of Justice

46. The Reich Citizenship Law and the Law for the Protection of German Blood and German Honour (by Reich Minister Dr. Frick)

As with so many other vital problems, it has been left to the National-Socialist Movement to realise the importance of finding a solution to the race problem for the German people.

According to what history and the theory of population have taught us, the continued existence of a nation depends essentially on keeping its blood pure and healthy. Even though external circumstances may influence the life of a people, whether that people can sustain its belief in the concept of the purity of blood must always be of vital importance. For it is on this peculiar quality of a people that its existence, its culture, its achievements etc., are based. If, on the other hand, a nation does not keep its blood pure, but absorbs elements of blood of a different kind, then a rift in its unity and completeness will necessarily appear in consequence, and its intrinsic nature will be lost.

In its programme, the National-Socialist Movement has already outlined directions which take this line of thought into consideration. Starting out from the fact that, in Germany, the race problem is the Jewish problem, it follows that members of the Jewish people must be excluded from exerting any influence whatsoever on the organic life of the German people. Points four to six of our Programme read as follows:

(4) Only a member of the fellowship of the people may be a citizen. And only if, regardless of creed, he has German blood in his veins, may he be a member of the fellowship of the people. Consequently, no Jew may be a member of the fellowship of the people.

(5) A person who is not a citizen should be able to live in Germany.

(6) Only a citizen has the right to determine leadership and laws of the State. We demand therefore that public offices of any kind whatsoever, whether in the Reich, the provinces or the community, may only be held by citizens of the Reich . . .

On the basis of these sentences from our Programme, the Reich Citizenship Law which, like the Reich Law of the Flag and the Law for the Protection of German Blood and German Honour, was unanimously accepted by the Reichstag at its gathering at the Party Rally of Freedom on September 15, 1935, regulates the future shape of political life in Germany: The German Reich belongs to the German people.

The Reich Citizenship Law distinguishes between the "national" and the "citizen of the Reich". By separating these two concepts, one of the main principles of the liberalistic era has been discarded. According to that principle, all nationals, regardless of race, religion etc., had equal rights and equal duties. Today formal membership of the German polity is no longer decisive in entitling one to the civic rights and for being called upon to do one's duty. Instead the concept of nationality serves primarily to distinguish Germans from aliens and stateless persons. The status of "national", therefore, is independent of the race to which the individual may belong. Rather, any one who, according to the regulations of the Reich Citizenship and Nationality Law, has acquired German nationality, and accordingly belongs to the protective commonwealth of the German Reich, is a German national.

Conversely, only a national who is entitled to full possession of political rights and duties is a citizen of the Reich. To achieve citizenship of the Reich is dependent, in particular, on two conditions. In principle, no one who is not of German or kindred blood (of German extraction) may become a citizen of the Reich; in addition, he must, by his demeanour, have manifested his will and suitability to serve the German people.

Since to be of German blood forms a condition for the acquisition of Reich citizenship, it follows that no Jew may become a citizen of the Reich. However, the same holds valid for members of other races whose blood is not akin to German blood, for example for gypsies and negroes.

German blood does not in itself constitute a race. Rather, the German people is composed of members of several races. But all those races have one peculiarity, and that is: their blood is compatible, and its intermingling does not—unlike blood that is not kindred—produce inhibitions and tensions.

Unhesitatingly, therefore, we may put on the same footing with German blood the blood of those peoples whose racial constitution is related to the German. That is the case consistently with the self-contained peoples of Europe. In every respect, kindred blood will be treated in the same way as German blood. For that reason, members of minority groups living in Germany, such as Poles, Danes etc., may become citizens of the Reich.

Citizenship of the Reich is acquired by the granting of a Patent of Reich Citizenship. Detailed conditions for the acquisition of this document will be determined in due course. In this context, we shall also outline ways in which evidence of the will and suitability to serve the German people will have to be adduced. As a rule, completion of compulsory Labour Service and of National Service will have to be demanded. Applicants must also have reached a specific age. It must be emphasised, however, that it is not by any means intended to restrict the granting of Reich citizenship to members of the N.S.D.A.P., that is to say, to a fraction of those who are German nationals. Rather, it is planned that the great mass of the German population should become Reich citizens. Exceptions will be made only in the case of persons who have committed offences against country or people; who have been sentenced to penal servitude, or in similar cases. This intention has already found expression in the First Directive to the Reich Citizenship Law of November 14, 1935. It is likely to be some considerable time before the final granting of Reich Citizenship, since this requires extensive administrative preparations. Therefore, and until further regulations concerning the Reich Citizenship Patent are published, all German nationals of German or kindred blood who held electoral rights when the Reich Citizenship Law came into force, that is to say, on September 30, 1935, or on whom provisional Reich Citizenship was conferred by the Reich Minister of the Interior in agreement with the Deputy Führer, will be deemed to be Reich Citizens. Provision for special conferment of Reich Citizenship had to be made in order to afford possession of Reich citizenship particularly to young people reaching maturity as well as to those who have newly acquired German nationality.

Just as regulations have been provided regarding the loss of final Reich citizenship, it has been necessary to create the possibility of withdrawing provisional Reich citizenship in case the holder should prove himself unworthy of it. This decision may be pronounced by the Reich Minister of the Interior in agreement with the Deputy Führer.

The Reich Citizen is the sole possessor of political rights, as directed by law. For that reason, it is he alone who is entitled to vote in political elections. Further, it is he alone who is entitled to hold public office. However, during the time of transition, the Reich Minister of the Interior may grant exceptions, individually or generally, for admission to public office, particularly for the purpose of enabling persons who, because of their age, are not yet in a position to acquire Reich Citizenship, to enter the Civil Service, particularly the training service.

Since a Jew cannot be a citizen of the Reich, a regulation was required to clarify once and for all who is to be deemed to be a Jew. This has been done in Article 5 of the First Directive to the Reich Citizenship Law.

It follows from the fact that a Jew cannot be a Reich citizen that he is excluded in every respect from participating in any affairs involving civic rights. Jewish civil servants at present in office will, therefore, have to resign; after December 31, 1935, they will officially retire; for those among them who fought at the front, special arrangements have been made to the effect that until they reach retirement age, they will continue to receive their last salary by way of pension.

The separation of the German people from the Jewish people, however, could not be confined to the province of civic rights. Separation in the personal field is of equal importance. We must emphatically prevent new Jewish blood being introduced into the German people. Consequently, both marital and extra-marital alliances between Jews and persons of German stock are forbidden and represent a punish-

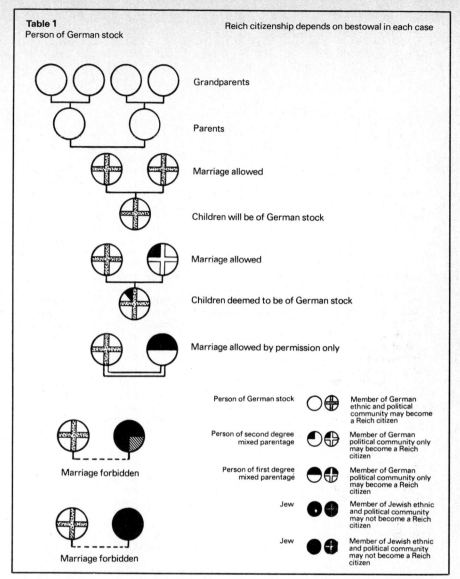

Table 1
Person of German stock

Reich citizenship depends on bestowal in each case

Grandparents

Parents

Marriage allowed

Children will be of German stock

Marriage allowed

Children deemed to be of German stock

Marriage allowed by permission only

Person of German stock — Member of German ethnic and political community may become a Reich citizen

Person of second degree mixed parentage — Member of German political community only may become a Reich citizen

Person of first degree mixed parentage — Member of German political community only may become a Reich citizen

Jew — Member of Jewish ethnic and political community may not become a Reich citizen

Jew — Member of Jewish ethnic and political community may not become a Reich citizen

Marriage forbidden

Marriage forbidden

able offence. Marriages contracted in contravention are null and void. In all other respects, however, the position of Jews regarding civic rights is unaffected. In particular, in economic life, they are subject only to legally fixed restrictions. In principle, those of mixed parentage must receive special treatment. As they are not Jews, they cannot be put on an equal footing with Jews; as they are not Germans, they cannot be put on an equal footing with Germans. And although, in principle, they have the possibility of acquiring Reich citizenship – as illustrated by the extension of provisional Reich citizenship to include persons of mixed parentage – they remain subject to the restrictions pronounced in legislation up to the

present time, as well as in regulations of the N.S.D.A.P. and its organisations. Thus in future entry to the Civil Service will no longer be open to them, nor will they be able to become members of the N.S.D.A.P. or its organisations. Economically, however, they are entirely on equal footing with persons of German stock. Further, insofar as persons of mixed parentage have been excluded from membership of organisations of all kinds, including the N.S.D.A.P., by dint of orders to that effect, such orders will become void as from January 1, 1936, unless they have received the consent of the Reich Minister of Justice in agreement with the Deputy Führer.

For the rest, care must be taken to bring about the disappearance

of persons of mixed origin as swiftly as possible. On the one hand, this has already been achieved by lumping together with the Jews persons of mixed parentage who tend overwhelmingly towards Judaism; on the other hand, it has been achieved by making marriage of persons of mixed parentage with two wholly Jewish grandparents and persons of German stock subject to permission. And although they are allowed to marry among themselves, according to medical science only a small number of offspring may be expected from such unions, if both partners each show half of the same composition of blood. Persons of mixed parentage with only one Jewish grandparent will be helped to become absorbed into

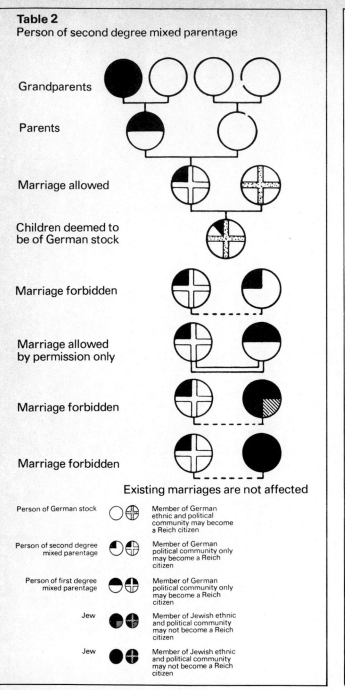

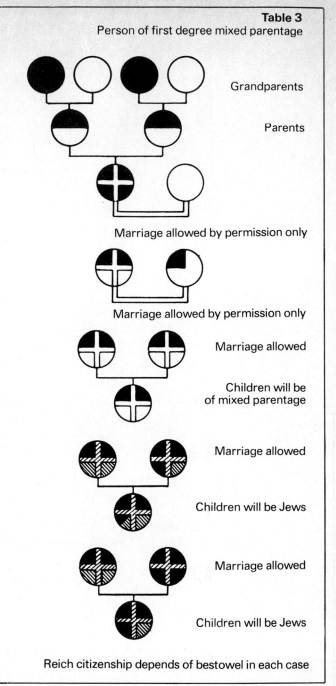

Germanity by marriage with persons of German stock, which is absolutely permissible. In order not to delay this process, marriage among themselves is forbidden.

The Reich Citizenship Law and the Law for the Protection of German Blood have not been framed for the purpose of placing members of the Jewish people in a worse position only because of their membership of that people. The elimination of Judaism from public German life and the prevention of further intermingling of races are, on the contrary, imperative necessities if the continued existence of the German people is to be safeguarded. The Jews in Germany are not to be deprived of the possibility of existing in Germany. German destiny, however, will in future be shaped solely by the German people.

Note
This article was published in the *Deutsche Juristen-Zeitung* on December 1, 1935.

47. Diagrammatic Survey of the Reich Citizenship Law and of the Law for the Protection of German Blood and German Honour

The law distinguishes between Jews, persons of mixed parentage, and persons of German stock. The distinguishing characteristic is the ethnic group to which the grandparents belong.

Those who have three or four wholly Jewish grandparents will be regarded as Jews.

Those who have one or two wholly Jewish grandparents will be regarded as of mixed parentage. In this context, a person with two Jewish grandparents is of first-degree mixed parentage; a person with one Jewish grandparent is of only second-degree mixed parentage.

Thus only a person who has no

Table 4   Person of first degree mixed parentage   Existing marriages are not affected

Exceptions

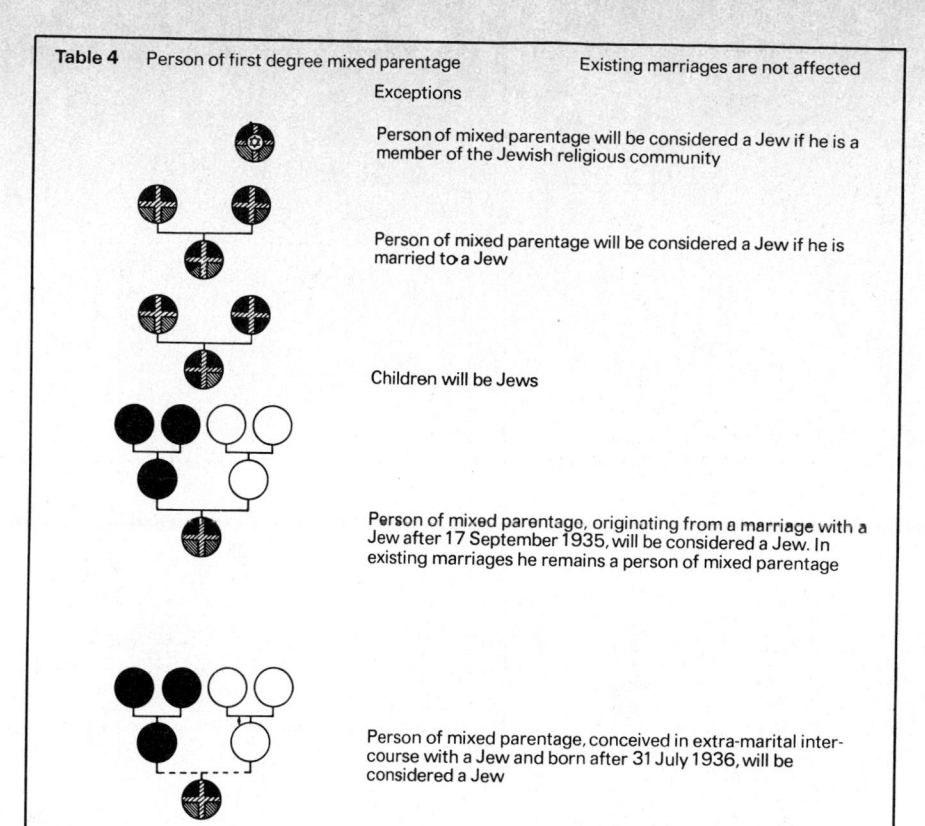

Person of mixed parentage will be considered a Jew if he is a member of the Jewish religious community

Person of mixed parentage will be considered a Jew if he is married to a Jew

Children will be Jews

Person of mixed parentage, originating from a marriage with a Jew after 17 September 1935, will be considered a Jew. In existing marriages he remains a person of mixed parentage

Person of mixed parentage, conceived in extra-marital intercourse with a Jew and born after 31 July 1936, will be considered a Jew

---

Table 5   Jew   Jews cannot become Reich citizens

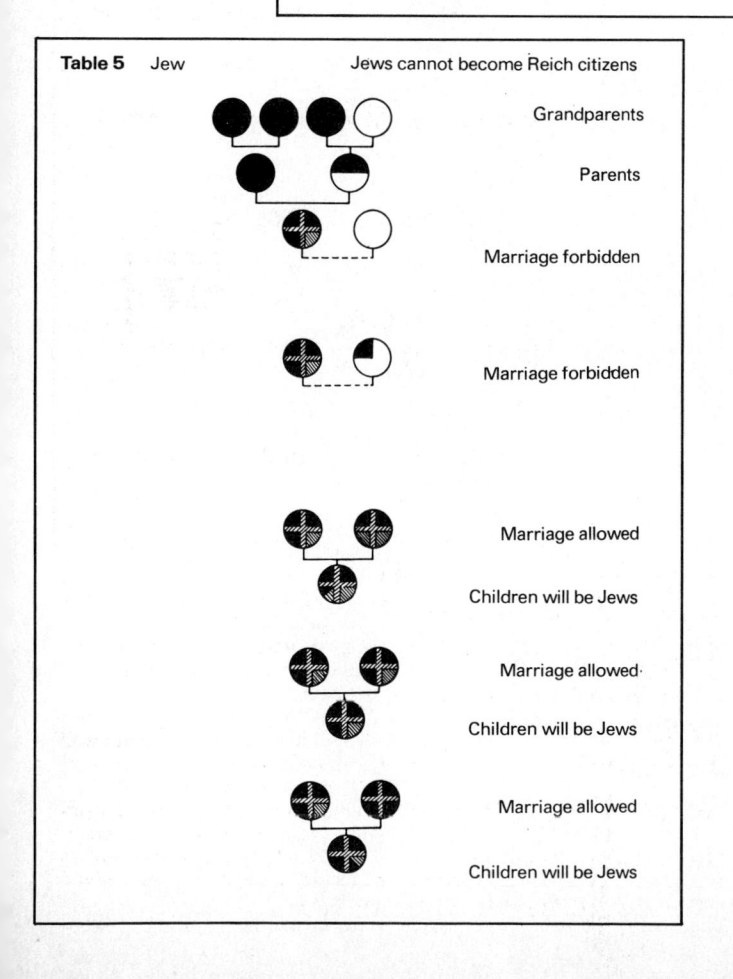

Grandparents

Parents

Marriage forbidden

Marriage forbidden

Marriage allowed

Children will be Jews

Marriage allowed

Children will be Jews

Marriage allowed

Children will be Jews

Table 6   Jew   Existing marriages are not affected

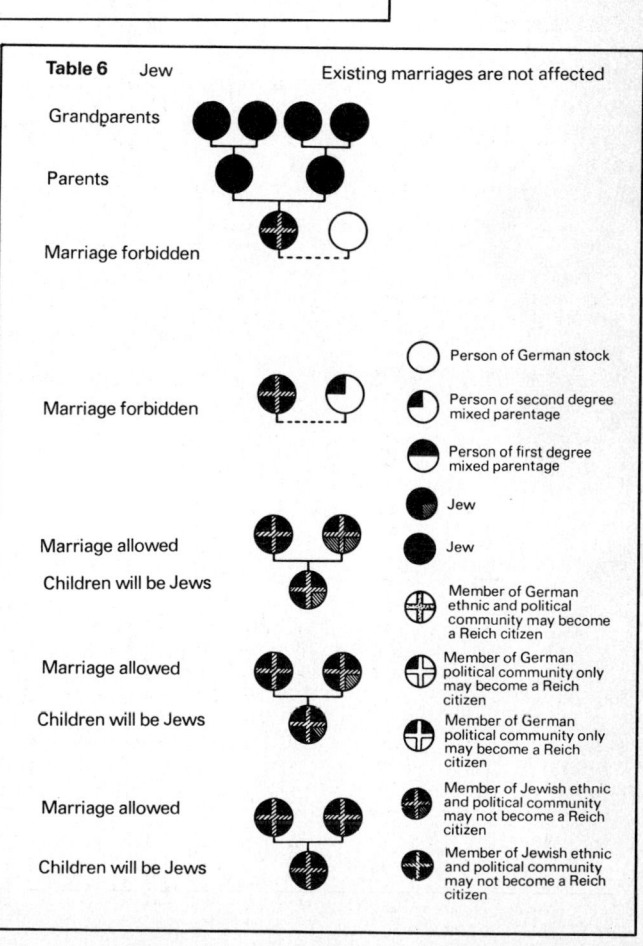

Grandparents

Parents

Marriage forbidden

Marriage forbidden

Marriage allowed

Children will be Jews

Marriage allowed

Children will be Jews

Marriage allowed

Children will be Jews

Person of German stock

Person of second degree mixed parentage

Person of first degree mixed parentage

Jew

Jew

Member of German ethnic and political community may become a Reich citizen

Member of German political community only may become a Reich citizen

Member of German political community only may become a Reich citizen

Member of Jewish ethnic and political community may not become a Reich citizen

Member of Jewish ethnic and political community may not become a Reich citizen

3219

Jews among his four grandparents can be considered to be of German stock.

Decisive for membership of Jewry is, naturally, not the religious but the ethnic factor. Thus a grandparent may be a Jew even though he belonged to a Christian religious community, or to no religious community at all. Needless to say, if a grandparent did belong to the Jewish religious community, he will immediately be regarded as wholly Jewish. The justification for this lies in the fact that, although at the time of the grandparents of the present generation there were Jews who left the Jewish religious community, there were conversely never any instances of persons not belonging to the ethnic community of the Jewish people entering the Jewish religious community. Thus the Jewish religious community was composed, at all times, only of those belonging both to the ethnic and religious Jewish community.

From the remarks by the Reich Minister of Justice it is clear who may be regarded as being of German stock. They are all those who originally formed the European peoples, or members of those peoples of mixed parentage.

A detailed account will be given below of different possibilities of marriage. In this connection, it must be emphasised, however, that only those conditions will be discussed which apply according to the Blood Law. The Law for the Preservation of Racially Healthy Marriage has not been included. Therefore, wherever marriage is contemplated, it will be necessary for the partners to find out whether, according to the law, there may not be health reasons which throw doubt on the advisability of their intended marriage.

Table 1:

Persons of German stock and kindred persons may marry each other unhesitatingly (Case 1). Children of such a marriage will unhesitatingly belong to the German ethnic and political community.

Similarly, persons of German stock may unhesitatingly marry a person of second-degree mixed parentage (Case 2). Children of such a union similarly belong to the German ethnic and political community. The proportion of Jewish blood in a child of such a marriage is so comparatively insignificant that in practical terms

it is of no importance, and there are thus no serious objections to the child's absorption into the German ethnic and political community.

However, things are different in the case of a person of German stock and a person of first-degree mixed parentage (Case 3). Here the proportion of Jewish blood is considerably higher than in Case 2. For that reason, whether pure German blood may be allowed to mingle with that of a person of mixed parentage has, in this instance, been made conditional upon special permission. The granting of such permission will depend on how long the family of mixed parentage has been living in Germany and on the attitude of its members towards the German people, that is to say, whether they have served in the German armed forces or whether they have supported the cause of the German community. Whether the children of a marriage which is conditional upon permission will have to be regarded as persons of mixed parentage, or whether they belong to the German or Jewish ethnic community, will have to be determined in each individual case.

Marriage between a German and a Jew is, of course, forbidden (Cases 4 and 5). If such a marriage takes place in contravention of

the law, it will be null and void.

Table 2:

A person of second-degree mixed parentage is unhesitatingly free to marry a person of German stock (Case 1). That fact had already been elaborated in Table 1 (Case 2). However, persons of second-degree mixed parentage are forbidden to marry each other (Case 2). The percentage of Jewish blood which is comparatively small in the parents, would be much higher in the children, and thus new persons of mixed parentage might be created. The absorption of persons of second-degree mixed parentage into the German ethnic community would be delayed.

Marriage between persons of second-degree mixed parentage and those of first-degree mixed parentage is allowed (Case 3). It is, however, subject to permission being granted. For this permission the same grounds apply as for permission of marriages between persons of German stock and persons of first-degree mixed parentage (cf. Table 1, Case 3).

Marriage between persons of second-degree mixed parentage and Jews is forbidden (Cases 4 and 5).

Table 3:

With persons of first-degree mixed

parentage only marriage to each other and with Jews is allowed (Cases 3, 4, and 5).

Marriage between persons of first-degree mixed parentage and persons of German stock is subject to permission (Case 1).

The same applies for marriage between persons of first-degree and those of second-degree mixed parentage (Case 2).

It has been possible to allow marriage between persons of first-degree mixed parentage without hesitation, because from experience these marriages result only rarely in offspring, thus minimising the danger of creating new persons of mixed parentage. By marrying a Jew (Cases 4 and 5), the person of first-degree mixed parentage, whose percentage of Jewish blood is, after all, still comparatively large, declares himself a member of the Jewish ethnic community. The children of such marriages will unhesitatingly be Jews. In contrast to the person of second-degree mixed parentage, such a person should not be prevented from making this declaration of belonging to the Jewish ethnic community, exactly because his percentage of Jewish blood is comparatively high.

Table 4:

A number of special cases have been provided for in connection with persons of first-degree mixed parentage, all of which have their inner justification in that very declaration of belonging to the Jewish ethnic community. For such a person of mixed parentage will unhesitatingly be considered a Jew if he belongs to the Jewish religious community or if he is married to a Jew. Therefore, a person of mixed parentage held to be a Jew is permitted to marry only Jews or persons of first-degree mixed parentage. The children of such a union will be Jews. In addition, persons of mixed parentage, born from a marriage with a Jew after September 17, 1935, will be regarded as Jews. In existing marriages the child will remain a person of mixed parentage. Correspondingly, a person of mixed parentage originating from extra-marital intercourse with a Jew and born after July 31, 1936, will be regarded as a Jew.

Tables 5 and 6:

Finally, Jews have only the possibility of marrying other Jews or persons of first-degree mixed parentage. Their children will in any case be Jews.